Fortress Introduction to
Salvation and the Cross

FORTRESS INTRODUCTION TO

Salvation and the Cross

David A. Brondos

Fortress Press ◆ Minneapolis

FORTRESS INTRODUCTION TO SALVATION AND THE CROSS

Cover image: Crucifixion from Saint Mark's Basilica, Venice, Italy.

Library of Congress Cataloging-in-Publication Data
Brondos, David A, 1958-
Fortress introduction to salvation and the cross / David A. Brondos.
   p. cm.
Includes bibliographical references and index.
ISBN 978-0-8006-6216-5 (alk. paper)
1. Salvation. 2. Jesus Christ—Crucifixion. I. Title. II. Title: Fortress introduction to
salvation and the cross.
BT751.3.B76 2007
234—dc22
                                    2007008173

Manufactured in the U.S.A.

11   10   09   08   07   1   2   3   4   5   6   7   8   9   10

In memory of Colin E. Gunton (1941–2003)

CONTENTS

Time Line   ix
Abbreviations   xii

Introduction   1
CHAPTER 1   Isaiah and the Redemption of Israel   5

CHAPTER 2   The Divine Plan of Salvation in the
                Writings of Luke   19

CHAPTER 3   Christ Crucified and Risen in the Letters
                of Paul   34

CHAPTER 4   The Redemption of "Man" in the
                Thought of Irenaeus   49

CHAPTER 5   Gregory of Nyssa and the Union of Divine
                and Human Natures   64

CHAPTER 6   Anselm and the Satisfaction of Divine Justice   76

CHAPTER 7   Christ as Redeemer from Sin, Death, and
                the Devil in the Thought of Martin Luther   88

CHAPTER 8   Christ Our Righteousness in John Calvin's
                Institutes   103

CHAPTER 9   Albrecht Ritschl and the Kingdom of God   116

CHAPTER 10   Karl Barth's Doctrine of Reconciliation   130

CHAPTER 11   Rudolf Bultmann and the Proclamation
                of the Word of the Cross   141

CHAPTER 12   Jon Sobrino and the Crucified People   154

CHAPTER 13   Salvation as Liberation from Patriarchy in
               the Thought of Rosemary Radford Ruether   169
Conclusion   183

Acknowledgments   185
Notes   187
Additional Resources   199
Glossary   211
Index   215

TIME LINE

BCE

c. 1000–c. 960   reign of King David in Israel
911   rise of (neo-) Assyrian Empire
c. 750–c. 690   prophet Isaiah
721   destruction of northern kingdom of Israel by Assyrians
715–687   reign of King Hezekiah in Judah
626   rise of (neo-) Babylonian Empire
586   Jerusalem falls to Babylonian king Nebuchadnezzar, who takes
                 people of Judah into exile
550   rise of Persian (Achaemenid) Empire
539   Persian king Cyrus allows exiles to return to Jerusalem and rebuild
                 temple
c. 427–c. 347   Greek philosopher Plato
400–300?   final redactions of Book of Isaiah
331   rise of Greek Empire under Alexander the Great
44   rise of Roman Empire
8–2?   birth of Jesus

CE

c. 27–c. 30   ministry of Jesus
c. 30   crucifixion of Jesus; day of Pentecost
c. 35–c. 65   missionary activity of Paul
64   persecution of Christians under Roman emperor Nero
70   destruction of Jerusalem during Jewish-Roman war
75–95?   composition of Luke and Acts
90–100   composition of New Testament writings ascribed to St. John
c. 130–202   Irenaeus
c. 150   rise of Valentinians, one of many Gnostic groups regarded as
                 heretical by Irenaeus in *Against Heresies*
185–c. 254   Origen
c. 297–373   Athanasius
303–305   final persecution of Christians under Roman emperor Diocletian

313	Diocletian's successor Constantine makes Christianity legal in Roman Empire
325	Council of Nicea condemns Arianism
c. 329–379	Basil of Caesarea
c. 329–c. 389	Gregory of Nazianzus
c. 331–c. 395	Gregory of Nyssa
354–430	Augustine
381	First Council of Constantinople defines Trinitarian doctrine
389–391	Roman emperor Theodosius I makes Christianity the state religion
610	birth of Islam under the prophet Mohammed
751	beginnings of Carolingian Empire in Europe, under which feudal society developed
1033–1109	Anselm of Canterbury
1079–1142	Abelard
1095–1099	first crusade to Holy Land
1483–1546	Martin Luther
1492	Christopher Columbus arrives in America; beginning of Spanish colonialism
1509–1564	John Calvin
1517	beginning of Protestant Reformation
1530	Confession of Augsburg
1541	Calvin begins efforts to make Geneva a model Christian city
1711–1776	Enlightenment thinker David Hume
1724–1804	Enlightenment thinker Immanuel Kant
1768–1834	liberal theologian Friedrich Schleiermacher
1787	Johann Philip Gabler delivers address outlining methodology of biblical theology
1809–1882	scientist Charles Darwin
1822–1889	Albrecht Ritschl
1884–1885	Berlin Conference regulates European colonization in Africa, leading to "scramble for Africa" among European imperial powers
1884–1976	Rudolf Bultmann

1889–1976	existentialist philosopher Martin Heidegger
1886–1968	Karl Barth
c. 1900	emergence of "social gospel" promoting the application of Christian principles to social problems such as poverty, inequality, and injustice
1914–1918	First World War
1933	Adolf Hitler comes to power in Germany
1936–	Rosemary Radford Ruether
1938–	Jon Sobrino
1939–1945	Second World War
1964–1971	emergence of Latin American liberation theology
1968	publication of *The Church and the Second Sex* by Mary Daly, a feminist critique of Christianity contributing to the emergence of Christian feminist theology
1980–1992	Civil war in El Salvador

ABBREVIATIONS

◆ ———————————————————————————————— ◆

1 Cor	1 Corinthians
2 Cor	2 Corinthians
2 Tim	2 Timothy
AARAS	American Academy of Religion Academy Series
ABC	Anchor Bible Commentary
AE	*Against Eunomius* (ch. 5)
AJT	*Asia Journal of Theology*
ATR	*Anglican Theological Review*
ATLAMS	American Theological Library Association Monograph Series
AUSS	*Andrews University Seminary Studies*
BHT	Beiträge zur historischen Theologie
BIS	Biblical Interpretation Series
BZNW	*Beihefte zur Zeitschrift für die neutestamentliche Wissenschaft und die Kunde der älteren Kirche*
CCP	Cambridge Companions to Philosophy
CCR	Cambridge Companions to Religion
CBQ	*Catholic Biblical Quarterly*
CC	*Christology at the Crossroads* (ch. 12)
CL	*Christ the Liberator* (ch. 12)
Col	Colossians
ConBNT	Coniectanea biblica: New Testament Series
CTJ	*Calvin Theological Journal*
CurTM	*Currents in Theology and Mission*
ECF	Early Church Fathers
EF	*Existence and Faith* (ch. 11)
EgT	*Eglise et théologie*
Eph	Ephesians
ESCT	Edinburgh Studies in Constructive Theology
EvQ	*Evangelical Quarterly*
FU	*Faith and Understanding* (ch. 11)
Gal	Galatians
GC	*Great Catechism* (ch. 5)
Gen	Genesis
GG	*Gaia and God* (ch. 13)
GOTR	*Greek Orthodox Theological Review*
Hor	*Horizons*
IBT	Interpreting Biblical Texts

ICC	International Critical Commentary on the Holy Scriptures of the Old and New Testaments
IR	*Introducing Redemption in Christian Feminism* (ch. 13)
Isa	Isaiah
JBL	*Journal of Biblical Literature*
JFSR	*Journal of Feminist Studies in Religion*
JL	*Jesus the Liberator* (ch. 12)
JSNT	*Journal for the Study of the New Testament*
JSNTSup	Journal for the Study of the New Testament: Supplement Series
JTS	*Journal of Theological Studies*
KM	*Kerygma and Myth* (ch. 11)
LC	*Large Catechism* (ch. 7)
LM	*The Life of Moses* (ch. 5)
LRPT	Library of Religious and Philosophical Thought
LW	*Luther's Works*
ML	*Mysterium Liberationis* (ch. 12)
MMT	Making of Modern Theology
MMTM	Makers of the Modern Theological Mind
ModTh	*Modern Theology*
NICNT	New International Commentary on the New Testament
NIGTC	New International Greek Testament Commentary
NovT	*Novum Testamentum*
NTG	New Testament Guides
NTT	New Testament Theology
OBC	*On the Baptism of Christ* (ch. 5)
OCT	Outstanding Christian Thinkers
OMM	*On the Making of Man* (ch. 5)
OSR	*On the Soul and the Resurrection* (ch. 5)
OV	*On Virginity* (ch. 5)
PC	*Primitive Christianity in Its Contemporary Setting* (ch. 11)
Phlm	Philemon
PL	Penguin Lives
PM	*The Principle of Mercy* (ch. 12)
PMast	Past Masters
ProEccl	*Pro Ecclesia*
PRS	*Perspectives in Religious Studies*
R&R	Religion and Reason
RevScRel	*Revue des sciences religieuses*
Rom	Romans
RSV	Revised Standard Version
SA	*Smalcald Articles* (ch. 7)
SBLAB	Society of Biblical Literature Academia Biblica
SC	*Small Catechism* (ch. 7)
SGT	*Sexism and God-Talk* (ch. 13)
SIMSVD	Studia Instituti Missiologici Societatis Verbi Divini
SJT	*Scottish Journal of Theology*
SNTSMS	Society for New Testament Studies Monograph Series
SVTQ	*St. Vladimir's Theological Quarterly*

ThStud	*Theological Studies*
TNT	*Theology of the New Testament* (ch. 11)
TPINTC	Trinity Press International New Testament Commentaries
WLS	*What Luther Says: An Anthology* (ch. 7)
WTJ	*Westminster Theological Journal*
WUNT	Wissenshaftliche Untersuchungen zum Neuen Testament
YSR	Yale Studies in Religion
ZNW	*Zeitschrift für die neutestamentliche Wissenschaft*

INTRODUCTION

When Christians speak of salvation, they tell a story. It is a story that stretches from even before the creation of the world to its final redemption, when the plan of salvation conceived by God from eternity is to come to fulfillment. While God's dealings of old with God's chosen people, Israel, play an important role in this story, ultimately it revolves around Jesus Christ and his death on the cross.

Yet, because over the centuries this story has been told in many different ways, we can also properly speak in the plural of Christian *stories* of salvation or redemption. These stories differ from one another in many respects. They define salvation in different ways, as well as the problem or plight from which we must be saved. They present a variety of interpretations of human history, generally beginning with a particular understanding of God's original intention in creation and ending with some vision regarding the "last things," that is, eschatology. What particularly distinguishes these stories of redemption from one another, however, is the way Christ and the cross are understood: while all Christians agree that Jesus' life, death, and resurrection "save" human beings in some sense, there are many different answers to the question of precisely *how* these events do so.

Related to this central question are many others. Christian thinkers have traditionally claimed that Jesus' coming and death on the cross were *necessary* for our salvation; but *why* could we be saved in no other way? Does Christ's work consist primarily of procuring divine forgiveness so as to save us from the *guilt* of sin, or is it aimed mainly at our *transformation* and deliverance from the *power* of sin? Do Christ's life, death, and resurrection in themselves "effect" some change in our human condition or in our relation to God, perhaps by making atonement for our sins or liberating us from the evil powers that oppress us and hold us in bondage? It has been common for Christian theologians to make a distinction between an "objective" salvation, involving the redemption of *the whole world* by Christ and his death, and the "subjective" appropriation of this salvation by individuals through faith. If we speak of an objective salvation, can we say that *all people* have been saved by Christ in some way, or is salvation limited only to those who respond in faith to what he has done? If a subjective response of faith is deemed necessary for salvation, is that faith sufficient in itself, or is something else also required, such as a life of love and obedience to God's will? Is our salvation a work of God alone from beginning to end, or does it depend in some way

1

on what *we* do as well? The different views regarding Christ's saving work also reflect different understandings of God. For example, while all Christians agree that God is love, some affirm that God also reacts with wrath toward our sin and must punish it, in contrast to others who reject the notion of a wrathful God from whom we must be saved.

Although human salvation is associated particularly with Christ's incarnation, life, death, and resurrection, it is also regarded as depending in some way on the work of the Holy Spirit as well as on the fellowship and ministry of the church, where the saving word is proclaimed and lived out. The sacraments of baptism and the Lord's Supper, or Eucharist, are also considered important for salvation. Yet the ways the Holy Spirit, the church, the word of God, and the sacraments are believed to contribute to our salvation tend to vary according to the understanding of the work of Christ adopted.

In the following pages, we will look at thirteen different interpretations of the Christian story of redemption revolving around Jesus Christ and his death on the cross. This work is intended not as a comprehensive treatment of the doctrine of salvation or the atonement but merely as a survey of the thought of several figures who have strongly influenced how salvation in Christ has been understood by Christians past and present. These thirteen figures have been chosen for consideration not because their work has had a greater impact on Christian thought than that of all others—indeed, many other figures have influenced equally, if not more so, the way Christians have understood Christ's saving work—but because together they offer us a rich variety of very different perspectives on the subject.

The objective here is not to present a general summary of the theological thought of each of the figures considered but only to examine the ways each one responds to the questions raised above concerning Christ and salvation. While it is important to take into account the scholarly discussion regarding their writings, an effort has been made to let all of these figures speak for themselves in their own words as much as possible. At the end of each chapter, the ideas of the figure under consideration are subjected to a brief evaluation. It must be observed, however, that this is a difficult task, given that Christians of different backgrounds and tendencies have reacted in conflicting ways to the ideas associated with each figure; what some consider to be virtues and strengths in the thought of any particular figure are often regarded by others as defects or weaknesses. The work ends with a brief conclusion that brings together its main arguments.

Among the criticisms that many today would make of all the figures considered—except the last one, Rosemary Radford Ruether—is that they use masculine pronouns to refer to both God and humanity, or "man." Many Christians today consider such a usage sexist, in that it contributes to the exclusion and oppression of women. To speak consistently of God as a male, a "he" but never a "she," and to use words such as *man, mankind,* and *men* to refer to people of both sexes, makes the male normative and provides a basis for justifying the domination of males over females. For this reason, throughout this work, the noninclusive language employed to refer to human beings in the English translations of the writings of the figures considered will be changed into gender-inclusive language. Of course, while this may help promote greater gender-inclusivity, it can also obscure the fact that the figures considered actually *do* regard the male as normative and thus can result in a slightly distorted representation of their thought. Several of these figures, however, use the word *man* in a special sense to refer simultaneously to one man in particular, to human beings collectively, to the human nature shared by all people, and to an abstract concept of humanity. Because this use of the word *man* is central to their understanding of salvation, in these cases, rather than replacing *man* with something more gender-inclusive, it will be placed in quotation marks ("man") so as to indicate that it is being used in this special sense. Though some may find it disagreeable, masculine pronouns will be used to refer to God throughout most of this work in accordance with the usage of the figures considered, simply because to attempt to change this would make it impossible to represent their thought faithfully and would result in a style that most readers would find somewhat laborious. Hopefully, however, the last chapter will make up for this by serving as a critique of the previous twelve chapters in this regard.

Finally, it is important to stress that the objective of this book is primarily *descriptive* rather than *prescriptive*. In other words, it does not attempt to argue in favor of any of the figures considered over against the others, so as to conclude that the ideas of one or another are "right," in contrast to the "erroneous" ideas of others. Instead, the main purpose here is to present as objectively as possible a wide variety of understandings of the Christian story of redemption so that the readers may grasp more fully the many different ways Christians have spoken of salvation in Christ. By gaining a deeper understanding of the many problems, questions, and issues involved, it is hoped that the readers may be enabled to develop their own views on the subject more clearly while at the same time gaining a greater appreciation of views that differ from their own as well as the difficulties inherent to all of these views.

CHAPTER 1

Isaiah and the Redemption of Israel

According to Christians, the story of salvation through Jesus Christ began long before his birth in Bethlehem. That story was seen as the continuation and fulfillment of a story that the people of Israel had been telling for centuries, found in the Hebrew Scriptures, which Christians have called the "Old Testament"; and outside of the Psalms, no Old Testament book is alluded to more frequently in the New Testament than the book of the prophet Isaiah, where all of the basic elements of the story of salvation told in ancient Israel can be found.

The book of Isaiah was named after the prophet "son of Amoz" (Isa 1:1), who was active in Jerusalem and Judah toward the end of the eighth century BCE; he is mentioned several times in the book as well as elsewhere in the Old Testament. However, it is widely recognized that parts of the book, most notably chapters 40–66, were written at least a couple of centuries later, since they speak to the situation of the Israelites living in exile in Babylonia during the sixth century BCE (chapters 40–55) and those who had returned from the exile after the Babylonian Empire was subjected to the Persian king Cyrus in the year 539 BCE (chapters 56–66).[1] While it is not clear whether an individual or a group or school edited the book and put it into its present form, the fact that it now comprises a single work means that we can still speak of "Isaiah" as the implied author, referring not to the eighth-century prophet but to the person or persons who concluded the editorial process.[2] What concerns us here is the story of redemption that can be discerned from the book as it now stands, rather than the various theologies and ideas that can be identified in the different stages of its redaction.

Israel's Sin

The book of Isaiah begins not with words of hope, consolation, or compassion but with a harsh rebuke of the people as well as a call to repentance:

Hear, O heavens, and listen, O earth; for the LORD has spoken: I reared children and brought them up, but they have rebelled against me. The ox knows its owner, and the donkey its master's crib; but Israel does not know, my people do not understand. Ah, sinful nation, people laden with iniquity, offspring who do evil, children who deal corruptly, who have forsaken the LORD, who have despised the Holy One of Israel, who are utterly estranged! . . . Wash yourselves; make yourselves clean; remove the evil of your doings from before my eyes; cease to do evil, learn to do good; seek justice, rescue the oppressed, defend the orphan, plead for the widow. . . . How the faithful city has become a whore! She that was full of justice, righteousness lodged in her—but now murderers! Your silver has become dross, your wine is mixed with water. Your princes are rebels and companions of thieves. Everyone loves a bribe and runs after gifts. They do not defend the orphan, and the widow's cause does not come before them. (1:2-4, 16-17, 21-23)

Here we see what Israel's sin consists of: injustice, oppression, and a lack of concern for those in need. These same ideas are repeated throughout Isaiah, where the people are accused of "grinding the face of the poor" (3:15), taking bribes and depriving the innocent of their rights (5:23), speaking lies, and "conceiving mischief and begetting iniquity" (59:4); "their feet run to evil, and they rush to shed innocent blood; their thoughts are thoughts of iniquity, desolation and destruction" (59:7). As Rainer Albertz has observed, these accusations are leveled primarily at the upper classes rather than at the oppressed themselves: "The LORD enters into judgment with the elders and princes of his people: It is you who have devoured the vineyard; the spoil of the poor is in your houses" (3:14).[3] At times, however, the people as a whole are accused of sin: "The LORD did not have pity on their young people, or compassion on their orphans and widows; for everyone was godless and an evildoer, and every mouth spoke folly" (9:17).

Closely tied to the sin of injustice is that of idolatry. "Their land is filled with idols; they bow down to the work of their hands, to what their own fingers have made" (2:8). While the relationship between injustice and idolatry may not seem immediately apparent, the two are closely connected. The law given by God to Israel contained many commandments aimed at promoting justice and providing for those in need. According to Isaiah, however, when the people abandon the Lord to serve other gods of their own making, they create for themselves their own religion characterized by cruel and oppressive practices. When they offer up sacrifices to their gods on the mountains and place statues of those gods in their homes, they make the righteous perish, "burn with lust," and even slaughter their own children as sacrificial offerings (57:1-9). Turning away from God thus involves turning away from God's law as well and replacing it with their own oppressive laws: "Ah, you who make iniquitous decrees, who write oppressive statutes, to turn aside the needy from justice and to rob the poor of my people of their right, that widows may be your spoil, and that you may make the orphans your prey!" (10:1-2).

In Isaiah, therefore, *sin* is understood in terms of abandoning and rebelling against God so as to set up one's own gods, and consequently disobeying God's commandments so as to practice evil and injustice; this involves forgetting and abandoning God (17:10; 43:22; 51:13). Sin is also a lack of trust in God: when threatened by enemies, the king and the people are rebuked by the prophet for putting their trust in other gods or in other people or nations, rather than in the Lord alone (30:1-17). Finally, God's people sin in that they "do not understand" (1:3); thus sin is not just a problem of the will but also a lack of knowledge on their part.

God's Love and God's Wrath

Throughout the book of Isaiah, we repeatedly encounter expressions of God's wrath at Israel's sin. When the people suffered from hunger, war, and other disasters, they often believed that God was angry at them: "Therefore the anger of the LORD was kindled against his people, and he stretched out his hand against them and struck them; the mountains quaked, and their corpses were like refuse in the streets" (5:25). Thus "devastation and destruction, famine and sword" were attributed to "the wrath of the LORD" and his "rebuke" (51:17-20).

According to Isaiah, a primary way that God punished Israel's sin was to send other nations, such as Assyria and Babylonia, to oppress the people. In 721 BCE, the Assyrians destroyed the northern kingdom of Israel and then ravaged the countryside of Judah before laying siege to Jerusalem. Later, in 586 BCE, the

Jehu, King of Israel, prostrating himself before King Shalmaneser III of Assyria (British Museum, London). Isaiah, like the Old Testament in general, interpreted Israel's subjection to foreign powers as divine punishment for Israel's sins.
Photo © Erich Lessing / Art Resource, NY.

Babylonians laid waste to Judah and Jerusalem, taking many of the leaders and people into exile in Babylon. These events were interpreted by the people of Israel and their prophets as divine punishment for their sins on the basis of their belief that God blesses and saves those who do good and obey God's commandments but punishes and destroys those who do evil. This belief is reflected in Isaiah's words to Israel in 1:19-20: "If you are willing and obedient, you shall eat the good of the land; but if you refuse and rebel, you shall be devoured by the sword; for the mouth of the LORD has spoken."

Yet, alongside the frequent expressions of intense anger on God's part and the graphic descriptions of the death and destruction endured by the inhabitants of Judah and Jerusalem as divine punishment, we also find numerous expressions of God's immense love and deep compassion for Israel. At times, these are very tender and moving, such as when God is spoken of as Israel's father (64:8), husband, and mother.[4] "You shall be called My Delight Is in Her, and your land Married; for the LORD delights in you, and your land shall be married. For as a young man marries a young woman, so shall your builder marry you, and as the bridegroom rejoices over the bride, so shall your God rejoice over you" (62:4-5; cf. 54:5). "As a mother comforts her child, so I will comfort you" (66:13). "But Zion said, 'The LORD has forsaken me, my Lord has forgotten me.' Can a woman forget her nursing child, or show no compassion for the child of her womb? Even these may forget, yet I will not forget you" (49:14-15).

It may seem surprising to encounter such expressions of intense anger and moving love alongside each other, often in the same immediate context. Yet, while these sentiments may seem to contradict each other, in the thought of Isaiah, God's wrath is rooted in God's love and mercy. This is true particularly with regard to God's anger at oppression: God's love for the poor, weak, needy, and oppressed moves God to react angrily when they are treated unjustly, so as to defend them and save them from their oppressors. God's wrath is also seen as fulfilling another loving purpose, that of purifying his people from their sin: rather than simply destroying or abandoning them when they sin, God attempts to correct the people by sending various afflictions upon them so as to bring them to see their evil ways and repent of their sin, just as a parent might do with a wayward child.[5] As precious metals are purified through fire, the same is to happen to Israel and Jerusalem, so that they may become righteous and faithful once more (1:24-26). "Whoever is left in Zion and remains in Jerusalem will be called holy . . . once the Lord has washed away the filth of the daughters of Zion and cleansed the bloodstains of Jerusalem from its midst by a spirit of judgment and by a spirit of burning" (4:3-4).

However, at times even when God sends suffering on the people, they refuse to repent and change: "Because of their wicked covetousness I was angry; I struck them, I hid and was angry; but they kept turning back to their own ways" (57:17). When this happens, if God's love will not let him abandon them, his only option is to chastise them further or else destroy a portion of them so that the few who remain are purified, as a righteous remnant (6:11-13; 9:8-16; 10:20-22).

According to Isaiah, because of God's love for his people, God wishes that it were not necessary to punish them, since his true desire is only to bless them. Isaiah presents God asking the people, "Why do you seek further beatings? Why do you continue to rebel?" (1:5), and elsewhere writes:

> Thus says the LORD, your Redeemer, the Holy One of Israel: I am the LORD your God, who teaches you for your own good, who leads you in the way you should go. O that you had paid attention to my commandments! Then your prosperity would have been like a river, and your success like the waves of the sea; your offspring would have been like the sand, and your descendants like its grains; their name would never be cut off or destroyed from before me. (48:17-19)

But why can God not simply forgive the people every time they sin, without punishing them? Implicit in some of these passages is the idea that there is an *intrinsic* relationship between sin and its consequences—that is, *in and of itself human sin brings pain, suffering, and other negative consequences upon people*. This stands in contrast to the idea of an *extrinsic* relationship between sin and its consequences; according to this idea, the negative consequences of sin do not follow immediately or naturally from it but are instead caused by God as punishment. The difference between these two ideas can be explained with the help of an illustration. If a mother tells her daughter not to put her hand into a flame but the girl does so and as a result is burned, there is an *intrinsic* relation between the girl's act and the suffering she endures; the pain she feels is the natural and inevitable consequence of touching the flame. However, if the girl puts her hand near the flame (without getting burned) and the mother sees it and consequently punishes her in some way, such as by scolding her or taking away some privilege, the relation between the girl's act and the suffering she endures as a result of the punishment she receives is an *extrinsic* one, since it is something brought about not by the act itself but by her mother, who elects to discipline her daughter to teach her not to do things that might harm her.

In Isaiah, on occasion, the idea of an intrinsic relation between the people's sins and the suffering they endure is hinted at; for example, in 65:2, God says that the people "walk in a way that is not good, following their own devices." In this case, God wants the people to stop doing what is not good for them; when God tells them to abandon their evil ways, he is warning them of the natural and inevitable consequences of their sinful actions, rather than threatening to punish them. However, the latter idea seems to be much more prevalent in Isaiah and the rest of the Hebrew Scriptures: when Israel suffers, it is not merely because the people's sins in themselves have negative consequences, both for themselves and for other people whom God also loves, but because God is punishing them in order to correct, discipline, and purify them. Nevertheless, the idea of divine punishment and correction makes sense only if an *intrinsic* relation between sin and its consequences is maintained at the same time: whether things go well or poorly for Israel does not depend solely on God or God's response to what Israel does; rather, God calls the people to repent and disciplines them, not for *God's own* sake but for *theirs*, since their sinful actions harm themselves and others whom God loves, such as the weak and needy.

The Salvation of Israel

The idea that God saves or redeems Israel is repeated frequently throughout Isaiah. This salvation is usually understood in collective terms: it has to do not with isolated individuals but with the people *as a whole*. Salvation involves experiencing God's blessings of abundance, well-being, freedom, peace, and joy, as well as being free from excessive heat, hunger, thirst, slavery, sadness, and sighing (49:8-10; 51:11). "He will give rain for the seed with which you sow the ground, and grain, the produce of the ground, which will be rich and plenteous. On that day your cattle will graze in broad pastures; and the oxen and donkeys that till the ground will eat silage, which has been winnowed with shovel and fork. On every lofty mountain and every high hill there will be brooks running with water" (30:23-25). Salvation also involves deliverance from enemies who oppress the people. Isaiah claims not only that Israel will be delivered from its subjection to other nations but that those nations and their kings will in turn be subjected in servitude to Israel, so that Israel becomes great in the eyes of all the earth (14:1-2; 60:10-16).

Yet is this salvation unconditional, or does it depend on what Israel does? On the basis of what we have seen previously, there is a *condition* for Israel to be saved, namely, that the people obey God's will: if they practice justice and righteousness and do good as God commands, they will enjoy God's blessing of salvation; but if they do evil and disobey God, they will face hardships, oppression, destruction, and death.[6] In many passages, however, salvation is spoken of as *unconditional*: no matter what Israel does, God will ultimately have mercy on his people and save them. These promises of salvation are rooted in God's love for Israel: his steadfast love and compassion will not let him utterly destroy them or abandon them definitively; nor will it let his wrath at their sins endure forever (49:14-15; 54:7-10; 57:16-19). The idea of forgiveness should be understood against this background: God forgives the people's sins when he saves them from the plights they suffer. While at times this forgiveness is seen as depending on Israel's behavior, elsewhere it appears unconditional. After punishing his people, God will forgive them their sins, not because of any merit of theirs but out of sheer grace: "I, I am he who blots out your transgressions for my own sake, and I will not remember your sins" (43:25; cf. 44:21-22).

At times, Israel's salvation and forgiveness are tied to sacrificial offerings to God. Isaiah repeatedly stresses, however, that in themselves these sacrifices and other similar rituals do not obtain divine forgiveness and acceptance, since if Israel continues to practice injustice and idolatry, God refuses to accept Israel's offerings, saying that they are a "burden" to him and that he is "weary of bearing them" (1:10-18; cf. 29:13-21; 58:5-7). This does not mean that Isaiah rejected outright the worship of God through sacrificial offerings and other practices, such as fasting.[7] In fact, a number of passages from Isaiah make it clear that Israel's sacrifices are pleasing to God, as long as the people are committed to doing God's will and sincerely repent when they sin (19:21; 43:23; 56:7). What must be stressed, however, is that ultimately what takes away sin is not sacrificial offerings themselves but doing what God commands, putting away idols, and serving him alone as God by keeping his ordinances: "Therefore by this the guilt of Jacob will be expiated, and this will be the full fruit of the removal of his sin: when he makes all the stones of the altars like chalkstones crushed to pieces, no sacred poles or incense altars will remain standing" (27:9). Only when Israel turns to God in justice and obedience will God accept their sacrifices and worship and respond favorably to the prayers for forgiveness and blessing they offer up to him together with those sacrifices.

Yet, while God *demands* from Israel a change of heart reflected in a life of obedience to his commandments, God also promises to graciously *give* them this change by bringing it about in them himself. God does this in part by correcting and disciplining the people, so as to purify a righteous remnant, and by teaching them his ways through those whom he sends. However, God also does this by giving them his Spirit so as to transform them internally: "I will pour my spirit upon your descendants, and my blessing on your offspring" (44:3); "this is my covenant with them, says the LORD: my spirit that is upon you, and my words that I have put in your mouth, shall not depart out of your mouth, or out of the mouths of your children, or out of the mouths of your children's children, says the LORD, from now on and forever" (59:21; cf. 29:24; 32:3-4).[8]

These passages, as well as a majority of the other passages in Isaiah that speak of salvation, use the future tense: God *will save* Israel. Yet this raises the question of whether salvation is understood as something to take place *in history* or *beyond history*. At times, it appears that salvation merely has to do with an improved situation for Israel *within history*: the people will dwell in peace and security in Jerusalem (or Zion) and Judah, enjoy life, and have all that they need. Even though life will be prolonged, for example, people will still ultimately die (65:20). At other times, however, it appears that salvation has to do with a totally new age, one radically different from the present: the bodies of the dead will be raised (26:19), people will be healed from all of their illnesses, all violence, war, and bloodshed will disappear (2:4), and nature itself will be transformed:

> The wolf shall live with the lamb, the leopard shall lie down with the kid, the calf and the lion and the fatling together, and a little child shall lead them. The cow and the bear shall graze, their young shall lie down together; and the lion shall eat straw like the ox. The nursing child shall play over the hole of the asp, and the weaned child shall put its hand on the adder's den. They will not hurt or destroy on all my holy mountain; for the earth will be full of the knowledge of the LORD as the waters cover the sea. (11:6-9)

The wilderness and the dry land shall be glad, the desert shall rejoice and blossom; like the crocus it shall blossom abundantly, and rejoice with joy and singing. . . . Then the eyes of the blind shall be opened, and the ears of the deaf unstopped; then the lame shall leap like a deer, and the tongue of the speechless sing for joy. For waters shall break forth in the wilderness, and streams in the desert; the burning sand shall become a pool, and the thirsty ground springs of water; the haunt of jackals shall become a swamp, the grass shall become reeds and rushes. (35:1-2, 5-7)

Elsewhere, Isaiah speaks of God creating "new heavens and a new earth," where there will be no more "sound of weeping" or "cry of distress," and where infants will all live a long, full life (65:17-25). But is all of this merely metaphorical language, or is it to be taken literally? Does Isaiah conceive of salvation in terms of the creation of a totally new world, radically different from the present one, or simply as the arrival of a time of greater prosperity and well-being within history? However these questions are answered, it should be stressed that for Isaiah and his contemporaries, the future hope still revolved around Jerusalem, or Zion, and the promised land: the idea is not that God's people will "go to heaven" to dwell in some spiritual, otherworldly paradise after they die but, rather, that they will live on earth in the land given them by God. Salvation, therefore, is conceived of in *corporal* and *material* terms, not just in spiritual terms: in the coming new age, people will still dwell in Jerusalem, live in houses, plant vineyards, and eat their fruit, thus enjoying physical pleasures along with spiritual well-being.

Israel, the Nations, and the Divine Plan

In accordance with the rest of the Hebrew Scriptures, the book of Isaiah affirms that God has chosen Israel from among all the nations of the earth to be his special people and to be the recipient of his blessings of salvation:

But you, Israel, my servant, Jacob, whom I have chosen, the offspring of Abraham, my friend; you whom I took from the ends of the earth, and called from its farthest corners, saying to you, "You are my servant, I have chosen you and not cast you off"; do not fear, for I am with you, do not be afraid, for I am your God; I will strengthen you, I will help you, I will uphold you with my victorious right hand. Yes, all who are incensed against you shall be ashamed and disgraced; those who strive against you shall be as nothing and shall perish. (41:8-11)

This passage and others contain several key ideas with regard to Isaiah's view of the relation between Israel and the nations. On the one hand, Israel repeatedly experienced suffering and oppression at the hands of other nations, such as Assyria, Edom, and Babylonia. While God is said to have used these nations for his purposes, God also promised ultimately to deliver Israel from their power and to destroy these nations for their own sins. Thus, for example, after calling Assyria the "rod of God's anger" chosen to punish sinful Israel (10:5-6), Isaiah

The Peaceable Kingdom (Edward Hicks, 19th century). Isaiah conceived of salvation as a new age in which peace and harmony would reign in nature: carnivorous beasts such as lions, leopards, and bears would feed instead on plants and coexist peacefully with lambs and calves, and all would be led by a little child (Isa 11:6-9; 65:19-25).
Photo © Art Resource, NY.

adds, "When the Lord has finished all his work on Mount Zion and on Jerusalem, he will punish the arrogant boasting of the king of Assyria and his haughty pride" (10:12). Elsewhere, God promises to take vengeance upon Israel's enemies for their oppressive ways and their mistreatment of Israel: "But thus says the Lord: Even the captives of the mighty shall be taken, and the prey of the tyrant be rescued; for I will contend with those who contend with you, and I will save your children. I will make your oppressors eat their own flesh, and they shall be drunk with their own blood as with wine. Then all flesh shall know that I am the Lord your Savior, and your Redeemer, the Mighty One of Jacob" (49:25-26).

On the other hand, however, Isaiah contains many promises of salvation with regard to the nations. In this respect, as indicated in the passage from 41:8-11 just cited, God chose Israel not merely for blessing and salvation but to be his "servant"; in fact, in virtually every passage where Israel's election is mentioned, the idea that Israel is to serve God is also stressed. Israel is to be "a light to the nations" and a "covenant" to them, as well as God's "witnesses" (42:6; 43:10). "Nations shall come to your light, and kings to the brightness of your dawn" (60:3). Furthermore, as the passage from 49:25-26 just quoted makes clear, one of God's ultimate objectives in pouring out his wrath on the nations is that they might learn that he alone is the all-powerful God and thus come to know and serve him, as Israel is to do.

Isaiah therefore conceives of a coming time of salvation in which people from all the nations will share in the salvation of Jerusalem and Israel.[9] They will flock to Jerusalem to worship in the temple there and will come to obey the law given by God to Israel: "In days to come the mountain of the LORD's house shall be established as the highest of the mountains, and shall be raised above the hills; all the nations shall stream to it. Many peoples shall come and say, 'Come, let us go up to the mountain of the LORD, to the house of the God of Jacob; that he may teach us his ways and that we may walk in his paths.' For out of Zion shall go forth instruction, and the word of the LORD from Jerusalem" (2:2-3; cf. 56:6-7). This salvation is spoken of as an eschatological banquet, in which both Israel and the nations will share "a feast of rich food" and "well-aged wines" and "the tears from all faces" shall be wiped away (25:6-8). Isaiah even speaks, in surprising fashion, of Assyria and Egypt as God's beloved chosen people, together with Israel: after "striking and healing" Egypt, God will "listen to their supplications," and then "Israel will be the third with Egypt and Assyria, a blessing in the midst of the earth, whom the LORD of hosts has blessed, saying, 'Blessed be Egypt my people, and Assyria the work of my hands, and Israel my heritage'" (19:22, 24-25).

In Isaiah, therefore, the idea that God will punish but then bless and save is applied not only to Israel but to all the nations. Nevertheless, God's promises of blessing still revolve around Israel and Jerusalem;[10] other peoples will be saved to the extent that they share in the salvation of Israel. For this reason, it is important that God purify and redeem Israel, because through them and the witness they are to give, he will bring redemption to other nations as well.

All of this means that, for Isaiah, God is the sovereign Lord in control of history; ultimately, God will accomplish his purposes and plans, no matter what either Israel or the nations do. Isaiah's affirmations that God is the Creator of all underscore this idea;[11] all people and all things are subject to him. In the case of human beings, God is like the potter and they are the clay, which God does with as he sees fit (45:9; 64:8). In fact, when it serves God's purposes, God may even use a prophet like Isaiah to make the people blind and deaf, so that they do not understand and consequently are not healed (6:9-13). While this idea no doubt sounds problematic, the reasoning appears to be that God is tired of the temporary and half-hearted repentance manifested by his people, on account of which he must delay punishing them; thus he desires that they *not* repent so that he may be justified in purifying them through punishment and in this way finally bring about a truly righteous remnant that will no longer turn back to sin.

Isaiah's understanding of God's sovereignty leads him to claim not only that God has the power to bring about either obedience or hardness of heart in his people but that God can also create and cause evil as well as good: "I form light and create darkness. I make peace and I create evil. I the LORD make all these things" (45:7).[12] In Isaiah, we find no allusions to any evil power, such as the devil or demonic spirits, inducing people to sin or bringing harm on them; evil and suffering are brought about either by human beings themselves through their actions or by God.

Of course, all of this raises once more the question of whether or not Israel's salvation depends on the people: if ultimately it is God who brings about in the people either the righteousness he requires or the sin he punishes, it would appear that, like the inanimate clay in the hands of the potter, human beings have no say in their salvation or condemnation. This tension is not resolved in Isaiah, who maintains the absolute sovereignty of God as the potter while nevertheless insisting that salvation depends on human beings' responding properly to God's love, mercy, and grace. Yet all of this must be seen in the context of the divine plan of which Isaiah repeatedly speaks, which involves the establishment of a righteous remnant of Israel so that it may serve as a light to draw other nations to God in order that they too may be saved: God's plan "has as its goal his lordship over all the earth through the realization of his holiness and dominion."[13] For Isaiah, as the creator of all things, God is in total control of history so that all of his purposes may be accomplished.

Savior Figures

According to Isaiah, in order to save his people, God raises up a number of savior figures. Perhaps the most important of these are the kings, including not only the kings of Israel or Judah, such as Hezekiah and other descendants of King David, but foreign kings, such as the Persian king Cyrus, who allowed those in exile in Babylon to return to Judah and rebuild Jerusalem and the temple; Isaiah even calls Cyrus God's "anointed" ("messiah" in Hebrew), which was a kingly title (44:28—45:7). In a number of passages from the first part of the book of Isaiah, God promises to raise up a king who will deliver his people from their oppressors and establish justice, equity, and peace in the land:[14]

> For a child has been born for us, a son given to us; authority rests upon his shoulders; and he is named Wonderful Counselor, Mighty God, Everlasting Father, Prince of Peace. His authority shall grow continually, and there shall be endless peace for the throne of David and his kingdom. He will establish and uphold it with justice and with righteousness from this time onward and forevermore. (9:6-7)

> A shoot shall come out from the stump of Jesse, and a branch shall grow out of his roots. The spirit of the LORD shall rest on him, the spirit of wisdom and understanding, the spirit of counsel and might, the spirit of knowledge and the fear of the LORD. His delight shall be in the fear of the LORD. He shall not judge by what his eyes see, or decide by what his ears hear; but with righteousness he shall judge the poor, and decide with equity for the meek of the earth; he shall strike the earth with the rod of his mouth, and with the breath of his lips he shall kill the wicked. (11:1-4; cf. 16:4-5)

Although these passages probably referred to specific kings in Israel's history, the things they promised never came fully to fruition under any king in the years before or after the Babylonian exile. Because these promises apparently remained unfulfilled, like many of the other promises of salvation and blessing found in Isaiah, they eventually came to be interpreted as referring to a future hope: God would send a Messiah figure or king descended from David to bring about the glorious new age he had promised.

The second part of the book of Isaiah speaks of another savior figure, who is simply called God's "servant." While at times the people of Israel or Judah as a whole are called God's servant, chosen by him to carry out his will, in several passages (often called the "servant songs," 42:1-4; 49:1-6; 50:4-9; 52:13—53:12), this servant is spoken of as an individual. His task is to bring Israel and the nations back to God. God promises to pour out his Spirit upon him, so that he will "faithfully bring forth justice" both for Israel and the nations throughout the world (42:1-4). Although one or more of these passages may originally have referred to a kingly figure (such as Cyrus),[15] the "servant" spoken of appears primarily to be a prophet, particularly since he speaks to others on behalf of God to bring them back to him and because he teaches the people (42:4; 49:5-6; 50:4; 53:11). A similar figure is spoken of in 61:1-11; as in 42:1, it is said there that God's Spirit will be poured out upon him and that, as God's anointed, he will be sent "to bring good news to the oppressed, to bind up the brokenhearted, to proclaim liberty to the captives, and release to the prisoners; to proclaim the year of the LORD's favor."

Significantly, a couple of these passages speak of the *suffering* of the servant. In 50:6, for example, the servant says: "I gave my back to those who struck me, and my cheeks to those who pulled out the beard; I did not hide my face from insult and spitting." The passage that particularly underscores the servant's suffering, however, is 52:13—53:12. There, the servant is described in the past tense as a "man of suffering" who was "despised and rejected" and "has borne our infirmities" as if stricken and afflicted by God; "he was wounded for our transgressions, crushed for our iniquities; upon him was the punishment that made us whole, and by his bruises we are healed." The song goes on to tell how he was silent in his afflictions like a lamb led to the slaughter and how he "poured out himself to death," making his life an "offering for sin" so as to bear the sin and iniquities of many and to make intercession for the transgressors.

This is one of the most difficult, complex, and controversial passages in the Hebrew Scriptures and has been understood in many different ways by both Jewish and Christian interpreters. While we can therefore hardly expect to do justice to it in this brief overview of Isaiah, it is important to examine the relationship that the passage establishes between the servant's suffering and the people's salvation. As noted previously, in the thought of Isaiah and much of the Hebrew Scriptures, suffering and oppression are sent by God as punishment for sin. In this case, however, rather than inflicting suffering upon the people themselves for their sins, God afflicts the servant, who unjustly suffers various calamities and, ultimately, death.[16] The innocent servant voluntarily endures these sufferings and the injustices done to him, offering himself up sacrificially for the people's sins and interceding to God for the wrongdoers. As a result, he is ultimately vindicated and exalted by God, and in the end many are made righteous.

Yet exactly how do the servant's sufferings bring wholeness, healing, and righteousness to others? While this is not entirely clear from the passage, it is important to stress once more that, like the rest of the Hebrew Scriptures, Isaiah repeatedly maintains that when God sends suffering upon people on account of their sins, his purpose is to purify them, bring them back to him in righteousness and obedience, and establish a righteous remnant. According to this idea, God punishes sin not *for his own sake* (that is, to satisfy some inner need of his own that sin be punished so that his own justice may be upheld) but *for the sake of his people* (that is, in order to discipline and correct them). Thus, in this passage, it is not the servant's sufferings and death *in themselves* that lead to the people's being made whole and healed and becoming righteous. As in the rest of Isaiah and the Hebrew Scriptures, the condition for people to be saved is not that they or some substitute (such as the "servant" or a sacrificial victim) be punished for their sins but that they turn back to God in obedience to live according to his will.

When read in the context of these beliefs, then, the sufferings and death inflicted by evildoers on the servant in accordance with God's will must be seen as resulting in salvation for others in that *they are thereby brought back to God*. Christoph Schroeder, among others, notes that the passage speaks of the impact that the servant's suffering has on the onlookers when they see that the servant has suffered unjustly on account of their sins rather than for his own: "They will confess their sins and this will ultimately create reconciliation among them."[17]

Evaluation

In many respects, Isaiah's teaching regarding salvation is grandiose and glorious. Particularly moving are the images he uses to describe the coming age of redemption as well as God's deep love and compassion for Israel; such images have inspired writers and artists from biblical times to the present.[18] Other aspects of Isaiah's thought, such as his insistence that there can be no worship that is pleasing to God unless it is accompanied by the practice of justice, mercy, and care for those in greatest need, are also timely and pertinent today.

However, Isaiah's teaching on salvation also raises many questions and problems. Perhaps the most serious of these has to do with the idea that God punishes sin by sending suffering, oppression, and even death upon people. This seems to lead to the view that when people suffer, it is because God is punishing or disciplining them for their sins; conversely, when things go well for people, it is thought that God is blessing them for having been obedient to his will. When a tragic event, such as the spread of AIDS or the mass extermination of Jews, Gypsies, Poles, homosexuals, and others at the hands of the Nazi authorities during the Second World War, is interpreted on the basis of such ideas, it is claimed that those who suffer are being punished by God for their sins or, perhaps, that God is attempting to discipline and purify them. Those who torture and kill others, as the Nazi authorities did, are also then viewed as God's instrument for punishing the guilty for their sins, just as Isaiah regarded the Assyrians as God's instrument for punishing sinful Israel. Most people today would find such ideas not only unacceptable but repulsive.

Equally problematic for modern thought is Isaiah's teaching that God's election and salvation have to do with entire nations. Such a claim has commonly been used to justify many injustices, including the oppression and domination of certain nations and peoples by others, as if God were on the side of the rich and powerful nations and were blessing them, perhaps as a reward for their piety, goodness, and righteousness. Isaiah's discussion regarding salvation also seems to leave open the questions of whether salvation is a work of God alone or of human beings as well, and whether it involves the creation of a radically new world *beyond* human history as we now know it or merely the arrival of a better world *within* history, perhaps as the result of a period of gradual progress and improvement in human living conditions. Thus, while there is no doubt much to be admired about Isaiah's understanding of salvation, it also involves a number of problems and tensions that are not easily resolved.

CHAPTER 2

The Divine Plan of Salvation in the Writings of Luke

Tradition ascribes the Third Gospel and the book of the Acts of the Apostles to Luke, "the beloved physician" whose name appears in several of the letters attributed to St. Paul (Col 4:14; 2 Tim 4:11; Phlm 24). While some scholars have questioned the veracity of that tradition, most agree that the Gospel and Acts are the work of a single author, probably a gentile Christian, who wrote during the second half of the first century CE.[1] Precisely because Luke adds a second volume to his Gospel, namely, the book of Acts, no other New Testament author can be said to give a more orderly and complete account of the story told by the first Christians regarding salvation in Jesus Christ.

Jesus' Birth and Ministry

Luke begins his story with a narration of events surrounding the births of John the Baptist and Jesus. The main point stressed throughout this narrative is that Jesus is the one sent by God to bring about the promises of salvation made to Israel, such as the ones mentioned in the book of Isaiah considered in the previous chapter. First Zechariah and then Mary sing a song of rejoicing over Jesus' coming as a mighty savior to redeem Israel and rescue them from their enemies in fulfillment of the promises made to Abraham and his descendants (Luke 1:54-55, 68-75), while the angel Gabriel announces to Mary that Jesus will receive "the throne of his ancestor David" and will reign over Israel as king forever (Luke 1:32-33). When Jesus is born, the angels similarly tell the shepherds that "a Savior, who is the Messiah, the Lord," is born to them in the "city of David" (Luke 2:11), and then Simeon rejoices at seeing Jesus the Messiah as an infant, since his coming means that the awaited "consolation of Israel" is at hand (Luke 2:25-35).

Jesus' ministry is preceded by that of John the Baptist, who calls the people to repentance in expectation of the salvation to be brought by Jesus. At the heart of John's message is that in order to participate in the coming salvation, it is not enough to be a descendant of Abraham according to the flesh, that is, a Jew; only those who "bear fruits worthy of repentance" (Luke 3:8) will be saved. In essence, this involves a redefinition of Israel: not all Jewish people belong to the Israel that will be saved, but only those who repent and live according to God's will and who manifest this by being baptized.[2] John also redefines what true obedience to the law consists of: what is necessary is not merely to keep the commandments of the law literally but to share with those in need and avoid practicing any type of injustice (Luke 3:10-14).

After being baptized by John and undergoing temptation in the desert, Jesus begins his ministry in Galilee. From the start, he defines the purpose of his ministry by citing Isaiah's words: "The Spirit of the Lord is upon me, because he has anointed me to bring good news to the poor. He has sent me to proclaim release to the captives and recovery of sight to the blind, to let the oppressed go free, to proclaim the year of the Lord's favor" (Luke 4:18-19). The things to which Jesus dedicates himself in his ministry include healing people from their ailments, casting out demons from the possessed, and teaching people about the coming of God's kingdom. Jesus also chooses disciples, training them and sending them out to carry out the same type of ministry as he does. What Jesus says and does demonstrates that God is with him to bring healing, wholeness, and salvation into the lives of others; thus he is the one chosen by God to save Israel, and many, especially his disciples, come to recognize him as the Messiah (Luke 9:20). In addition to graciously offering that salvation to others, however, he also calls them to repentance, defining this repentance as a new life characterized by loving others and forgiving them, practicing justice and mercy, and sharing with those in need.

What Jesus does and says generates conflict, primarily with the religious leaders. As Jack Kingsbury has shown, at the heart of this conflict is the question of authority.[3] For Luke, Jesus is one who teaches with authority (Luke 4:32), casts out evil spirits with authority (Luke 4:36), and even exercises authority over the winds and the water (Luke 8:25). Many of the religious leaders respond to Jesus' mighty deeds by claiming that his power comes from Satan rather than God (Luke 11:14-20). On a couple of occasions, the religious leaders question Jesus' authority openly, becoming upset when he declares the sins of a paralytic forgiven (Luke 5:18-26) and asking him at the temple by what authority he teaches and performs healings (Luke 20:1-8).

Closely tied to the question of Jesus' authority is his interpretation of the Mosaic law. Jesus says and does a number of things that appear to demonstrate a lack of respect for the Mosaic law, as if he were above that law in some way. In particular, he is accused of violating the Sabbath commandment or of letting his disciples do so (Luke 6:1-11; 13:10-17; 14:1-6). According to Luke, Jesus responds by insisting that he is "Lord of the sabbath" and that he is not in fact violating the Sabbath commandment, since he is doing what is lawful on the Sabbath by saving life and restoring others to wholeness. For his part, Jesus accuses his opponents of violating the law by oppressing others and not practicing justice and mercy (Luke 11:39-46).

Zacchaeus in the Mulberry Tree (Detail from the pulpit of Archbishop Maximian, Museo Arcivescovile, Ravenna, Italy). According to Luke, Jesus' acceptance of "sinners" and tax-collectors such as Zacchaeus generated controversy; Jesus, however, insisted that he had come to "seek out and save the lost" (Luke 19:10) and "to call not the righteous but sinners to repentance" (Luke 5:32).
Photo © Erich Lessing / Art Resource, NY.

At the heart of these controversies are two different ways of interpreting the law. For Jesus, true observance of the law involves practicing the principles underlying the law, such as justice and mercy. What the law really commands is to "do good" and "save life" (Luke 6:9); thus any interpretation of the law that does not fulfill these principles in reality runs contrary to the law or its spirit. In contrast, Jesus' opponents adhere to their tradition in interpreting the law and are particularly concerned about observing carefully the letter of the law. For them, Jesus is one who violates the law and teaches others to do the same.

For this same reason, the religious authorities repeatedly become upset when Jesus has fellowship with men and women whom they consider "sinners" (Luke 5:30; 7:34, 39; 15:2; 19:7). The authorities interpret this openness to people who do not observe the law properly as a lack of concern on Jesus' part for the fulfillment of the law. Yet, once more, because Jesus interprets the law in terms of the need to show God's love and mercy to others, particularly those undeserving of that love, in his mind he is upholding rather than violating the law. In fact, he repeatedly speaks of God's love for those considered "sinners" and tells parables, such as those of the lost coin, the lost sheep, and the prodigal son, to underscore the idea that God is a God of love and mercy who is anxious to accept and forgive sinners who have not kept the law yet repent (Luke 15:1-32).

Jerusalem and the Cross

Luke presents much of Jesus' ministry as taking place on the way to Jerusalem. From chapter 9 of Luke's Gospel, Jesus embarks on the journey to Jerusalem in order to be "taken up" there (Luke 9:51). Immediately, he also begins to tell his disciples what will take place there: "The Son of Man must undergo great suffering, and be rejected by the elders, chief priests, and scribes, and be killed, and on the third day be raised" (Luke 9:22). He repeats words like these throughout the journey, but the disciples do not understand (Luke 9:44-45; 17:25; 18:31-34).

The idea of Jesus' rejection at the hands of the religious authorities and inhabitants of Jerusalem runs throughout the rest of Luke's Gospel (as well as Acts). In Luke 13:31-33, Jesus is told by some Pharisees to go elsewhere because Herod is seeking to kill him; he responds: "Go and tell that fox for me, 'Listen, I am casting out demons and performing cures today and tomorrow, and on the third day I finish my work. Yet today, tomorrow, and the next day I must be on my way, because it is impossible for a prophet to be killed outside of Jerusalem.'" The idea is that Jesus will die like the prophets before him, who were killed by Israel's leaders in their own time (Luke 11:49-51). However, Jesus' words also indicate his commitment to carrying out his ministry to the end: he will not run or hide but will continue his work. In fact, after his glorious entry into Jerusalem, Jesus is presented as continuing to carry on his teaching activity at the temple, undaunted by the threats posed by his enemies (Luke 19:47; 20:1; 21:37; 22:53).

Jesus also foretells his rejection in a couple of parables. In Luke 19:11-27, he tells a parable about a nobleman who is to be crowned king but who is visited by a delegation of his fellow citizens who tell him that they do not want him to rule over them. Then, in Luke 20:9-19, Jesus tells a parable about a man who planted a vineyard and leased it to tenants. When this man repeatedly sent his servants to collect his share of the produce, the wicked tenants mistreated the servants and sent them away empty-handed. Finally, the owner sent his son, but the tenants killed him. Clearly, the idea conveyed by this parable is that Jesus will be killed in the same way that the prophets before him had been killed; like the nobleman and the son of the vineyard owner, Jesus will be rejected by Israel's leaders.[4] Yet, at the end of the parable, Jesus cites Psalm 118:22—"The stone that the builders rejected has become the cornerstone"—to affirm that his rejection will lead to his becoming the foundation of something new.

After Judas arranges to inform the Jewish authorities where and when they can find Jesus without a crowd being around, Jesus celebrates a last supper with his disciples and then goes to the Mount of Olives with several of them, where he is arrested after spending time in prayer. The Jewish council tries Jesus, condemns him for claiming to be the Messiah and God's Son, and hands him over to the Roman procurator Pontius Pilate as a subversive who perverts others with his teaching and is against the emperor. Pilate sends Jesus to King Herod, who in turn sends him back to Pilate. Though Pilate claims to find nothing wrong in him, under intense pressure from the Jewish authorities and the crowd gathered there, he sentences Jesus to death by crucifixion. The crucifixion takes place on Golgotha, outside of Jerusalem, and then Jesus is buried (Luke 22:1—23:56).

Jesus' Exaltation and the Mission to Israel and the World

On the third day after Jesus' crucifixion, the first day of the week, some of the women who had followed Jesus come to the tomb to anoint his body. However, they are met by two men in dazzling clothes (later spoken of as "angels," Luke 24:23), who tell them that Jesus has risen; they in turn tell the disciples, who are amazed (Luke 24:1-12). Later that day, on the road to the village of Emmaus, Jesus appears to some disciples who initially do not recognize him. He then reveals himself to them, and after they return to Jerusalem, he reveals himself to the other disciples as well (Luke 24:13-43). According to Luke, who continues the story in the book of Acts, some forty days later Jesus takes his disciples to a mountain outside of Jerusalem. When they ask Jesus, "Lord, is this the time when you will restore the kingdom to Israel?" he tells them that it is not for them to know the times or periods that God has determined and then commissions them to be his witnesses to Jerusalem, Judea, Samaria, and "the ends of the earth" once they have received the Holy Spirit. Jesus then ascends into heaven (Luke 24:49-53; Acts 1:3-11).

On the day of Pentecost, the Holy Spirit descends on the disciples, who then proclaim to those present the same basic message that is later repeated throughout the book of Acts by the apostles: although the Jewish authorities and inhabitants of Jerusalem had killed Jesus, God had raised him and made him "Lord and Messiah," exalting him to heaven and then pouring out the Holy Spirit on his followers through Jesus (Acts 2:1-41). Those who wished to partake of the coming salvation needed to "repent and be baptized" (Acts 2:38); many did so, and in this way the "church" was formed. For Luke, the church is the community of believers who live under Jesus in faith, devoting themselves "to the apostles' teaching and fellowship, to the breaking of bread and the prayers," and to having "all things in common" (Acts 2:42-47).

According to Luke, Jesus' disciples (especially Peter and John) continued to proclaim this same basic message, as well as to effect a number of healings, but encountered the same resistance on the part of the Jewish authorities and many of the people that Jesus had faced (Acts 3:1—5:42). In Acts 6:8—7:60, another of Jesus' disciples, Stephen, is tried by the Jewish council and then put to death by stoning. Shortly thereafter, the risen Jesus appears to Saul, who was among those persecuting Jesus' followers, and Saul himself becomes a follower of Jesus (Acts 9:1-35). Luke dedicates more than half of the book of Acts to the ministry carried out by Saul, who is generally called by his other name, Paul. Paul's ministry follows the same basic pattern as that of the apostles before him: he initially proclaims the gospel regarding Jesus to the Jews, and although some of them come to believe, many (particularly the authorities) reject his proclamation and seek to kill him.

Yet, while many Jews refuse to accept the gospel, the church begins to grow among non-Jews, or Gentiles. The first Gentile convert is Cornelius, to whom Peter is sent: while Peter is preaching at Cornelius's house, the Holy Spirit descends upon Cornelius and he is baptized, together with other Gentiles, so as to form part of the church (Acts 10:1-48). Initially, many of Jesus' Jewish followers are hesitant to admit believing Gentiles into the church, and some begin to insist that such Gentiles need to convert first to Judaism, observing the Jewish law and undergoing circumcision (in the case of males; Acts 11:1-18; 15:1). However, when the apostles and leaders of the church meet in Jerusalem to settle the question, they decide that this is not necessary and that Gentiles can be accepted as they are as long as they observe certain dietary regulations and refrain from fornication (Acts 15:2-33).

Throughout most of Acts, the fierce persecution encountered by the apostles and the rejection of the gospel they proclaim on the part of many Jews is said to have as its consequence the spread of the gospel throughout the world and the incorporation of many Gentiles into the church.[5] The openness to uncircumcised Gentiles manifested particularly in Paul's missionary activity eventually led to his arrest at the temple in Jerusalem, where some Jews who had heard him elsewhere accuse him of "teaching everyone everywhere against our people, our law, and this place" (Acts 21:28). Paul is later put in prison and sent to Caesarea and then to Rome to be tried (Acts 23:1—28:31). The book of Acts ends with Paul under house arrest in Rome, where he continues to preach about Jesus. The result of his efforts, however, is essentially the same: some Jews believe, while others do not. After condemning the latter for their hardness of heart, Paul tells them, "Let it be known to you then that this salvation of God has been sent to the Gentiles; they will listen" (Acts 28:30).

The Divine Plan

A central theme in both Luke's Gospel and Acts is that the story of salvation just outlined had been foretold by the prophets of Israel in ancient times and, thus, that all the events that took place formed part of a divine plan established long before Jesus' coming.[6] While the fulfillment of the Scriptures is mentioned throughout Luke's Gospel and Acts, it is particularly stressed with regard to Jesus' passion and death. As noted above, Jesus tells his disciples before his crucifixion that "everything that is written about the Son of Man by the prophets will be accomplished" (Luke 18:31). Similarly, during the Last Supper, he says to them, "For I tell you, this scripture must be fulfilled in me, 'And he was counted among the lawless'; and indeed what is written about me is being fulfilled" (Luke 22:37). After his resurrection, the angels tell the women, "Remember how he told you, while he was still in Galilee, that the Son of Man must be handed over to sinners, and be crucified, and on the third day rise again" (Luke 24:6-7). Then the risen Jesus tells the disciples on the road to Emmaus, "'Oh, how foolish you are, and how slow of heart to believe all that the prophets have declared! Was it not necessary that the Messiah should suffer these things and then enter into his glory?' Then beginning with Moses and all the prophets, he interpreted to them the things about himself in all the scriptures" (Luke 24:25-27). That same night, he tells the disciples gathered in Jerusalem, "'These are my words that I spoke to you while I was still with you—that everything written about me in the law of Moses, the prophets, and the psalms must be fulfilled.' Then he opened their minds to understand the scriptures, and he said to them, 'Thus it is written, that the Messiah is to suffer and to rise from the dead on the third day, and that repentance and forgiveness of sins is to be proclaimed in his name to all nations, beginning from Jerusalem'" (Luke 24:44-47).

These same ideas are repeated in Acts. On Pentecost, Peter cites several passages from the Hebrew Scriptures to argue that they foretold Jesus' resurrection and exaltation, as well as the outpouring of the Holy Spirit, and then tells the inhabitants of Jerusalem, "This man, handed over to you according to the definite plan and foreknowledge of God, you crucified and killed by the hands of those outside the law" (Acts 2:23). Later, the disciples rejoice at the release of Peter and John and pray to God, "For in this city, in fact, both Herod and Pontius Pilate, with the Gentiles and the peoples of Israel, gathered together against your holy servant Jesus, whom you anointed, to do whatever your hand and your plan had predestined to take place" (Acts 4:27-28). In other passages, the fulfillment of the Scriptures through Jesus is also proclaimed (Acts 8:27-35; 13:27-39, 44-48; 17:2-3; 18:28).

In a number of these passages, Luke uses the Greek word *dei*, which means "it is necessary," to speak of what "must" happen according to God's plan foretold in the Scriptures. According to these passages, however, the Scriptures foretold not only Jesus' coming, ministry, passion, death, and resurrection, as well as the outpouring of the Holy Spirit, but also the rejection of the gospel on the part of many Jews and the subsequent mission to the Gentiles by apostles such as Paul. The idea that from the start God had intended Gentiles to form part of his people is reflected in Acts 13:46-47, where Paul tells the unbelieving Jews in Antioch of Pisidia: "It was necessary that the word of God should be spoken first to you. Since you reject it and judge yourselves to be unworthy of eternal life, we are now turning to the Gentiles. For so the Lord has commanded us, saying, 'I have set you to be a light for the Gentiles, so that you may bring salvation to the ends of the earth.'" Luke then continues: "When the Gentiles heard this, they were glad and praised the word of the Lord; and as many as had been destined for eternal life became believers" (Acts 13:48; cf. 18:5-6). Luke also uses the word *dei* to speak of the necessity of Paul's sufferings (Acts 9:16) and his going to Rome to bear witness there before the emperor (Acts 23:11; 27:24). Acts ends, as well, with the claim that the rejection of the gospel on the part of the Jews had been foretold by the prophet Isaiah (Acts 28:25-27). Thus, for Luke, everything that took place from the birth of Jesus to the proclamation of the gospel throughout the world formed part of a divine plan revealed in ancient times to God's prophets; and an important part of this plan was the rejection of Jesus and the gospel by many from Israel.[7]

Jesus, the Cross, and Salvation

It has often been said that Luke does not ascribe any theological significance to Jesus' death.[8] Outside of presenting Jesus' words over the bread and wine at the Last Supper—"This is my body, which is given for you," and "This cup that is poured out for you is the new covenant in my blood" (Luke 22:19-20)—as well as having Paul speak of the "church of God that he obtained with the blood of his own Son" (Acts 20:28), Luke never seems to link salvation or forgiveness to the cross. Instead, he compares Jesus' death to that of the prophets before him who were also rejected, persecuted, and put to death.

In fact, throughout Luke's Gospel and Acts, salvation and divine forgiveness are spoken of as something that could have been brought about *without* Jesus' death. Luke mentions that on the way to Jerusalem, a number of Jesus' followers "supposed that the kingdom of God was to appear immediately" (Luke 19:11), that is, before anything might happen to Jesus. Similarly, before recognizing the person accompanying them as Jesus, the disciples on the road to Emmaus express their sadness over Jesus' death, saying, "We had hoped that he was the one to redeem Israel" (Luke 24:21). According to these passages, God could have brought in the awaited kingdom and redemption of Israel through Jesus at any moment; there was nothing preventing God from doing so. Similarly, just as Jesus freely forgave sins during his ministry, and just as in Jesus' parable the waiting father graciously forgave his prodigal son (Luke 15:11-32), so there was no reason why God could not forgive sins without Jesus' suffering and dying. As in Isaiah, all that was necessary for the awaited salvation to arrive was that God will it to arrive.

What purpose, then, did Jesus' death have? And in what way was it salvific? As observed above, for Luke, Jesus' death was comparable to the deaths of the prophets yet was also necessary for the divine plan of salvation to be carried out. While that plan contemplated first and foremost the salvation of Israel, which required that Jesus go to Israel's capital, Jerusalem, to proclaim the gospel and teach there about the kingdom of God, it also contemplated the inclusion of people of other nations from around the world; and for Jews and Gentiles to participate in the promised salvation, they first needed to be brought to faith and repentance, as Luke repeatedly emphasizes. For this reason, Jesus could not merely stay in Galilee if the awaited redemption of Israel and the nations was to come through him.

At the same time, however, the consequence of carrying out his ministry in Jerusalem was that he would be killed. While he might have fled or hidden to escape that fate, this would have involved putting an end to his activity for the kingdom. Of course, God might have brought the kingdom in through him "immediately," as some were expecting; but that would have meant that there would be no opportunity for the mission to the Gentile nations to be carried out through the apostles. According to Jesus, God did not want the kingdom to come yet (Acts 1:6-8). The parable of the ten pounds, which Jesus told when some were thinking that the kingdom was to come immediately, stresses that there was still much work to be done before the kingdom might come (Luke 19:11-27). For Luke, then, it was necessary not only for Jesus' disciples but for Jesus himself to be active in carrying on that work on behalf of the kingdom.[9]

Thus, in order for God's plan of salvation to be carried out, the only alternative was for Jesus to die. According to this plan, he would then be raised and the mission first to Jews and then to Gentiles around the world would be carried out by the apostles. Jesus would also be raised and exalted to a position of divine authority at God's right hand (Luke 22:69; Acts 2:33; 5:31; 7:55-56), so as to pour out the Holy Spirit on his followers, thereby empowering them for the task given them, before returning in glory to save them.

The affirmation ascribed to Paul concerning the "church of God that he obtained with the blood of his own Son" (Acts 20:28) should be understood against the background of these ideas. By giving up his Son so that this plan might be carried out and people from around the world might hear the gospel and be incorporated into the church through faith and baptism, God obtained the "church" that he had desired. Yet the allusion to Jesus' "blood" should be understood as a reference not simply to Jesus' death but to his having been killed for his prophetic activity; he died because he insisted on carrying out a ministry of teaching and calling others to repentance, that is, because of his work to bring about a new community of people that came to be known as the "church." In other words, God obtained the church not merely through Jesus' *death* but through *all* of the activity oriented to founding a new community of righteous people that *led* to Jesus' death. God had sent his Son not so that he might die, as if that were the objective or would accomplish something in itself, but to carry out the ministry aimed at establishing the church, which would result in his death because of the rejection of many. Jesus' faithfulness to this task led to his death but also to the church.

Jesus' words over the bread and wine at the Last Supper should be understood against the background of this same story. When he speaks of his body "given for you," the "you" should be seen as referring not merely to the disciples gathered there but to the future community of believers as a whole. Jesus was giving up his body, representing his life or himself, "for" them in the sense that he was giving himself over to death so that they might some day attain salvation and God's kingdom through him. It is this that he anticipates at the Last Supper, looking forward to the day when the disciples would eat and drink at his table in his kingdom (Luke 22:30). By giving up his life rather than attempting to "save" it (Luke 9:24), and consequently being raised by God, he would also be able to be present among them in a new way, as the story of the risen Jesus' appearance to the disciples on the road to Emmaus illustrates; they recognized him in the breaking of the bread (Luke 24:30-31). Thus, just as Jesus was giving his body not only *for* his disciples but *to* them, from then on Jesus would be able to give himself to them in a new way, by continuing to work among them and pouring out God's Spirit on them, so that they and others might attain the kingdom.[10]

The idea of Jesus offering himself up to God sacrificially on their behalf may also be present in Jesus' words "given for you"; he was not only giving himself over *to death* but offering himself, his body, or his life up *to God*. If this is the case, however, there is no need to read back into his words any ideas of his dying in the place of his followers, as if God demanded his death in order to forgive them. Rather, the idea is that Jesus was offering himself up to God with the petition that what he had lived and died for might become a reality; just as he had sought the salvation of others throughout his ministry, so he continued to seek that salvation for them from God in his death. God's raising Jesus would then be understood as a favorable response to that petition, in effect granting Jesus what he had asked for by raising and exalting him so that he might return to bring about for others the salvation he had sought for them in life and death.

Ideas closely related to these appear to be behind Jesus' words "This cup that is poured out for you is the new covenant in my blood." Jesus sought that everything that had been promised in the covenant with Israel but had not been fulfilled might become a reality through him: his followers would have access to God and to the salvation and forgiveness God had promised through him as a result of his giving up his life and consequently being raised and exalted to God's right hand. They would thus live as members of a new covenant people under him, doing God's will as now defined, not simply by the law of Moses, but by Jesus himself. All of this would result from Jesus' willingness to give up his life. Those who ate of the bread and drank of the cup "in remembrance" of Jesus would thus be symbolizing or expressing that they formed part of the new covenant people for whom Jesus had lived and died.

Jesus' words over the cup may also communicate the idea that his death resembled a covenant sacrifice, such as that presented by Moses in Exodus 24:3-8. There Moses poured out sacrificial blood and sprinkled it on the people, calling it "the blood of the covenant." Just as in the Hebrew Scriptures, covenants were generally established through sacrifices, so the new covenant would be established through the sacrificial death of Jesus. From then on, the things the Jewish people sought at the temple and through obedience to the law under the old covenant, such as salvation and forgiveness of sins, would be found in Jesus under the new covenant following his death, resurrection, and ascension to God's hand. For this reason, in Acts, forgiveness of sins is consistently associated with the *risen, exalted* Jesus.

It is important to stress, however, that in order to understand the significance of Jesus' death in Luke's Gospel and Acts, it must be seen in the context of both the ministry that preceded it and the resurrection and exaltation of Jesus that followed upon it. Jesus' death was "for others" because his *life* had been "for" them and because, once risen and exalted, he would continue to be active on their behalf until the final redemption came through him. Thus it would be not *his death itself* that would save them and bring them forgiveness but *all* that he had done *before* his death and would continue to do *after* his death. Ultimately, for Luke, it is the *risen, exalted* Jesus who saves; however, all that Jesus did in the past through his ministry and his faithfulness unto death to that ministry also makes this salvation possible.

Salvation, Faith, and Repentance

In general, Luke understands salvation in the same way as the book of Isaiah. It has to do first and foremost with the people of Israel, who would be redeemed from their enemies (Luke 1:71); a glorious new age would be inaugurated, and the righteous would be raised from the dead to share in that new age (Luke 14:14; 18:30; 20:27-39; Acts 4:2; 17:18-32). All of this lies in the future and will come to pass when Jesus returns in glory. Peter tells his fellow Jews that God will "send the Messiah appointed for you, that is, Jesus, who must remain in heaven until the time of universal restoration that God announced long ago through his holy prophets" (Acts 3:20-21). According to this idea, salvation is something yet to come.[11]

Yet, for Luke, salvation through Jesus was not merely a future hope but something already realized during Jesus' ministry. Jesus tells both a woman whose sins he has declared forgiven and a woman who touched him so as to be healed from hemorrhages she has suffered for twelve years, "Your faith has saved you" (Luke 7:50; 8:48 in Greek). The same words are addressed to a Samaritan leper cured by Jesus and to a blind man whose sight Jesus restores (Luke 17:19; 18:42). Elsewhere, Luke speaks of people delivered from possession by demons (Luke 8:36) and a girl raised by Jesus from the dead as being "saved" (Luke 8:50). When Zacchaeus the tax collector decides to restore to others what he has unjustly taken, Jesus says, "Today salvation has come to this house, because he too is a son of Abraham. For the Son of Man came to seek out and to save the lost" (Luke 19:9-10). On the cross, those mocking Jesus recognize that "he saved others" (Luke 23:35), evidently referring to his healings. For Luke, then, salvation through Jesus has to do not only with the age to come but with the present age, and it involves being delivered from various types of suffering and oppression on both a physical and spiritual plane. This understanding of salvation leads Luke to pay special attention to the marginalized in his Gospel, such as women, the poor, and the "sinners"; it is these whom Jesus has come to save.[12]

Like salvation, the coming of God's kingdom is spoken of as both a present reality and a future hope: while in one sense that kingdom will come only when Jesus returns in power and glory, in another sense it is already present. Jesus tells his followers, "If it is by the finger of God that I cast out the demons, then the kingdom of God has come to you" (Luke 11:20); when asked by the Pharisees when the kingdom of God is to come, he replies, "The kingdom of God is not coming with things that can be observed; nor will they say, 'Look, here it is!' or 'There it is!' For, in fact, the kingdom of God is among you" (Luke 17:20-21). He also compares the kingdom to a mustard seed that grows little by little, or to yeast slowly leavening dough (Luke 13:18-21). Thus the blessings associated with the kingdom of God are attained both in the present and in the future. Yet precisely how these two ideas are to be reconciled is not clear, leaving open the same question we noted with regard to Isaiah, namely, whether the salvation to come is to be understood primarily as taking place *within* history or *beyond* it.

For Luke, salvation and the coming of the kingdom are inseparable from Jesus' person. This is because, as Messiah and Son of God, Jesus is God's chosen instrument to bring the awaited salvation, "the one ordained by God as judge of the living and the dead" (Acts 10:42). For this reason, Luke regards faith in Jesus as necessary for salvation. Just as those who believed in Jesus during his ministry were "saved" in various ways, so also those who now come to faith in him as Lord, Son of God, and Savior are promised salvation (Acts 2:38; 4:12; 10:43; 13:39; 16:29-31). Those who believe in Jesus are baptized and thereby come to form part of his community or church, where they obtain God's gifts of forgiveness and the new life of the Spirit.

Of course, Luke also repeatedly stresses that repentance is necessary for salvation.[13] Just as Jesus during his ministry called on others to repent (Luke 5:32; 11:32; 13:1-5), following his death and resurrection the apostles consistently proclaim the need for repentance (Luke 24:47; Acts 2:38; 3:19; 5:31; 17:30; 20:21). However, this repentance is to be understood not simply in terms of remorse for one's sins but as a total change of heart and a new life of obedience to God's will as revealed by Jesus. It is those who obey Jesus' words—loving their enemies, doing good, and forgiving others rather than judging or condemning them—who will receive a reward, obtain forgiveness, and be spared judgment and condemnation (Luke 6:35-37, 46-49). They must lose their life for Jesus' sake, take up their cross daily, and follow him (Luke 9:23-26). Repentance for Luke comprises all of this.

While such repentance is, thus, something demanded by Jesus and the apostles, Luke also stresses that it is a *gift*, made possible by the Holy Spirit. After hearing that the Holy Spirit was poured out on Gentiles such as Cornelius, the Jewish believers rejoice that "God has given even to the Gentiles the repentance that leads to life" (Acts 11:18), just as God had previously given Israel repentance through Jesus: "God exalted him at his right hand as Leader and Savior that he might give repentance to Israel and forgiveness of sins" (Acts 5:31). At the same time, Luke teaches that God gives the Holy Spirit "to those who obey him" (Acts 5:32). The idea, therefore, is that repentance and obedience are *demanded* by God and at the same time graciously *given* by God; and all of this takes place through faith, which is also both a gift from God and something God demands.

Luke thus agrees with the Jewish idea that justification or forgiveness of sins depends on one's repenting and living righteously in accordance with God's will. In itself, this has not changed as a result of Jesus' coming. However, because obedience to God's will has now been redefined through Jesus and his teaching, justification and forgiveness are seen as mediated through him. When Paul proclaims to the Jews that "through this man forgiveness of sins is proclaimed to you," and "by this Jesus everyone who believes is justified from all those things from which you could not be justified by the law of Moses" (Acts 13:38-39), the idea is that, previously, under the Jewish law, the people were not able to attain divine forgiveness and justification, either because they were not able to fulfill the law sufficiently and attain the righteousness necessary before God or because God had intended forgiveness and justification to come through Jesus rather than through the Jewish law. Now that Jesus has come, however, that has changed, because God *gives* the necessary repentance to people and, through Jesus' teaching and the Holy Spirit's power, enables them to live as he intended, practicing true righteousness.[14] For the same reason, the understanding of sin also changes in Luke's writings: no longer is it simply disobeying God's law; rather, it has become refusing to believe in Jesus, since the promised salvation is seen as inseparable from him as the one ordained by God as Savior. Thus, for Luke, to reject Jesus is to reject God himself (Luke 10:16).

Evaluation

The story of salvation told by Luke is from beginning to end a very *Jewish* story, and it reflects many of the same ideas found in the book of Isaiah. As mentioned earlier, Luke follows Isaiah in speaking primarily of the redemption of *Israel*,[15] though this redemption embraces the nations or Gentiles as well, and in ascribing a primary role to the Messiah descended from David, who is not only a king but God's servant. Luke, of course, goes beyond Isaiah in identifying this Messiah as Jesus of Nazareth and regards him as more central to Israel's redemption than Isaiah had regarded the Messianic king. However, it is evident that much continuity exists between Luke and Isaiah as well as among the rest of the Old Testament writings.

Yet there are also some significant differences between the stories of Luke and Isaiah. Luke's writings, for example, contain repeated references to personal forces of evil, such as the demons and the devil, who is also called Satan and "Beelzebul, the ruler of the demons" (Luke 11:15; cf. Luke 4:1-13; 8:12; 10:17-18; 13:16; 22:3, 31; Acts 5:3; 10:38; 26:18). These forces oppress people and cause various maladies and suffering. The devil is also presented as tempting people and inciting them to sin, often by entering into their hearts (Luke 22:3; Acts 5:3). Such ideas are not found in Isaiah and most of the Hebrew Scriptures yet had apparently become fairly common in the Judaism of Jesus' day as it is reflected in Luke's Gospel and other Jewish and Christian writings of the period. Although Jesus consistently shows himself to be stronger than these forces, the idea that they are somehow conquered or overcome in Jesus' death and resurrection is not to be found in Luke's writings. While Jesus does celebrate Satan's downfall in Luke 10:18, this is associated with the ministry carried out by Jesus' disciples *before* he dies and is glorified.

Christ Raising the Daughter of Jairus (James Jacques Joseph Tissot, Ann Ronan Picture Library, London). For Luke, salvation involves not only a future hope but a present reality as Jesus brings healing and wholeness into the lives of those who have faith in him.
Photo © HIP / Art Resource, NY.

Although the idea of a divine plan is present to some extent in the book of Isaiah, this idea is developed much further in Luke's writings. It becomes somewhat problematic, however, in that it appears that some type of "fate" or "destiny" is involved and because it is not always clear to what extent the events that take place are caused by God or even by Satan. In particular, Jesus' death is said to take place according to God's will, as his prayer in the Garden of Gethsemane makes clear: "Father, if you are willing, remove this cup from me; yet, not my will but yours be done" (Luke 22:42). The repeated claim that the Scriptures foretold all that would happen to Jesus also underscores this idea. At the same time, however, Judas's betrayal of Jesus is ascribed to Satan's entering into him (Luke 22:3). These ideas stand alongside the affirmation that sinful human beings were responsible for Jesus' death, particularly the Jewish authorities and the inhabitants of Jerusalem (Acts 2:23; 3:13-15; 4:27-28; 5:30; 7:52; 10:39).[16] The book of Acts claims repeatedly not only that they were the ones who killed Jesus but that they acted out of ignorance: "Because the residents of Jerusalem and their leaders did not recognize him or understand the words of the prophets that are read every sabbath, they fulfilled those words by condemning him" (Acts 13:27; cf. 3:17). While Luke never says or implies that God had his Son killed, as if God were ultimately responsible for Jesus' death, he does maintain that it took place according to God's will and predetermined plan and, thus, that God *allowed* evildoers to kill his Son. All of this raises the question of the extent to which those who had Jesus crucified can be blamed for his death, since they were unwittingly carrying out a divine plan.

Luke also differs from Isaiah in that he does not regard suffering and oppression in the present age as God's punishment for the sins committed by human beings. Jesus rejects the notion that those who perish suddenly are "worse sinners" than others (Luke 13:1-5) as well as the belief that success and wealth in the present age are given by God as a reward to those who are more righteous than others (Luke 18:24-27). In fact, he teaches the exact opposite: those who follow Jesus in doing God's will and obeying his commandments will face suffering and persecution in the present age, as Jesus did, as well as poverty and hunger, while those who enjoy wealth, fullness, and laughter will be condemned (Luke 6:20-26). In contrast to Isaiah, therefore, suffering is not necessarily a sign of God's wrath or punishment for sin in the present, just as prosperity is not necessarily a sign of God's blessing. The blessings promised to those who obey God's will, like the punishment allotted to those who sin and disobey God, will come to pass fully only in the coming age, following the final judgment of all by Christ.

Finally, while Luke certainly speaks of salvation in collective terms, he differs from Isaiah in emphasizing more the *personal* aspect; what ultimately matters is not one's nationality or descent from Abraham but repenting and believing in Jesus personally. God's election and salvation have to do with people of many nations who come to form part of the church, rather than one particular people or nation. Nevertheless, Luke does not go the further step of seeing *all people* as having been saved in some objective, universal sense through Jesus; salvation is confined to those who repent and believe. This possibility is now open to people of every tongue and nation thanks to the proclamation of the gospel "to the ends of the earth" (Acts 1:8).

CHAPTER 3

Christ Crucified and Risen
in the Letters of Paul

Following his encounter with the risen Jesus on the road to Damascus some four or five years after the events surrounding Jesus' crucifixion in Jerusalem, Paul of Tarsus dedicated his life to building up the church that he had previously sought to destroy. As "apostle to the Gentiles," Paul played a vital role in the expansion of the church beyond the limits of Judaism, traveling throughout the Roman Empire to establish and strengthen Christian communities in one city after another. Facing countless hardships and fierce opposition from Jews, Greeks, and even other believers in Christ, Paul preached the gospel faithfully and tirelessly for well over two decades before dying the death of a martyr in Rome sometime around 65 CE.[1]

Reconstructing the story of redemption told by the apostle Paul is extremely difficult for several reasons. First of all, considerable doubt exists regarding precisely which of the letters bearing Paul's name were actually written by him. Many Pauline scholars doubt that 1 and 2 Timothy and Titus, called the "Pastoral Epistles," were composed by Paul, and serious questions exist as well with regard to Ephesians, Colossians, and 2 Thessalonians.[2] Whether or not Paul is the author of all of these writings, generally known as the "deuteropauline" letters, they must still be regarded as Pauline in some sense, since if they were not written by Paul himself, they appear to be the product of some type of Pauline circle or school. Thus we can still ascribe all of these letters to "Paul" as the "implied author," because in one way or another they are "Pauline."

For our purposes here, a more serious problem with Paul's letters is that the way they were written makes it difficult to discern clearly the story of redemption on which they are based. Paul nowhere presents the story revolving around Jesus in any orderly fashion, in the way that Luke and the other Evangelists do; nor does he offer any detailed systematic summary of that story. Paul's letters are occasional documents, written to respond to specific situations, questions, and problems that arose in the lives of the churches and individuals to whom they are addressed. Precisely because these churches and individuals had already been instructed in the faith and thus were well acquainted with the story of redemption told by Paul and other Christians, when Paul alludes to that story, and particularly to Jesus' death, he uses brief formulas: Jesus "was handed over to death for our trespasses and was raised for our justification" (Rom 4:25); "Christ died for us" (Rom 5:8); "we have been justified by his blood" (Rom 5:9); "we were reconciled to God through the death of his Son" (Rom 5:10); "Christ died for our sins in accordance with the Scriptures" (1 Cor 15:3); "he died for all" (2 Cor 5:15); "in him we have redemption through his blood, the forgiveness of our trespasses" (Eph 1:7).

The problem with brief formulas such as these is that all kinds of ideas can be read back into them. In fact, precisely because these formulas lend themselves to varied interpretations, Paul's letters have been cited in support of many different understandings of Christ's redemptive work, including most of those that we will examine throughout the rest of this book. This makes it very difficult to consider Paul's teaching regarding salvation through Christ in a short chapter such as this, because there have been seemingly endless interpretations of Paul's teaching on the subject, each of which claims to be grounded in Paul's thought.

As I have argued elsewhere in detail, however, in order to attempt to understand what Paul's letters say regarding salvation in Christ, we must look not only to those letters themselves but to the story of redemption told by the first Christians as we can best reconstruct it from the Synoptic Gospels and Acts.[3] Although Paul wrote several decades before Luke, a close look at the writings of each reveals that the story we have discerned in Luke's Gospel and the book of Acts provides many of the elements necessary to interpret Paul's teaching, particularly the brief allusions to Jesus' death so characteristic of the letters attributed to Paul.

Creation and God's Eternal Plan

For Paul, the story of redemption begins even before the creation of the world. It seems clear that Paul believed that God's Son, whom he identifies with Jesus, existed before creation, although precisely how he conceived of this preexistence is not entirely evident from his letters.[4] In a couple of passages, he sees creation as a work not only of God but of Christ, "through whom are all things and through whom we exist" (1 Cor 8:6); "all things have been created through him and for him" (Col 1:16). In some way, therefore, God's Son was destined from eternity to play a central role in the history of the created world.

Paul also speaks of a plan conceived by God before creation. This plan embraced not only the election of Abraham and his descendants but the eventual adoption of people from other nations throughout the earth to be God's people through Christ as well (Rom 9–11; Gal 3:8-16; 4:4-5). According to Ephesians, God "chose us in Christ before the foundation of the world to be holy and blameless before him in love. He destined us for adoption as his children through Jesus Christ, according to the good pleasure of his will" (Eph 1:4-5; cf. 2 Tim 1:9; Titus

1:1-3). This involved being "predestined to be conformed to the image of his Son" (Rom 8:29). The Scriptures foretold not only the coming of God's Son but his crucifixion and resurrection (1 Cor 2:6-8; 15:3-5), as well as the sending out of apostles into the world following these events. Paul speaks of all of this as a "mystery hidden for ages in God who created all things" (Eph 3:9) but that is now disclosed and revealed to the saints and apostles (Rom 16:26; Eph 1:4-12; 3:1-12; Col 1:26). This mystery embraces Christ himself and the gospel concerning him, all of which was foretold by the prophets, as well as the adoption of the Gentiles as members of God's people (Rom 1:1-6; 16:25-26; Eph 3:5-6; Col 1:26-27; 2:2). It should be noted, however, that when Paul speaks of predestination or election, he probably has in mind the election not of specific *individuals* but of a *people* of whom individuals come to form part through faith and obedience. Just as God had chosen Israel as his people, God had also chosen the church.

For Paul, this divine purpose or plan is yet to be consummated through Christ: it is "a plan for the fullness of time, to gather up all things in him, things in heaven and things on earth" (Eph 1:10). Christ, now risen and exalted, is subjecting all things to himself and in the end will establish his lordship over every ruler, authority, and power, so as then to reunite all with God: "When all things are subjected to him, then the Son himself will also be subjected to the one who put all things in subjection under him, so that God may be all in all" (1 Cor 15:24-28).

Sin and Evil

According to Paul, creation and humanity as a whole have become subject to sin, death, and evil since the time of the first human being, Adam. Humanity now lives in the "present evil age" (Gal 1:4), in which sin and evil predominate; "there is no one who is righteous, not even one," since "all have sinned and fall short of the glory of God" (Rom 3:10, 23). Paul never addresses the question of whether, before creation, God foresaw the entrance of sin and evil into the world, though perhaps this might be inferred from the idea that God apparently foresaw the salvation of human beings from sin and death through his Son; nor does Paul ever use the word *fall* to refer to the situation that came over the world as a result of what Adam and Eve did. He does, however, attribute the fact that all people sin and die to Adam's sin: "Sin came into the world through one man, and death came through sin, and so death spread to all because all have sinned" (Rom 5:12; see vv. 13-19). At least in part, Paul also attributes the sins of Adam and the rest of humanity to the activity of the devil, or Satan, and the other forces of evil who wage war against human beings by tempting, deceiving, and oppressing them, thereby leading them to fall into sin (1 Cor 7:5; 2 Cor 2:11; 11:3; Eph 6:11-18; 1 Thess 3:5; 2 Thess 2:9-10; 1 Tim 2:14-15; 3:6-7; 2 Tim 2:26). What is not clear is to what extent human sin results from the influence of these evil forces; while these forces might be blamed for blinding and deceiving human beings, Paul also regards human beings as responsible for their own actions. For this reason, all

Saint Paul Discussing with Jews and Gentiles (Victoria and Albert Museum,
London). According to Paul's gospel, "there is no longer Jew or Greek,
there is no longer slave or free, there is no longer male and female,"
since all believers "are one in Christ Jesus" (Gal 3:28).
Photo © Erich Lessing / Art Resource, NY.

will be judged and held accountable for what they have done (Rom 2:5-16; 1 Cor
4:5; 2 Cor 5:10; 2 Tim 4:1).

Neither is it clear from Paul's letters precisely how he conceived of the relation
between Adam's sin and that of his descendants, as well as the extension of death
to all. Once again, the fact that all will be judged according to their deeds means
that Adam alone cannot be held responsible for the sin of all. However, did Paul
think that, as a result of Adam's sin, some type of alteration had taken place in
human nature, such as the introduction of some malignant power or sinful inclination into it that induces people to sin? Paul does make the distinction between
"sin" as a power and "sins" as acts of disobedience. In Rom 7:7-23, for example,
Paul says that the "sin" dwelling in him causes him to commit sins, even contrary
to his own will. If sin was introduced as a power into human nature, was this a
direct consequence of Adam's act? Did all human beings instead become sinners
because Adam in effect subjected himself to slavery under Satan, so that now all of
his descendants are also in Satan's bondage? Or was the relation between Adam's
sin and the sin of his posterity one of *imitation*, so that all human beings now sin
merely because they have learned to do so from those who precede them?

Similar questions arise regarding the relation between Adam's sin and the
death of all. Is the fact that all people die to be attributed to Satan, who now has

human beings under his power because of the sin of Adam or his descendants? Is death instead the punishment or penalty inflicted on human beings by God for their sin? In this case, according to the distinction mentioned in chapter 1, the relationship between sin and death would be an *extrinsic* one: when God told Adam and Eve that they would die when they sinned, God was advising them of how he would *punish* their sin (perhaps using the forces of evil as his agents to carry out his sentence). Or did Paul regard the relation between sin and death as an *intrinsic* one? If so, then he would have considered God's words to Adam and Eve in the garden a *warning* of the natural and inevitable consequences of their disobedience. To speak in these terms involves positing the existence of some natural law, either in the universe as a whole or in human nature itself, according to which human sin *in and of itself* eventually produces death in human beings. Even if the existence of such a natural law is posited, however, this must still be attributed ultimately to God, who established the laws inherent in the created order. In that case, sin still leads to death because God *willed* death to be the consequence of sin.

It is not entirely clear, then, how Paul believed that Adam's sin had resulted in all other human beings' sinning and dying. These questions are essential, however, for considering how Paul believed Christ brought about human salvation. Was Christ's task that of delivering human beings from some type of evil power that had inhered in the human flesh that all share, or perhaps that of overcoming the devil and the forces of evil who subjected them to sin and death? Was Christ's purpose that of bringing some type of divine teaching or revelation to human beings so that they might no longer follow Adam's example? Or did Christ come to save human beings from a punishment imposed by God or God's law on those who are guilty of sin and disobedience? All of these ideas have been attributed to Paul.

Paul appears to stress the idea that both Jews and Gentiles are subject to sin's power in order to insist that salvation can therefore not come through the law, since because of sin the law cannot be kept fully (Rom 3:9-31; 7:7-25; Gal 3:10-26). For this reason, it is senseless for believing Gentiles to attempt to gain salvation by observing the law of Moses. The plight of Gentiles, then, is the same as that of Jews, since both need to be delivered from sin's power in order to be saved; for Paul, this can occur only through Christ and the Holy Spirit.

Salvation through Christ

Throughout his letters, Paul seems virtually to ignore much of the material we find in the Gospels regarding Jesus' teaching and ministry. Nowhere does he refer explicitly to any of Jesus' healings, miracles, or parables; allusions to Jesus' teaching are also extremely scarce. He does, however, speak fairly frequently of Jesus' birth or coming as well as of his death and resurrection. This has led many Pauline scholars to conclude that, for Paul's teaching regarding salvation, the earthly or "historical" Jesus was relatively unimportant. Rather, what truly mattered was the coming, death, and resurrection of Jesus as the eternal Son of God.[5]

In recent years, these ideas have been challenged. Many have argued that, even though explicit allusions to Jesus' ministry and teaching are rare, what Jesus did and said during his ministry does play an important role in Paul's thought.[6] In this case, the reason that Paul rarely mentions such material as we find in the Gospels is not that it was unimportant for him or that he was unacquainted with it but, rather, that he considered it unnecessary to make explicit reference to it because he assumed that his readers were well acquainted with it.

If this is the case, then we should expect Paul's answer to the question of how Jesus saves people to be essentially the same as that which we found in Luke's writings. There, we saw that Jesus saves primarily by bringing about in his followers a new life in the context of the community he founded and then by returning in power and glory to establish definitively the kingdom of God that he had announced and manifested in his ministry.

With regard to this second idea, substantial evidence from Paul's letters suggests that it was a prominent part of the gospel he proclaimed. Paul repeatedly refers to the second coming of Christ and anticipates it as the time of the ultimate fulfillment of all of God's promises of salvation. Christ will return from heaven to raise the dead, destroy all sin and evil, and bring about the redemption of all of creation, which "will be set free from its bondage to decay and will obtain the freedom of the glory of the children of God" (Rom 8:21).[7] In essence, for Paul, *this is how Jesus Christ saves.*

At times, however, Paul seems to speak of salvation as a present reality.[8] He uses the past tense to affirm that believers have already been redeemed, justified, and reconciled to God (Rom 5:9-10; 2 Cor 5:18; Gal 3:13) and writes that "if anyone is in Christ, there is a new creation: everything old has passed away; see, everything has become new!" (2 Cor 5:17). In the deuteropauline letters, it is said that believers have already been raised with Christ and that God "has rescued us from the power of darkness and transferred us into the kingdom of his beloved Son" (Col 1:13).[9] While some Pauline scholars have argued that Paul proclaimed that the awaited new age had already arrived in some sense, it seems preferable to understand his language as indicating simply a present experience of many of the blessings associated with the coming age, such as "righteousness and peace and joy in the Holy Spirit" (Rom 14:17), as well as a certainty regarding the future based on what has already taken place in Christ: because Christ has now been raised and exalted to God's right hand, from where he will one day return to save and redeem his people, it can be said that believers were *already* saved and redeemed when Christ was glorified, since his glorification ensured his future return in glory for them. Paul's idea, then, is that "in hope we were saved," since believers can now be certain that they will be redeemed from their bondage together with all of creation (Rom 8:19-25).

Faith, Works, and Justification

What is necessary to participate in the promised salvation? Like Luke and the rest of the New Testament, Paul makes salvation dependent on faith: "If you confess with your lips that Jesus is Lord and believe in your heart that God raised him from the dead, you will be saved" (Rom 10:9). He also teaches that salvation is a divine gift, not a human achievement: "For by grace you have been saved through faith, and this is not your own doing; it is the gift of God—not the result of works, so that no one may boast" (Eph 2:8-9). At the same time, however, Paul consistently teaches that all people will be judged on the basis of their works: God "will repay according to each one's deeds. . . . There will be anguish and distress for everyone who does evil, the Jew first and also the Greek, but glory and honor and peace for everyone who does good, the Jew first and also the Greek. . . . For it is not the hearers of the law who are righteous in God's sight, but the doers of the law who will be justified" (Rom 2:6, 9-10, 13). Here and elsewhere, Paul appears to insist on the need to obey God's law in order to be saved (for example, 1 Cor 7:19) and says that he does not "overthrow" God's law but upholds it (Rom 3:31).[10] These statements stand alongside others in which he insists that "a person is justified by faith apart from works prescribed by the law" (Rom 3:28) and that "no human being will be justified in [God's] sight by works of the law" (Rom 3:20). Thus Paul appears to claim that one must do the works prescribed by God's law in order to be saved and justified, and yet that salvation and justification are gracious gifts of God given *independently* of such works.

Resolving this apparent contradiction in Paul requires distinguishing between the *letter* and the *spirit* of the law. Paul makes this distinction explicitly in three passages: Rom 2:29, where he contrasts literal and spiritual circumcision, the latter of which is a "matter of the heart"; Rom 7:6, where he says that believers are "discharged from the law" so as to "serve in the newness of the spirit and not the oldness of the letter" (RSV); and 2 Cor 3:5-6: "Our competence is from God, who has made us competent to be ministers of a new covenant, not of letter but of spirit; for the letter kills, but the Spirit gives life." Because believers live under the new covenant established through Christ and his death, they are no longer obligated to observe literally everything that the Mosaic law prescribed, such as circumcision, the Sabbath, and the prescriptions concerning clean and unclean food (Rom 14:1-23; Gal 4:9-11; 5:2-6; Col 2:16).

Nevertheless, believers are still required to fulfill the *spirit* of the law, practicing righteousness, mercy, and love. In Rom 13:9-10 and Gal 5:14, Paul speaks of love as the fulfillment of the law, and elsewhere he refers to the "law of Christ" (1 Cor 9:20-21; Gal 6:2), which is probably a reference to Jesus' own teaching on the need to love God and neighbor in order to keep the commandments.[11] Thus, while believers are "free from the law" in the sense that they no longer need to observe all of the prescriptions of the law of Moses as they live in the new covenant, they are still under the law of Christ and must fulfill the "just requirement of the law" (Rom 8:3) or its spirit as "slaves of righteousness" (Rom 6:18-19).

Yet, while Paul teaches that believers must live in accordance with God's will in order to be saved and justified—that is, accepted as righteous by God—he also speaks of this new life as something produced not by believers themselves but by God: through Christ and the Holy Spirit, God graciously brings about in believers the life of righteousness he demands. The "just requirement of the law" is fulfilled in those "who walk not according to the flesh but according to the Spirit" (Rom 8:4). The idea is similar to Luke's affirmation that God "gives" repentance to those who believe (Acts 5:31; 11:18). The Holy Spirit produces good fruits in them, pours God's love into their hearts, and guides and leads them (Gal 5:16-25; Rom 5:5; 8:14), enabling them to "become obedient from the heart to the form of teaching" entrusted to them, which is no doubt an allusion to what Christ taught (Rom 8:17). While a new life of righteousness thus is necessary for people to be saved, this is brought about not through their own deeds or merits but solely by the grace of God as they look to God and Christ in faith; as Paul tells the Philippians, "It is God who is at work in you, enabling you both to will and to work for his good pleasure" (Phil 2:13).

Of course, as in Luke's writings, God's grace is also manifested in the forgiveness of sins granted to believers through Christ, which is necessary because they continue to sin (1 Cor 6:1; 8:12; 2 Cor 2:7-11; 13:2; Phil 3:12). Because they are still in the present evil age and in the flesh, they are not yet perfect; the "good work" begun in them by God will be brought to completion only in the day of Jesus Christ (Phil 1:6). Through faith and the Spirit, they still "eagerly wait for the hope of righteousness" (Gal 5:5). Thus they do not *earn* God's forgiveness or their justification through their obedience; rather, their acceptance before God is due solely to God's grace and mercy through Christ. Yet the reason God forgives them is their relation to Christ their Lord; it is "in him" that believers have forgiveness of sins (Col 1:14; Eph 1:7).

Jesus' Death "for Us"

If people are saved by believing in Christ so as to receive through him both forgiveness of sins and the new life of righteousness God requires, what role does his death play? To answer this question, we must return to the overarching story of salvation that we saw in chapter 2. According to that story, Jesus died because his ministry and teaching generated conflict and opposition among many, particularly the Jewish religious leaders. Although Paul never affirms such an idea explicitly, he is aware that Jesus was crucified by the "rulers of this age" (1 Cor 2:8) and that the Jewish authorities acted to have Jesus put to death; when Paul writes that they "killed both the Lord Jesus and the prophets" (1 Thess 2:15), he is comparing Jesus' death to that of the prophets, who were also put to death for their prophetic activity.

While Paul rarely alludes to Jesus' ministry, he was at least aware that Jesus had dedicated himself to teaching. He also seems to refer to Jesus' ministry in Rom 15:8, where he says that Jesus became "a servant of the circumcised on

St. Paul Disputing in Damascus (Cappella Palatina, Palermo, Italy). For Paul, suffering and dying with Christ involves enduring the same persecutions Christ did on account of the gospel. On numerous occasions, such as when he had to flee Damascus by being let down in a basket through an opening in the city wall by night (Acts 9:23-25), Paul faced danger and death on account of his witness to Christ. Photo © Alinari / Art Resource, NY.

behalf of the truth of God in order that he might confirm the promises given to the patriarchs." Obviously, if Paul knew that Jesus carried out a ministry in relation to others, he must have believed that Jesus was seeking their salvation in some way through that ministry. Yet Paul also speaks of Jesus' seeking the salvation of others in his *death*: he died so that others might "live no longer for themselves" but for him (2 Cor 5:15), in order to set believers "free from the present evil age" (Gal 1:4), and so that "the blessing of Abraham might come to the Gentiles" and they might "receive the promise of the Spirit through faith" (Gal 3:13-14; cf. Rom 15:9). In Rom 14:9, Paul affirms that "Christ died and lived again, so that he might be Lord of both the dead and the living," while in 1 Thess 5:10 he states that Jesus "died for us, so that whether we are awake or asleep we may live with him."

For Paul, then, Jesus was clearly seeking something in his death: that others might enter into the life of the coming age, that they might live for him rather than for themselves, and that the promises of salvation made by God might be fulfilled. For the most part, these were things that Jesus had sought also in his life and ministry. Yet the allusions to the Gentiles in Rom 15:9 and Gal 3:14 also point to the idea we saw in chapter 2, namely, that Jesus died so that a new covenant embracing not only Jews but non-Jews might be founded through him and that there might be a time in which the gospel would be proclaimed around the world so that Gentiles might be incorporated into the new covenant people. Like Luke, Paul knows of the tradition regarding the Last Supper, when Jesus spoke of the new covenant in his blood (1 Cor 11:24).

In fact, the idea found in Luke that the rejection of Jesus and the gospel as proclaimed by the apostles led to the mission to the Gentiles is also present in Paul's letters. We have already noted Paul's affirmation of a divine plan or "mystery" now revealed that contemplated the salvation of Gentiles through the work of the apostles, such as Paul. Paul also follows Luke in regarding the rejection of the gospel by the people of Israel as part of this divine plan, especially in Romans 9–11, where he speaks of Jesus as the stone over whom the Jewish people have stumbled (9:32-33). This idea is similar to that found in the parable of the wicked tenants in Luke 20:9-19, where Jesus teaches that, following his rejection and death, the kingdom would be given over to others, and then concludes that the stone that is rejected will become the cornerstone of something new. In Rom 11:11-12, Paul draws the same conclusion regarding Israel: "Through their stumbling salvation has come to the Gentiles, so as to make Israel jealous." He then goes on to describe the "mystery" in the following terms: "A hardening has come upon part of Israel, until the full number of the Gentiles has come in. And so all Israel will be saved; as it is written, 'Out of Zion will come the Deliverer; he will banish ungodliness from Jacob.' 'And this is my covenant with them, when I take away their sins'" (11:25-27). Here we see once more the idea of the (new) covenant, which is related to the Gentiles "coming in."

All of this suggests the same basic understanding of Jesus' death that we identified in Luke's writings: Jesus gave himself over to death so that a new covenant might be established through him and so that God's plan of incorporating people from around the world into the church through the proclamation of the gospel might be carried out, in order that they might find there forgiveness, salvation, and reconciliation with God. Thus, when Paul writes that "while we were enemies, we were reconciled to God through the death of his Son" (Rom 5:10), his reference to reconciliation must be seen against the background of what he affirms regarding the Jews in Rom 11:15: "Their rejection [of the gospel] is the reconciliation of the world." In other words, people from around the world are now reconciled to God through faith thanks to the fact that Jesus was willing to suffer the rejection of those who crucified him, giving up his life so that there might be a new covenant and the gospel might be proclaimed throughout the world. Of course, this reconciliation is also due to the work of the apostles, such as Paul, who have been entrusted with the "ministry of reconciliation" (2 Cor 5:18-19). However, it is important to note that Paul does not say that *Christ's death itself* reconciled people to God; rather, they were reconciled to God *through* Christ's death, in that it led to a new situation in which people now may find reconciliation with God, forgiveness, and salvation through Christ. As they live under him as members of the new covenant community, practicing righteousness and obedience to the law of Christ empowered by the Holy Spirit, they are pleasing and acceptable to God and thus are no longer under God's wrath but at peace with God. They are now included as members of the community of those he reconciled to God through his faithfulness unto death to his mission.

For Paul, then, this is what Jesus was seeking in life and death: to bring into existence an obedient, righteous people composed of both Jews and Gentiles who would be pleasing to God. When threatened with the cross, Jesus did not run or hide, attempting to avoid such an accursed death, but instead offered himself and his life up to God with the implicit petition that what he had lived and died for might come to pass through him. In this sense, Jesus' death was sacrificial. Seeking the "interests of others," he "humbled himself and became obedient to the point of death—even death on a cross"; and because of this, he was raised by God and exalted to God's right hand, so that now he can return some day as Lord to bring in the kingdom he lived and died for (Phil 2:1-11; 3:20-21). Thus, by being obedient unto death to the task given him, he attained for others the salvation he had sought for them, since now that he has been given all power and glory, that salvation is certain to take place through him. For this reason, Paul affirms that salvation and redemption are now to be found "in him" (Rom 3:24; Eph 1:7; Col 1:14) yet are also something Jesus obtained for others through his death or blood, since this led to his being raised for them as Savior.

In considering how Jesus' death is "for" others, it is important to note two aspects of his work, which can be labeled "Godward" and "humanward." The former has to do with Jesus' activity *in relation to God on behalf of others*; in the past, he "loved us and gave himself up for us, a fragrant offering and sacrifice *to God*" (Eph 5:2), and in the present he "intercedes for us" at the right hand of God (Rom 8:34; cf. 2 Cor 3:4; Col 3:17). Jesus' "humanward" work consists of what he does *in relation to human beings on behalf of God*: this includes the teaching and ministry he carried out in the past and his present activity of strengthening, nourishing, and comforting believers, dwelling in them, and answering their prayers (Rom 10:12; 2 Cor 13:5, 8; Gal 2:20; Eph 3:17; 4:32; 5:29; Phil 4:13; 2 Thess 2:16; 1 Tim 1:12). It also includes his future activity of raising them from the dead and bringing them into the kingdom. While Jesus' death no doubt has a *humanward* aspect for Paul, in that it provides an example for believers to imitate and reveals God's love to them, it also has a *Godward* aspect; in the latter sense, it is sacrificial, though it must be remembered that sacrifices were essentially *offerings to God accompanied by prayers*. In this sense, Jesus offered himself up to God along with an implicit petition that the salvation of others to which he had dedicated his life might become a reality through him. This petition was, in essence, granted when God raised and exalted Jesus so that he might complete the work of saving human beings that he had begun during his ministry.

Paul's language concerning the salvific nature of Jesus' death can and should be understood against the background of these ideas. Believers were reconciled to God, redeemed, and justified through Jesus' death or blood in the sense that he obtained these things definitively on their behalf through his faithfulness unto death, thanks to the fact that God raised him as a result of that faithfulness. Jesus gave up his life so that others might come to live under the new covenant as members of the church, where they now find reconciliation with God (and one another), redemption, and justification in him (Rom 3:24; 5:8-11; 2 Cor 5:18-19; Eph 2:16). In this sense also, Jesus "died for our sins according to the Scriptures" (1 Cor 15:3; cf. Gal 1:4), since he died so that the divine plan of salvation foretold in the Scriptures might be carried out, according to which people from around the world would come to receive forgiveness of sins through him once he had been raised (see 1 Cor 15:17). Jesus was "put forward as an expiation by his blood" (Rom 3:25 RSV) in that God gave him over to death so that both Jews and Gentiles might now find forgiveness of sins through him as their mediator. Thus forgiveness, as well as the redemption and justification of believers, was ensured when Jesus offered up his life sacrificially on behalf of others seeking their salvation and God responded by raising his Son so as to make certain that what Jesus had sought in life and death might come to pass through him. Believers now have access to God through him yet were also "brought near in the blood of Christ," in that he obtained that access for them by giving up his life sacrificially (Eph 2:16-18).

Because Jesus had dedicated his life to forming around himself a righteous, obedient people, it can be said that he "gave himself for us that he might redeem us from all iniquity and purify for himself a people of his own who are zealous for good deeds" (Titus 2:14). Here the objective is not just that people be redeemed from their sins but that they live in a righteous, pure manner. The same idea seems to be present in Rom 5:18-19, where Jesus' act of righteousness and obedience (in death) is said to lead to many others being made righteous and receiving justification, as well as in 2 Cor 5:21, where Paul writes that "for our sake [God] made him to be sin who knew no sin, so that in him we might become the righteousness of God": Jesus died, and God "gave him up for all of us" (Rom 8:32), so that many might now come to live a new, righteous life and obtain justification through Jesus as members of the community he founded through his life and death. In this way, his death leads to their justification and new life. Similarly, by sending his Son and giving him up to death, God "condemned sin in the flesh," since Jesus' death, resurrection, and the gift of the Spirit have made it possible for believers to "walk not according to the flesh but according to the Spirit," fulfilling the "just requirement of the law" (Rom 8:3-4). By "becoming a curse for us" when he gave himself over to the accursed death of the cross, Jesus "redeemed us from the curse of the law," attaining for believers the redemption that the Mosaic law had promised but was unable to give, since it is now to come through him. He died so that the promises of blessing made to Abraham and the gift of the Spirit might now be given not only to Jews but to Gentiles who through faith are incorporated into the church founded as a result of Jesus' death (Gal 3:13-14).

It is important not to read later theological ideas into a number of these passages, particularly the ones just cited. To say that God made Jesus sin (2 Cor 5:21), or that Jesus underwent the curse pronounced on those who hang on a tree (Gal 3:13), is not to affirm that he died *in the place* of others as their substitute. Rather, God treated his Son as a sinner in that God did not rescue him from death but, rather, gave him up and let him undergo the curse pronounced on those hanging on a tree, so as to ensure that others may now find salvation, justification, forgiveness, and redemption in him; this occurs as they are incorporated into the community of faith. In that sense, Jesus' death was "for" others. Through his death, he became the "one mediator between God and humankind" (1 Tim 2:5), since he was consequently exalted to God's right hand. Yet he also "gave himself a ransom for all" (1 Tim 2:6) in the sense that, in exchange for the giving up of his life, he obtained the redemption of others, because that is now to come through him.

The language and brief formulas employed by Paul to speak of Jesus' death, then, can be understood according to the same basic story told by Luke. Paul never speaks of Jesus' death as having some salvific "effect" nor affirms that Jesus' death or blood saved, redeemed, justified, or reconciled people with God; rather, he says that these things occurred *through Jesus' death*, in that when Jesus gave up his life and was consequently raised by God, they became a certainty.

Furthermore, it is important to note that, for Paul, only those who would come to faith were actually redeemed through Christ's death. The conditional nature of their reconciliation with God is evident, for example, in Col 1:22-23, where Paul tells the Colossians that Jesus has reconciled them through his death "provided that you continue securely established and steadfast in the faith, without shifting from the hope promised by the gospel that you heard"; thus only if they believe and remain steadfast are they among those who were reconciled to God through Jesus' death. While occasionally Paul speaks of the salvation of "all," at times this seems to refer only to all believers.[12] However, because Jesus went to the cross seeking that people from throughout the world might come to form part of the church that would be established through his death, he can also be said to have died for all people. Thus it can be said that those who were "objectively" redeemed through Christ's death were all those who would "subjectively" come to faith; and Christ's hope was that "all" might eventually come to faith and thus be saved.

In Col 1:16, Jesus' death on the cross is also seen as a victory over the evil powers: "He disarmed the rulers and authorities and made a public example of them, triumphing over them" in the cross. While this verse speaks of this victory as something already accomplished, elsewhere Paul sees it as a future event (Rom 16:20; 1 Cor 15:24-28) and speaks of the struggle against the forces of evil as something still going on in the present (Eph 6:11-17). Thus the idea seems to be that Jesus' death, resurrection, and exaltation ensure the future defeat of the evil powers, since this defeat is now certain to occur through him; in the meantime, they are still active.

"With Christ" and "in Christ"

Paul's letters speak not only of Christ dying "for" others but of others suffering, dying, and rising "with Christ": Paul and others have "died with Christ" (Rom 6:8) and been "crucified with Christ" (Gal 2:19-20) and were "buried with him in baptism," when they were "also raised with him through faith in the power of God" (Col 2:12; cf. 3:1; Eph 2:4-6; Rom 8:17; 2 Tim 2:11). Many Pauline scholars have claimed that Paul intended his words to be taken literally: believers actually participate in Christ or in his death and resurrection through some type of real union with him, so that what is true of Christ is true of all.[13]

If Paul's language is interpreted on the basis of ideas found in the Gospels, however, his words should be understood only in a metaphorical sense: those who take up their cross daily and give up their lives as Jesus' followers (Luke 9:23-24) can be said to have "died" with Jesus. Because this commitment to "die" to their previous way of life and begin a new way of life was symbolized and expressed in the rite of baptism, it can be said that they died with Christ when they were baptized, putting off the old person they were and becoming a new person (Eph 4:22-24; Col 3:5-10). Because of this, they can be certain that they will be raised by Christ and, in fact, can be said to have already been raised with Christ when he was raised, since his resurrection ensured theirs; this is because God raised Christ to life so that he might return in glory to raise believers to life as well. In the meantime, however, they must suffer and die with him in the sense of experiencing the same sufferings and same type of death that he endured.

Closely related to Paul's "with Christ" language is his affirmation that believers are "in Christ," which occurs repeatedly throughout his letters. This idea has also been understood literally by some, as if believers were actually "in" Christ in some spatial or mystical sense.[14] It seems preferable, however, to take Paul's language metaphorically or figuratively: believers are "in Christ" in the sense that, by virtue of their faith, they are in a relationship with Christ that involves living under his lordship and identifying with him in his life, sufferings, death, and resurrection.

Paul also refers to the community of believers or church as the "body of Christ" in several passages: "For as in one body we have many members, and not all the members have the same function, so we, who are many, are one body in Christ, and individually we are members one of another" (Rom 12:4-5; cf. 1 Cor 12:12-27; Eph 1:22-23; 4:12; 5:23-32; Col 1:18). For Paul, the church is a community where believers live united to Christ and to one another, sharing the particular gifts that they have received through the Holy Spirit and building one another up in various ways. Both baptism and the Lord's Supper are interpreted as signifying, symbolizing, and commemorating this union with Christ and his body (1 Cor 10:16-17; 11:29; 12:13; Gal 3:27; Eph 5:25-32).

Evaluation

The story of redemption told by Paul, like that of Luke, is still in essence a *Jewish* story. It revolves not only around Jesus, the promised Messiah and Son of David coming from Zion (Rom 1:2-4; 9:5; 11:26), but around God's chosen people, Israel, and the fulfillment of the divine promises made of old found in the Hebrew Scriptures. As in Jewish thought, to share in the coming era of redemption, it is necessary to fulfill the law and be circumcised, though in a *spiritual* rather than a *literal* sense, and to live under a covenant. For Paul, it is still "all Israel" that will be saved, though he redefines this Israel to also include Gentiles, who are branches grafted onto the olive tree representing Israel (Rom 11:17-27). Together with believing Jews, Gentile believers are now "children of Abraham" and constitute the "Israel of God" and the "true circumcision" (Rom 9:6-8; Gal 3:29; 6:16; Eph 2:11-22; Phil 3:3). In the end, the dead will be raised and all will be judged. The unrighteous will face God's wrath and condemnation, while believers will be delivered from that wrath (Rom 2:5-12; 5:9; 1 Thess 1:10).

Just as Paul is in close continuity with the Jewish story of redemption, so is he also in continuity with the story of redemption we discerned in Luke's writings. Paul understands the eternal divine plan or "mystery" in basically the same terms as Luke, and while he never asserts explicitly that Jesus' death was necessary for human beings to be saved, he probably agreed with Luke's idea that Jesus had to die so that the divine plan might be carried out. Paul also reflects the same tension found in Luke's writings between present and future salvation, understands fulfillment of the law of Moses in accordance with Jesus' teaching as Luke presents it, and maintains that forces of evil, such as the devil and demons, oppress human beings.

Nevertheless, certain elements of Paul's thought go beyond what we find in Luke and Isaiah. In particular, Paul speaks of sin and death as powers that dominate and enslave human beings on both an individual and a universal level, and he sees the two as closely related. The figure of Adam is also significant for Paul's story of redemption. In contrast, Adam is scarcely mentioned in the Hebrew Scriptures outside of the book of Genesis and is also virtually absent from the story of redemption found not only in Luke's writings but in the New Testament as a whole. Paul also uses language regarding the significance of Jesus' death that goes beyond what we find in Luke's writings. However, on the basis of what has been argued above, it seems clear that Paul's understanding of the role played by Jesus' death in human salvation is essentially the same as that of Luke.

CHAPTER 4

The Redemption of "Man" in the Thought of Irenaeus

The spread of the Christian faith among Gentiles, who were for the most part unacquainted with the Jewish faith and worldview of Jesus' first followers, made it inevitable that the early Christian story of redemption would begin to be told in very different ways in the period after the New Testament was composed. In certain cases, that story became virtually unrecognizable. Some, for example, transformed Christ into a mythical figure, one among many divine beings called "Aeons" who existed before creation. Others maintained that "Christ" was a separate being who had descended upon the man Jesus at his baptism to reveal divine truths to human beings but then had departed from Jesus before his crucifixion since, as a divine spiritual being, he was incapable of suffering. A variety of stories like these began to circulate among many who claimed to be faithful to the teaching of the apostles.

Toward the end of the second century, a presbyter of the Christian church at Lyons named Irenaeus composed a lengthy work commonly known as *Against Heresies,* intended to counteract the influence of these "perverse mythologists" and "heretics," as he refers to them, and to present "the only true and life-giving faith, which the Church has received from the apostles and imparted to her children," which is "one and the same" throughout the world (1.10.1-2; 3.Preface; 3.1.1; 4.1.1).[1] Only certain passages of the Greek original of this work survived; the work in its entirety was preserved only in a Latin translation. Relatively little is known about Irenaeus's life and death and the context in which he wrote. It is thought that around 202 CE he died as a martyr, like many Christians during the first three centuries of the church's existence, since in addition to the challenges the church faced from the so-called heretics within its own ranks, it faced persecution of various types from those on the outside.

Although Irenaeus's objective in *Against Heresies* was not to put forward a systematic presentation of the Christian faith as he understood it, few if any of the other Christian writings of the first three centuries provide a more complete summary of the ways the story of redemption in Christ was told in the period following the composition of the New Testament writings. The fact that Irenaeus strove to present not merely his own ideas and beliefs but those found in the tradition handed down to him makes his work especially valuable. At the same time, however, his reliance on a variety of traditions produced a range of ideas that are often difficult to reconcile with one another. As Dennis Minns observes: "He evidently did not notice that the ideas and formulations which he borrowed from different sources were sometimes inconsistent with one another, or contradictory." This has made it virtually impossible for interpreters to produce a neat and orderly presentation of all of the aspects of Irenaeus's thought; he "was not a systematic theologian, but a polemicist."[2]

Creation and Its Goal

Following ideas found in the writings of Paul and Luke, Irenaeus speaks of a divine plan of salvation conceived by God before creation. To refer to this plan, Irenaeus uses the Greek word *oikonomia*, which has often been translated as "economy," though its meaning is that of a purposeful arrangement, system, or plan.[3] This plan contemplated both the creation of the world and the redemption or "recapitulation" of all things; Irenaeus apparently borrowed the word *recapitulation* from Eph 1:10, which speaks of God's "plan for the fullness of time, to gather up ('recapitulate') all things in [Christ], things in heaven and things on earth." Thus, from the start, this plan revolved around God's eternal Son or Word (*Logos* in Greek, John 1:1), through whom all was created and in whom all is to be "gathered up."

While Irenaeus no doubt speaks of the creation and redemption of the world in general, his primary interest lies with "man." As we shall see below in greater detail, Irenaeus's doctrine of salvation revolves around his understanding of "man"; and because he uses the word in several different senses, his thought cannot be understood properly if we substitute "man" with terms that are gender-inclusive, such as *humanity* or *humankind*. Irenaeus follows Gen 1:26 in affirming the creation of "man" in God's "image and likeness" but distinguishes between the two terms. As Eric Osborn notes, the image "includes the physical and intellectual qualities with which man is born" and which "cannot be lost," while the likeness "may be identified as reason and freedom or as the incorruption which flesh will finally receive."[4] This likeness is dependent on the obedience of "man" to God; it was lost when Adam sinned but is recovered through Christ and God's Spirit.

Even though Irenaeus regarded both creation and "man" as originally "perfect" in some sense, he also conceived of the original human being, Adam, as imperfect, in that he was like an infant who still needed to grow and mature to become what God intended (4.38.1). Interpreters of Irenaeus have struggled to understand exactly how creation and Adam can be regarded as perfect and imperfect at the same time, but the idea may be that creation is "perfect in that it is destined for perfection. That is, it is relatively perfect: created for an eschatological perfecting."⁵

Unfortunately, rather than living according to God's likeness, Adam disobeyed God when, together with Eve, he was deceived by the devil in the form of a serpent in paradise (5.21.1–2; 5.23.1; 3.22.4; 3.23.8). As a result, together with his descendants, Adam fell under the power of the devil and sin and was expelled from paradise and subjected to death. In one sense, this subjection to death was the work of the devil, but in another, it was the decree of God. God's desire, however, was not to punish "man" but to avoid that "man" might "continue a sinner forever" (3.23.6). Thus death was a merciful judgment on God's part, since God's objective was that the fallen condition of human beings might some day come to an end through death and that they might then be transformed into something else, in accordance with God's original intention.

What remains unclear is whether Irenaeus regarded Adam's sin as an inevitable part of the divine economy or plan. While he never addresses that question directly, he does seem to maintain that God's Son would have become flesh whether or not Adam had sinned, since "Christ would still have been the model of humankind's creation in the image and likeness of God, and he would have offered humanity his fellowship and instruction."⁶ The fall into sin, therefore, seems not to have been entirely tragic in Irenaeus's mind, since it was partially a result of the imperfection of humanity in its original state and because it made it possible that the "man" who had sinned might still be transformed and perfected in the future rather than remaining forever in his fallen state.

All of this makes Irenaeus's understanding of salvation and eschatology somewhat different from what we find in the New Testament. Brian Daley rightly notes: "Salvation, for Irenaeus, is not so much God's unexpected intervention in history to rescue his faithful ones from destruction as it is the end-stage of the process of organic growth which has been creation's 'law' since its beginning. So eschatology, in the apocalyptic sense of the expectation of a wholly new age, is replaced in Irenaeus' theology by a grand, continuous conception of salvation-history."⁷ Undoubtedly, Irenaeus foresees the coming of a glorious new age and even employs much apocalyptic imagery to describe it. Yet he sees history more as a gradual progress to perfection that is some day to be consummated. Irenaeus also seems at times to conceive of the salvation of believers in terms of a new, immortal life in heaven or paradise rather than on earth (5.36.1–2), in contrast to ancient Judaism.

The Salvation of "Man" through Christ

According to Irenaeus, God has acted in Christ to "redeem man" (3.18.7), "vivify man" (3.18.7), effect "the correction of man" (3.23.1), and "once for all restore man sound and whole in all points" (5.12.6), thus "bringing man to perfection" (4.11.1). Yet how does the incarnation, life, death, and resurrection of God's Son accomplish this? Irenaeus answers this question in several ways in *Against Heresies*. At

Crucifixion of Christ with Two Thieves (S. Sabina, Rome). For Irenaeus, Christ "hung upon the tree, that he might sum up all things in himself" (5.18.3), uniting humanity and creation as a whole to God.
Photo © Alinari / Art Resource, NY.

times, he presents the same basic story of salvation found in Paul, Luke, and the rest of the New Testament, speaking of Jesus' passion, death, and resurrection as fulfilling Old Testament prophecy, and anticipating Jesus' second coming in glory, when the final consummation will take place.[8] However, he also speaks of at least three other ways in which Christ saves human beings: by joining God to "man," by rescuing "man" from the devil's power, and by revealing God to "man."

According to the first of these ideas, Christ "caused man to cleave to and to become one with God" (3.18.7), "attaching man to God by his own incarnation" (5.1.1) and "assimilating man to himself, and himself to man" (5.16.2). The Word of God was "made man" to bring "man" and God into "friendship and concord, and present man to God" (3.18.7) as well as to "accustom man to receive God, and God to dwell in man" (3.20.2). Irenaeus's language of recapitulation is closely tied to this idea: Christ "recapitulated man in himself" (5.14.2), that is, "the whole human race from the beginning to the end" (5.23.2).[9] This involves assuming "man" in all of his different stages and ages, from birth to death (2.22.4), so as to restore him to God's likeness.

But who or what is this "man" to whom Irenaeus repeatedly refers? The word *man* (Greek *anthrōpos*, Latin *homo*) can be used in several ways. Most commonly, it refers to a particular human being, in which case it is often preceded by an indefinite article in English: "*a* man." In the passages just cited, however, it is obvious that this is not the word's meaning, since it was not just *one particular man* who was redeemed, vivified, and restored to friendship with God. "Man" can also be a collective noun, in which case it is equivalent to "humankind" or the plural "men and women." This would seem to be the meaning in many of the preceding quotes, since the idea is that "humankind" as a whole, comprising all men and women, has been redeemed and saved. Yet in some of these and other passages from Irenaeus, the word *man* appears to refer neither to a particular man nor to humankind in general. At times, for example, it seems necessary to translate *homo* as "human nature," such as when Irenaeus speaks of "man being swallowed up in God" when Christ had "become man" (3.19.3), or claims that St. Paul "adopted the term 'flesh and blood' with regard to the Lord Jesus Christ, partly indeed to establish his humanity" (literally "his 'man,'" 5.14.1). Here "man" refers not to a particular man nor to women and men in general but, rather, to some*thing* possessed by Christ, that is, human nature. In fact, in *Against Heresies*, we often find the Latin neuter pronoun *quod* used to refer to "what" God's Son took: it behooved him "that he should himself be made *that very same thing (quod)* which he was, that is, man" (3.18.7).

A closer look at Irenaeus's language regarding "man," however, reveals that when he uses the term, often he has in mind not a particular man, humankind collectively, or human nature, but something similar to what the "idea of man" was in Platonic thought.[10] According to Plato's theory of ideas, eternal "forms" or "ideas" exist independently of the particulars that participate or share in them and therefore must be distinguished from the particulars. At the same time, however, the idea or form is somehow present in all the particulars, so that the particulars are all included or comprehended in the idea or form. In this way of thinking, there is an eternal "form" or "idea of man" that is distinct from all particular men and women yet at the same time includes them all. Precisely how this "idea of man" relates to concrete, particular women and men, of course, is a problem that neither Plato nor his successors were able to resolve to the satisfaction of all. Equally problematic is how this "idea of man" can be said to be "real": "he" or "it" is ultimately an abstraction, existing only in either divine or human thought or in some ideal realm that transcends our material world, even though this "man" somehow includes within "himself" or "itself" all those men and women who do live in the material world.

Thus, when Irenaeus writes that "the Word of God was made man, assimilating himself to man, and man to himself" so that "man might become precious to the Father" (5.16.2), and that the Word "dwelt in man" so as "to accustom man to receive God, and God to dwell in man" (3.20.2), he clearly does not mean merely that God's Son was made one man in particular in order to assimilate himself to that particular man and accustom him to receive God; but neither does he mean that, at the incarnation, God's Son became "humankind" or dwelt in all men and women collectively or that he was made human nature as a whole. In both of these passages, Irenaeus speaks of this "man" as some*one* (rather than some*thing*) who is precious to God and actually lives, knows, disobeys, thinks, and gives thanks. Irenaeus writes of this "man" as if "he" were an actual person in other passages as well, using the singular even though he clearly does not have one particular man in mind: this "man" was unable to reform himself (3.18.2) and is able to glorify God, express opinions, make suppositions, boast, and acquire knowledge and understanding (for example, 3.20.1–2; 5.15.3; 5.21.3). This makes it difficult to claim that for Irenaeus *homo* and *anthrōpos* refer simply to human nature, since such personal characteristics could hardly be ascribed to human nature. Rather, Irenaeus must have in mind some type of abstract "man" who actually exists, thinks, speaks, and acts yet who must be distinguished from concrete, individual women and men and humankind collectively, since he is one "man," not many men and women. The idea, then, is that, through his incarnation, Christ was joined to all other human beings by virtue of the fact that they are all one "man," that is, something equivalent to the Platonic idea of man in whom all particular women and men are included. Because of this connection, when the "man" that Christ became (or was made) was accustomed to receive God and assimilated to him, all men and women collectively were at the same time accustomed to receive God and assimilated to him.

Several passages, however, make it clear that, for Irenaeus, this "man" does not always include or comprise all women and men collectively; rather, it encompasses only *some*, namely, believers.[11] In relating how Christ "passed through every age," thus "not despising or evading any condition of man" (2.22.4), he writes that Christ "came to save all through means of himself—all, I say, who through him are born again to God," thus limiting this salvation to baptized believers. Elsewhere, referring to those who assert that Christ was a mere man, Irenaeus claims that they "are in a state of death, having been not as yet joined to the Word of God the Father, nor receiving liberty through the Son"; "not receiving the incorruptible Word, they remain in mortal flesh" (3.19.1). God will "receive those who believe in him into incorruption" but "shall righteously shut out into the darkness which they have chosen for themselves, those who do not believe" (4.6.5). Yet, if the Word was joined to "man" and thus "caused man to cleave to and to become one with God" so as to bestow incorruptibility on him (3.18.7), and if God "has afforded help to man, and restored him to his own liberty" (3.23.2), evidently this "man" did not include the heretics and other unbelievers, since they have *not* been joined to God, made incorruptible, or restored to liberty. All of this must be taken to mean that, for Irenaeus, the "man" who has been redeemed, set free from bondage, restored to health, and joined to God is neither one particular man alone nor all human beings collectively, since "he" is distinct from them. Therefore, this "man" exists as an abstraction or idea. While "man" in general has been saved "potentially" or "in principle," in order for that salvation to become "actual," particular men and women must believe and be baptized; only those who do so come to be joined to this redeemed "man." If this is the case, however, then this redeemed "man" must also be distinguished from the fallen "man," since the latter embraces *all* women and men while the redeemed "man" includes only those who come to faith.

Furthermore, if what actually saves and transforms human beings is the union of the earthly and heavenly in Christ's incarnation, then it would appear that Christ's real work of salvation was already completed when he became incarnate as a man to unite the immortal divine nature to the fallen human nature. In this case, it is not clear what role Christ's life, death, and resurrection play in uniting the divine and the human. Perhaps the best answer to this problem is to say that, according to Irenaeus, through his death Christ "recapitulates" the death of "man" in that he assumes all aspects of the existence of "man," including death, to restore the "whole man": Christ "hung upon the tree, that he might sum up all things in himself" (5.18.3).

Irenaeus's understanding of redemption as the "blending and communion of God and man" (3.20.4) also raises the question of what this union entails. At times, it appears that Irenaeus does not have in mind merely some type of restored relationship of friendship and communion between God and humanity but instead conceives of the divine nature as some type of incorruptible and immortal substance that, when brought into contact with the substance of human nature, made it immortal and incorruptible as well. He seems to maintain such an idea, for example, when he writes that in Christ, "the righteous flesh has reconciled that flesh which was being kept under bondage in sin, and brought it into friendship with God" (5.14.2); here it is some*thing*, "flesh," rather than some*one*, that is reconciled with God. This would appear almost magical, as if the union of God to "man" at the incarnation automatically brings about the union and reconciliation of God with all women and men independently of any subjective response on their part.

The idea of a union between two substances, the divine and the human, seems to be reflected in Irenaeus's understanding of baptism and the Eucharist. The communication of the Holy Spirit in the water of baptism serves to "join us to God" in the same way that water is mixed with dry wheat to form a "compacted lump of dough" (3.17.2); thus, in baptism, the divine substance is united to our human substance to transform it. The bread of the Eucharist "is no longer common bread" but consists of "two realities, earthly and heavenly; so also our bodies, when they receive the Eucharist, are no longer corruptible, having the hope of resurrection to eternity" (4.18.5). This can be understood in the sense that the Eucharist contains some divine or heavenly substance that, when ingested, makes human bodies incorruptible, as if some mysterious biological or chemical process were involved.

Irenaeus's claim that the Holy Spirit joins believers to God raises a further problem, namely, how the work of the Spirit relates to that of Christ. Irenaeus regards the Son and the Spirit as the "two hands" of God, both of whom play a role in creation and redemption (4.Preface.4; 5.6.1; 5.28.4). However, at times it is not clear how the work of each is distinct: Is "man" united to God by the Holy Spirit, who became "commingled and united with flesh" (4.31.2), or by Christ through the incarnation? Irenaeus's idea may be that the Spirit first had to be united to Christ's righteous flesh in order to become accustomed to dwelling in human flesh as a whole, and for that flesh to become accustomed to receiving the Spirit (3.17.1; 4.20.5). Yet Irenaeus also teaches that it is the Word of God who, by dwelling in "man" directly, accustomed man "to receive God, and God to dwell in man" (3.20.2), and that the Spirit himself prepares believers for incorruption, as they are "little by little accustomed to receive and bear God" (5.8.1). Thus, at times, Irenaeus seems to ascribe to the Holy Spirit some of the same saving activities that he assigns to Christ.

The *Christus Victor* Idea

A second understanding of Christ's saving work involves the liberation of human beings from their bondage to Satan. Adam had become a "vessel in [Satan's] possession" and was held under his power as his captive," together with "man" as a whole (3.23.1). However, through Christ, "he who had led man captive, was justly captured in his turn by God," while "man, who had been led captive, was loosed from the bonds of condemnation" (3.23.1). By "waging war against our enemy, and crushing him who had at the beginning led us away captives in Adam," Christ "trampled upon his head" (5.21.1). This understanding of Christ's work has been labeled the *Christus Victor* idea, thanks primarily to the book by Gustav Aulén published under that same name in English in 1931.[12]

Yet precisely how did Christ defeat the devil and thus deliver humanity from the power of sin and death? While at times it may appear that Christ simply "binds" or overpowers the devil by virtue of his superior strength (3.21.1; 4.33.4; 5.21.3), Irenaeus insists that God acted in conformity with justice:

> And since the apostasy tyrannized over us unjustly, and, though we were by nature the property of the omnipotent God, alienated us contrary to nature, rendering us its own disciples, the Word of God, powerful in all things, and not defective with regard to his own justice, did righteously turn against that apostasy, and redeem from it his own property, not by violent means, as the [apostasy] had obtained dominion over us at the beginning, when it insatiably snatched away what was not its own, but by means of persuasion, as became a God of counsel, who does not use violent means to obtain what he desires; so that neither should justice be infringed upon, nor the ancient handiwork of God go to destruction. (5.1.1)

As we shall see in chapter 5, it later came to be taught that God had tricked Satan, offering him his own Son in exchange for the liberation of the human beings under Satan's power. Satan acceded to this exchange, unaware that he would be unable to retain Christ under his power because of Christ's divinity, by virtue of which he rose from the dead. In this way, God did not use violence or force against Satan but acted in accordance with justice. Irenaeus never speaks explicitly of God dealing with Satan in this way; rather, he implies that it was

Burial Niches with Fresco of Christ Pantocrator (catacomb of S. Callisto, Rome). For Irenaeus, Christ is the "all-powerful one" (Pantocrator) who, by defeating the devil, has delivered human beings from death and restored them to immortality.
Photo © Erich Lessing / Art Resource, NY.

Christ's obedience that led to his victory over Satan (5.21.2-3).[13] Irenaeus may instead have had in mind another idea found in ancient Christian thought: that Satan had no right to inflict death on Christ since he was perfectly righteous and obedient and thus did not deserve to die. Consequently, when Satan exceeded his rights by putting Christ to death, God was justified in taking away from Satan the human beings who had fallen under his power. One other possibility is that for Irenaeus, Christ brought the "man" whom he had assumed at the incarnation back into conformity with God's will; and because all men and women are included in that "man," humanity in general has been restored to obedience and thus delivered from death and the devil. In any case, strictly speaking, it is Christ's *resurrection* that defeats Satan, rather than Christ's *death* per se; the cross is salvific only in that it leads to the victory obtained when Christ rose from the dead.

The *Christus Victor* understanding of Christ's work raises some of the same problems as Irenaeus's idea that Christ effects salvation by uniting the divine to the human. If "man" in general, "who had been led captive in times past," has been "rescued from the grasp of his possessor" (5.21.3) and "loosed from the bonds of condemnation" (3.23.1), then are not *all* people saved? Or is it only those who come to faith who have been rescued, so that the rest remain under the devil's power? Irenaeus never affirms the latter idea. Once again, while he stresses the need for faith in order to attain redemption, it is not clear how he can say that "man" as a whole was rescued from the devil's power. Irenaeus thus affirms an objective, universal liberation involving *all* people while at the same time maintaining that ultimately only *some* are subjectively freed from their bondage. This understanding of salvation also appears to be automatic. It is as if human beings, who are under Satan's power by virtue of what Adam did, merely stand by passively while Christ and Satan struggle to see who will be the victor and obtain "man" as the "spoils" or "goods" (3.23.1–2). And if it is maintained that Christ's victory over Satan merely made it *possible* for human beings to turn from sin back to God, then it is not clear in what sense they have actually been rescued. If they continue to sin, do they not remain under Satan's power, so that they have *not* been redeemed by Christ?

Other criticisms have also been leveled against the *Christus Victor* idea. Above all, it appears too mythical: rather than human beings being responsible for Jesus' death, the culprit is considered to be Satan, or perhaps even God himself, who offers his Son to Satan in exchange for human beings as a whole. The idea of some type of struggle in which Christ actually uses chains to bind Satan also seems quite fanciful. Furthermore, if Satan has already been bound, why does he apparently continue to be active in the world, and why has evil not already disappeared? Can we simply attribute all human sin to what Adam did or to the power of Satan? Or are human beings themselves responsible for the sins they commit?

Christ as Teacher and Revealer

The third way that Irenaeus presents Christ as saving human beings is by revealing God to them. This he did through his teaching as well as the "example of piety, righteousness and submission" he provided (2.22.4; 4.6.4–5; 4.20.7). While the creation in general reveals God, "much more does that revelation of the Father which comes through the Word, give life to those who see God" (4.20.7). For Irenaeus, Jesus' death also serves to impart knowledge to human beings and draw them back to God in love: "The Lord suffered that he might bring those who have wandered from the Father, back to knowledge and to his fellowship" (2.20.3; cf. 4.37.7).

In contrast to the other understandings of Christ's work found in Irenaeus, his work of revelation and teaching cannot be regarded as bringing about some automatic change in humanity as a whole or in the human situation in general; people are saved only to the extent that they respond properly to what Christ reveals and teaches. For this reason, some have argued that the idea of Christ teaching human beings and revealing God to them is actually at the heart of Irenaeus's doctrine of salvation: neither the union of God and "man" nor liberation from the devil's power *in themselves* redeem human beings; rather, Christ's incarnation and victory over the devil merely *make it possible* for human beings to turn back to God in obedience to be healed, united to God, and restored to incorruption.[14]

Nevertheless, at times, Irenaeus's language does reflect a belief that the incarnation of Christ and his victory over the devil had actually *effected* the "union and communion" of God and "man" (5.1.1) and the redemption of "man" as a whole, rather than merely making these things *possible*.

Irenaeus's doctrine of the church seems to be most closely tied to this understanding of Christ's saving work. While the church is undoubtedly the body of Christ, in which believers are united to God and freed from Satan's power, for Irenaeus the primary task of the church appears to be that of preserving and transmitting the revelation received from Christ and proclaimed by the apostles.[15] The church, "having received this preaching and this faith . . . , carefully preserves it" (1.10.2) and fulfills its mission in the world as it "preaches the truth everywhere" (5.20.1).

In a couple of passages, Irenaeus briefly alludes to a fourth understanding of Christ's work, according to which Christ turns away God's anger and obtains forgiveness of sins.[16] He writes that Christ "fulfilled the law, by performing the offices of the high priest, propitiating God for men, and cleansing the lepers, healing the sick, and himself suffering death, that exiled man might go forth from condemnation" (4.8.2). Here, just as the high priest's work involved both a *Godward* aspect of propitiating God through sacrifices and a *humanward* aspect of healing others, so Christ is said to have carried out the same work. Elsewhere, however, Irenaeus ties Christ's work of forgiveness to his work of revelation: he refers to Christ's divine authority to forgive sins and claims that "by remitting sins, he did indeed heal man, while he also manifested himself who he was" (5.17.3). Although the allusion here appears to be to the forgiveness offered by Christ to sinners during his lifetime, Irenaeus continues by citing Col 2:14, regarding the "bond which stood against us with its legal demands" being nailed to the cross, to affirm that "as by means of a tree we were made debtors to God, [so also] by means of a tree we may obtain the remission of our debt."

In neither of these passages does Irenaeus provide us with a clear explanation of how Christ or his death obtained remission of sins for human beings. It does appear, however, that the remission of sins through Christ merely makes possible the healing of "man" and reveals God to women and men. Thus, for Irenaeus, forgiveness is a *precondition* to salvation, rather than constituting salvation itself, since salvation involves a process by which human beings are actually changed and transformed.

The Necessity of Christ

Associated with each of the three main understandings of salvation in Irenaeus is an argument for the necessity of God's work in Christ. With regard to the first, Irenaeus argues:

> Unless man had been joined to God, he could never have become a partaker of incorruptibility. . . . For by no other means could we have attained to incorruptibility and immortality, unless we had been united

to incorruptibility and immortality. But how could we be joined to incorruptibility and immortality, unless, first, incorruptibility and immortality had become that which we also are, so that the corruptible might be swallowed up by incorruptibility, and the mortal by immortality, that we might receive the adoption of sons? (3.18.7—3.19.1; cf. 4.33.4)

Related to this argument is the claim that it was not possible for "man" to receive divinity and perfection into himself without first gradually being "accustomed" to God dwelling in him, because "man" was "yet an infant." By nature, "man" had to be created "inferior" to God and grow to perfection gradually, rather than being perfected from the outset or all at once (4.38.1; cf. 3.20.2; 5.8.1).

The *Christus Victor* idea in Irenaeus is also tied to an argument for necessity: it was necessary for the "enemy" to be "fairly" or "legitimately vanquished" (3.18.7; 5.21.1, 3) and "in a manner consonant to reason," without resorting to violence (5.1.1). This implies that other ways of vanquishing the devil might have been "unfair" or "illegitimate" and therefore unfitting for God.

Irenaeus also argues that it was not possible for God to be revealed to human beings or for human beings to have knowledge of God except through God's Son: "For in no other way could we have learned the things of God, unless our Master, existing as the Word, had become man. For no other being had the power of revealing to us the things of the Father, except his own proper Word. For what other person 'knew the mind of the Lord,' or who else 'has become his counsellor'?" (5.1.1; cf. 4.6.1, 7). Irenaeus brings all of these arguments together elsewhere, claiming that it was impossible for "man" who had "fallen under the power of sin" to "reform himself" and overcome the one who had conquered him; thus the "Word of God" had to become "man" so as to consummate "the arranged plan of our salvation" (3.18.2; cf. 4.33.4). In addition, he argues that God could not have let his creation go to ruin and destruction, since this would have involved God's own defeat, which by definition is impossible: if God had abandoned "man" to death, "God would have been conquered, and the wickedness of the serpent would have prevailed over the will of God" (3.23.1; cf. 4.38.3–4; 5.1.1).

When compared to the arguments found in the New Testament for the necessity of Christ's work, Irenaeus's arguments clearly are fundamentally different. While Irenaeus is in agreement with the New Testament in claiming that it was necessary for the divine plan (or "economy") of salvation to be carried out, he goes further in claiming that *it was not possible for God to save "man" in any other way than by God's Son himself becoming "man."* Nowhere in the New Testament do we find such a claim stated explicitly.[17] In addition, Irenaeus's argument for necessity differs from the New Testament in that it focuses almost exclusively on the need for God's Son to become incarnate, rather than the need for him to suffer, die, and rise.

The primary difference between the arguments for necessity in the New Testament and those presented by Irenaeus, however, is that the latter are based on certain definitions of *nature*. Many of Irenaeus's arguments revolve around the nature of "man," which is incapable of receiving the immortality, incorruptibility, and perfection inherent to the divine nature without first being joined and accustomed to these things, or which is incapable of freeing itself from the power of sin, death, and the devil. Yet, ultimately, all of these arguments are based on Irenaeus's understanding of the *divine* nature. God could not make "man" perfect from the beginning, since *by nature* God must be superior and "man" inferior (4.38.1). Because God alone is *by nature* immortal, incorruptible, and perfect, the only way for mortal, corruptible, and imperfect "man" to share in these qualities is to be united to the divine nature, which is something that could be accomplished only by God through the incarnation of God's Son. Because God is *by nature* just, reasonable, and nonviolent, it was necessary for God to treat the devil fairly, acting through persuasion in a way consonant with reason. It was impossible for God to be revealed to "man" without Christ, the eternal Word or Logos of God, since *by nature* only God can reveal God.

In reality, all of these arguments ultimately impose some type of limitation on God: the divine nature, the created human nature, or the nature of the world in general limit God, making it impossible for God to do certain things. Undoubtedly, Irenaeus repeatedly argues that God is all-powerful and thus subject to no type of necessity or limitation (3.8.3; 4.38.2; 5.4.2). On several occasions, he also quotes the words attributed to Jesus in the Gospels, according to which for God nothing is impossible (2.10.4; 4.20.5; 5.5.2). Yet the fact that Irenaeus does in fact subject God to necessity and limit God's omnipotence in order to argue for the necessity of Christ becomes evident when we examine Irenaeus's arguments against the background of the ancient Jewish and early Christian understanding of God's omnipotence.

In ancient Jewish and early Christian thought, immortality was something that God would bestow on human beings at the end time, when God raised them from the dead. There was no need to join the immortal divine nature to the mortal human nature previous to that, or for God to become human in order to bestow immortality on human beings, ideas that would, at the very least, have sounded strange to Jewish ears; nor did human beings have to become accustomed gradually to receive immortality or the divine nature into themselves, especially since being raised from the dead so as to die no longer was not understood in terms of coming to partake of divinity or being joined to the divine nature. Similarly, it was believed and expected that God could destroy the powers of sin and death, as well as overthrow the devil, simply with his word, by *fiat*. While, in ancient Judaism, it was recognized that human beings were incapable of saving themselves and freeing themselves from the powers of sin, death, and evil, there was no reason why God needed to do these things through a Messiah. God might simply pour out the Holy Spirit directly on human beings to transform them and change their hearts, just as God would eventually do when they were raised from the dead. God's powers of revelation were also unlimited; God could reveal whatever he wished to human beings by any means he chose. In fact, Irenaeus's recognition that the Word or Logos revealed many things to many people in different ways even before the incarnation, and that God also reveals through the Holy Spirit, who is equally God and able to comprehend and communicate the things of God (1 Cor 2:11), would seem to undermine the claim that there was no other way for God to be revealed except by the Word becoming "man."

Irenaeus's understanding of God thus implies that God is not omnipotent, since God is subject to certain limitations and therefore is not free to save the world in any way he wishes. Even to subject God to a certain understanding of "justice" in order to claim that God must act justly is to limit God; justice does not define God but, rather, is defined by God. The same must be said with regard to God's nature: in ancient Jewish thought, God is not subject to the divine nature, so that God must by necessity act in accordance with that nature; it is God who defines God's nature, not God's nature that defines God. To subject God to either the divine nature or the nature of the created order is a characteristic of Platonism, where the eternal ideas or forms, together with matter, exist prior to God and limit what God can do. Irenaeus's argument that God could not have created "man" perfectly from the beginning seems to reflect the same difficulty, since it implies that there is something in human nature itself, if not in the divine nature, that made it impossible for God to have bestowed perfection on human beings from the start.

When viewed against this background, then, it is clear that Irenaeus's arguments for the necessity of God's Son becoming "man" are based on an understanding of God that both the Jews in antiquity and the first Christians would have found problematic. Although the Christians no doubt maintained that Christ's coming and death, together with other events, were necessary for human salvation, this was only because they believed that God's salvific plan or purpose for human beings as foretold in the Scriptures had to be carried out. This was not because God was under some obligation to accomplish this plan but simply because God had willed it to be so.

Evaluation

Irenaeus's *Against Heresies* gives clear evidence that, by the end of the second century, the stories of redemption told not only by the so-called heretics but by the "orthodox" Christians, such as Irenaeus himself, differed in many respects from the story told by the first Christians. Undoubtedly, we can identify the basic components of the early Christian story in Irenaeus's work, including virtually everything seen previously in our examination of the thought of Isaiah, Luke, and Paul. Yet standing alongside those ideas are other ones that clearly have come from other sources and are difficult to reconcile with the essentially *Jewish* story that we find in the New Testament.

Among the most significant of these differences is the understanding of "man" that we find in Irenaeus. The New Testament never speaks of the salvation or redemption of "man" in the way that Irenaeus does, as an abstract entity or a Platonic idea embracing all men and women, or as a "human nature" in which all particular human beings share; nor do we find in the New Testament the notion that Christ's coming, death, and resurrection have had some mysterious effect on all human beings collectively, liberating them from Satan's power or uniting them to God as a whole. This kind of universal language raises the problem of reconciling the affirmation that *all people* have been saved objectively by Christ with the claim that only those who come to faith are saved; it also presents an understanding of salvation that contradicts reality, in that the world and humanity in general appear to be just as much under the influence of evil forces and as separated from God as they were before Christ's coming. Irenaeus's understanding of a gradual growth toward perfection on the part of humanity is also difficult to reconcile with the apocalyptic worldview found in much of Scripture (for example, Rom 8:19-23), in which the situation of the world is characterized by decay and disintegration rather than improvement. In this worldview, eschatological redemption is brought about by God or Christ coming from outside or above the world to save it, rather than through a lengthy process within history culminating in the perfection of humanity. Although both of these ideas are found in Irenaeus, it is not at all clear that he has succeeded in resolving the apparent contradiction.

Irenaeus introduces several other ideas and concepts not found in the New Testament, such as the "accustoming" of God to "man" and "man" to God through Christ and the Spirit, and the union of heavenly and earthly realities or substances in the Eucharist. At times, even when he uses Pauline language such as "recapitulation," he goes far beyond what Eph 1:10 affirms regarding the eschatological summing up of all things in Christ; Paul nowhere speaks of all the different stages of "man" being recapitulated in Christ, as if all human beings were included in Christ and the life of each were repeated in his own. Similarly, while Irenaeus follows the New Testament in employing the language of necessity with regard to Jesus' coming, life, death, and resurrection, the arguments for necessity he presents are fundamentally different from what we encounter in the Gospels. Undoubtedly, many of Irenaeus's ideas regarding sin and salvation can be read back into the New Testament passages that lend themselves to a variety of interpretations due to their brief, formulaic nature. Yet it seems clear that there is much in Irenaeus that is not directly based on New Testament thought, which still reflects a worldview and understanding of history that are primarily Jewish, revolving around not only Christ but the people of Israel and such figures as Abraham, Moses, and David, all of whom play only a minor role in *Against Heresies*. In Irenaeus, we see that this worldview and understanding of history and salvation are gradually being left behind so as to be replaced by ideas and concepts drawn from the Hellenistic world. Rather than seeing this only as something to be criticized, however, it can be considered the inevitable consequence of the penetration of the gospel into a context that was in many ways distinct from the Jewish context in which Christianity originally arose.

CHAPTER 5

Gregory of Nyssa and the Union of Divine and Human Natures

◆

No period in the church's history has been more decisive and eventful than the fourth century. That century began with the most intense and widespread persecution that the church had ever faced, ordered by the Roman emperor Diocletian. Only about seven years after this persecution ended in 305 CE, the new emperor Constantine legalized Christianity in the empire, later adopting the Christian faith himself and overseeing many aspects of the church's life. By the end of the century, Christianity had become the state religion of the Roman Empire and the tables had turned: instead of pagan authorities persecuting Christians, it was now Christians who persecuted those who practiced the traditional pagan religions.

After the persecution of the church ended, differences over faith and doctrine that had been left unresolved in the midst of the struggle for survival in the previous centuries became painfully evident. Arius, a presbyter from Alexandria, began to teach that the Son of God had been created by God the Father rather than being of the same substance or essence as God. When Constantine convened a general council of bishops at Nicea in 325, Arius's position was condemned; yet the conflict continued and even grew, despite the council's resolution, and was not resolved until the end of the century.

The question of Jesus' humanity also began to be debated when Apollinarius, the bishop of Laodicea, seemed to deny that Jesus had been fully human. His position was condemned in another general council of bishops, that of Constantinople in 381. This council affirmed the full divinity and full humanity of Jesus as the incarnate Word of God as well as the full divinity of the Holy Spirit. This laid the basis for the doctrine of the Trinity, according to which there are three divine persons, Father, Son, and Holy Spirit, who share a single substance or essence as one God.

The fourth century produced a number of outstanding theologians, chief among them Athanasius (c. 297–373), who led the struggle against Arianism, and the three Cappadocian Fathers, Basil of Caesarea (c. 329–379), his close friend

Gregory of Nazianzus (c. 329–389), and Basil's younger brother Gregory of Nyssa (c. 331–395). While any of them would be an ideal subject for this study, Gregory of Nyssa is particularly appropriate because, as the last of the four, he reflects and develops many of the ideas found in the others in spite of the inevitable differences among them.

The Creation of "Man"

The doctrine of creation is crucial to the story of salvation told by Gregory, and he dedicates much attention to it. Gregory follows the Christian Scriptures and tradition in ascribing creation not only to the activity of God but to that of God's Word, his Son, who existed together with the Father from eternity, as well as the Holy Spirit. At the same time, however, he looks to the creation account in Genesis to develop a fairly complex doctrine of the creation of human beings that revolves around the concept that lies at the heart of his understanding of salvation: *nature*, both divine and human.

According to Gregory, God's intention from the beginning was that human beings might live in communion with God. "Man" was "born for the enjoyment of divine good"; God "made man for the participation of his own peculiar good" and so that "the earthy might be raised up to the divine" (*GC* 5, 6).[1] Life in paradise was to be a perfect existence in which God and humanity would be one; human beings would live eternally, free from passions and emotions, contemplating the goodness and beauty of God, in a kind of blessed angelic existence (*OSR*).

When Gregory affirms that God made "man," however, he means that God created not merely *one* man, the first man, Adam, but, rather, the *human nature in which all particular individuals share*. This reflects an idea considered in the previous chapter, namely, that there is a single human nature common to all people. This nature is something like a Platonic idea of "man" in that it is a universal that is present in all particulars yet is in some sense independent of them; strictly speaking, "it" is a some*thing* rather than a some*one*, a "what" rather than a "who."[2]

For Gregory, in fact, this human nature was created before Adam himself was. Gregory speaks of a kind of "double creation" of "man" on the basis of Gen 1:27: "So God created man in his own image, in the image of God he created him; male and female he created them" (RSV). Gregory separates the first part of this verse from the second, interpreting the passage to mean that God originally made "man" in some ideal sense before actually creating Adam and Eve: "Man, then, was made in the image of God; that is, the *universal nature*, the thing like God; not part of the whole, but all the fulness of the nature together was so made by omnipotent wisdom" (*OMM* 22.4). The man Adam (who as a single man would constitute only "part of the whole") was created *after* the human nature common to all women and men: "The image of God, which we behold in universal humanity, was consummated then; but Adam did not yet exist" (*OMM* 22.3). It

Icon of Saint Gregory of Nyssa.
Image © Holy Transfiguration Monastery, Brookline, Mass.

is not clear whether, for Gregory, this universal "man" or human nature existed merely as an idea or in a real sense;[3] but only after the creation of human nature were the first man and woman actually formed from the earth and the distinction between male and female established.

In this ideal state, "man" or human nature was perfect and immortal, endowed with reason and intellect, to be able to contemplate God's goodness and beauty, as well as with free will. This is what distinguished human nature from the "lower nature" of the animals, characterized by irrationality and subjection to passions. At the same time, God foresaw precisely the "full number" of human beings that would eventually come into existence out of this one universal human nature (*OMM* 22.4–5). However, God also foresaw that "man" would fall into sin: "As he perceived in our created nature the bias towards evil, and the fact that after its voluntary fall from equality with the angels it would acquire a fellowship with the lower nature, he mingled, for this reason, with his own image, an element of the irrational" (*OMM* 22.4). Only after God had made the distinction between male and female did he tell Adam and Eve to "multiply, and replenish the earth." In reproducing, they obeyed not the divine, rational element in their nature but the irrational, animal element subject to passion; had the sexual distinction not been introduced into human nature, human beings would have reproduced in a different way, perhaps like the angels, and lived free from fleshly passions (*OV* 12).

Of course, all of this raises the question of why God created human nature with a "bias towards evil" in it beforehand, and also whether the "irrational element" introduced by God into human nature made it inevitable that human beings would fall into sin. In some way, God appears to be responsible for making a flawed humanity that would eventually sin. Partially in response to this problem, Gregory insists that it was necessary for human beings to have free will from the start (*OV* 12; *GC* 7, 21, 30–31); God could not "enslave" the human will, which by nature needed to be free. Nevertheless, the question remains as to whether sin was inevitable in the human nature as created originally by God.

Sin and the Fall

For Gregory, humanity as a whole fell into sin when Adam and Eve succumbed to temptation in paradise under the influence of the devil in the form of a serpent.[4] Having "for choice the good and the beautiful lying all around him in the very nature of things," the first man "wilfully cut out a new way for himself against this nature, and in the act of turning away from virtue, which was his own free act, he created the usage of evil." In this way, the "habit of sinning" entered into the life of "man," who "lost the blessing of being an image of the imperishable deity" and "clothed himself instead with a perishable and foul resemblance to something else" (*OV* 12). This affected the nature of humanity as a whole: "Since by a motion of our self-will we contracted a fellowship with evil, and, owing to some sensual gratification, mixed up this evil with our nature like some deleterious ingredient spoiling the taste of honey, and so falling away from that blessedness which is involved in the thought of passionlessness, we have been viciously transformed" (*GC* 8). Evil thus became like a disease fixed in human nature (*GC* 29).

As a result of this sin, death was introduced into human nature, making it no longer immortal. This death affected both the body and the soul. The death of the body involves the mortality and the corruption or decay that became characteristic of human existence, as well as the separation of the soul from the body. By making the body mortal, God made it possible for it to be transformed from its present condition into a new one through death and resurrection. The death of the soul, however, consists of the alienation and separation from God that took place the same day Adam sinned (*AE* 2.13; cf. 8.5). In reality, the soul remained immortal according to its nature, as it had been before the fall; but like the skins with which Adam and Eve clothed themselves after their sin, death was provisionally "made to envelope the nature created for immortality" (*GC* 8). Along with death, of course, came a life of pain and suffering in which all are subject to the passions of the irrational nature.

God's intention in subjecting humanity to suffering and death, however, was not to *punish* human beings or exact retribution for their sin but to *purify* and *correct* them. God's love sought to draw back "that which belongs to him from the ruins of the irrational and material" and "to get the good separated from the evil and to attract it into the communion of blessedness" (*OSR*). This would happen as human beings suffered the consequences of their sin, since they would thereby realize their need to turn back to God as the source of life and all that is good.

The Work of Christ

For Gregory, the only way for humanity to be delivered from its plight was for God's Son to become human, taking upon himself our fallen human nature. "Our diseased nature needed a healer. Man in his fall needed one to set him upright" (*GC* 15). By "putting on our sinful nature" (*LM*), the Son of God brought together divine and human nature; and because all individual human beings share in the one human nature common to all, this involves the healing of all: "He who holds together nature in existence is transfused in us. . . . He was transformed throughout *our nature*, in order that our nature might by this transfusion of the divine become itself divine" (*GC* 25). According to Gregory, when human nature

> had fallen away to evil, and come to be in the destruction of death, he by his own agency drew it up once more to immortal life, by means of the man in whom he tabernacled, taking to himself humanity in completeness, and . . . mingled his life-giving power with our mortal and perishable nature, and changed, by the combination with himself, our deadness to living grace and power. . . . He who is immutable came to be in that which is mutable, to the end that altering it for the better, and changing it from the worse, he might abolish the evil which is mingled with our mutable condition, destroying the evil in himself. For "our God is a consuming fire," by whom all the material of wickedness is done away. (*AE* 5.4)

Gregory follows Irenaeus in claiming that human salvation was not possible without the incarnation of God's Son: "In no other way was it possible for our body to become immortal, but by participating in incorruption through its fellowship with that immortal body" (*GC* 37). Because salvation involves the union of the divine and human natures in Christ, it was also necessary for Christ to be both fully divine and fully human; had he been less than divine, or only partly human, humanity would not have been joined in its entirety to God. For this reason, Gregory rejects both the doctrine of Arius, according to which the Son of God is not fully God, and the doctrine of Apollinarius, who taught that Christ lacked a human spirit or mind, since this part of him was only divine, thus implying that Christ was not fully human.

However, if human nature was already changed and transformed through its union with the divine nature when God's Son became human, what need was there for Christ to live, die, and rise again? Gregory answers this question by claiming that the divine nature had to descend to the full depths of the fallen, mortal human nature through death in order to raise up that nature. Thus "the human nature is renewed by becoming divine through its conmixture with the divine" in the same way that a pocket or bubble of air, when "dragged down by some weighty body and left in the depth of the water," consequently "rises quickly" back up to the surface, bringing up with it water that is "raised up together with the air in its upward rush" to make a splash at the surface; "so too, when the true life that underlay the flesh sped up, after the passion, to itself, the flesh was raised up with it, being forced upwards from corruption to incorruptibility by the divine immortality" (*AE* 5.5). Furthermore, since death involves the separation of body and soul, Christ "separated his soul from his body" at his death so that the divine life inherent in his soul might then kindle and inflame his body once more like a fire hidden under a pile of wood ignites the wood from below, "fostering into life that which had been brought to death" (*AE* 5.5). By being infused with the divine life in this way, the fallen, mortal body was restored to immortality.

This is how Gregory understands Christ's resurrection: it involves the reuniting of the human body and soul separated in death. In this way, Christ "reestablished in himself that nature which death had divided" so that human nature might become immortal once again:

> For when our nature, following its own proper course, had even in him been advanced to the separation of soul and body, he knitted together again the disunited elements, cementing them, as it were, together with the cement of his divine power, and recombining what has been severed in a union never to be broken. . . . For as the principle of death took its rise in one person and passed on in succession through the whole of human nature, in like manner the principle of the resurrection life extends from one person to the whole of humanity. (*GC* 16)

As is evident here, for Gregory, Christ's resurrection had a universal effect on humanity as a whole, automatically restoring the principle of the resurrection life in all people; the fallen body and soul restored by Christ were not merely his own, but the one universal body and soul in which all particular human beings share.[5]

Elsewhere, Gregory provides another argument for the necessity of Jesus' death: since "death is rendered necessary by the birth," "he who had determined once for all to share the nature of man must pass through all the peculiar conditions of that nature," including the condition of death, which had come to characterize that nature. Gregory then continues:

> Since, then, there was needed a lifting up from death for the whole of our nature, he stretches forth a hand as it were to prostrate man, and stooping down to our dead corpse he came so far within the grasp of death as to touch a state of deadness, and then in his own body to bestow on our nature the principle of the resurrection, raising as he did by his power along with himself the whole man. For since from no other source than from the concrete lump of our nature had come that flesh, which was the receptacle of the Godhead and in the resurrection was raised up together with that Godhead, therefore just in the same way as, in the instance of this body of

ours, the operation of one of the organs of sense is felt at once by the whole system, as one with that member, so also the resurrection principle of this member, as though the whole of humankind was a single living being, passes through the entire race, being imparted from the member to the whole by virtue of the continuity and oneness of the nature. (*GC* 32)

Gregory also understands Christ's death in terms of a ransom paid to the devil. Reflecting the language of Irenaeus, Gregory says that God acted without violence and according to justice in delivering humanity from the devil's power. Just as a master must agree to a certain price in order to free his slaves, so also the devil was offered a ransom in exchange for liberating the whole of humanity that was under his rule. This ransom was God's Son himself, whom the devil apprehended when the Son died and descended into the realm of the dead. However, because God's Son was in human flesh, the devil was not aware of his divine power, which made him stronger than death, and was thus deceived:

> In order to secure that the ransom in our behalf might be easily accepted by him who required it, the deity was hidden under the veil of our nature, that so, as with ravenous fish, the hook of the deity might be gulped down along with the bait of flesh, and thus, life being introduced into the house of death, and light shining in darkness, that which is diametrically opposed to light and life might vanish.[6] (*GC* 24)

The idea of a ransom paid to the devil in exchange for the liberation of humanity was told in different ways in antiquity.[7] As noted in chapter 4, some claimed that even though the devil justly held human beings under his power because they had willfully submitted to him, when he took the life of the sinless Son of God he acted unjustly. Therefore, God was no longer under obligation to treat the devil fairly and was justified in taking humanity back from him. Others claimed that when the devil took God's Son in death in exchange for sinful humanity, he did not realize that the Son was all-powerful and immortal because he was God and that he would therefore be unable to retain the Son under his power. When God's Son subsequently rose from the dead to conquer death, the devil lost everything. In both cases, the idea is that God treated the devil justly, without wrenching humanity violently away from him. However, it appears that God did so by deceiving the devil. One of the strongest critics of these ideas was Gregory of Nazianzus, who rejected the notion that Jesus' blood should constitute a ransom paid by God to the devil to redeem human beings (*Oration* 45.22).

In reality, however, Gregory's idea seems to be that when the devil devoured Christ like a "ravenous fish," he unwittingly brought the immortal divine nature present in Christ into contact not only with the fallen human nature of the human beings he held under his power but with his own nature or self. According to Gregory, this was similar to the way a medicinal antidote might secretly be mixed into food and given to a sick person to eat, for that person's own good. Thus, although this involved deception on God's part, the devil himself benefited from God's action, since not only humanity but the devil himself was transformed by

Eleventh-century Byzantine Fresco of the Nativity (Karanlik Kilise, Cappadocia, Turkey). In Gregory's thought, by becoming incarnate in our human nature, the Son of God has united humanity to God and made us participants in the divine nature.
Photo © Gilles Mermet / Art Resource, NY.

coming into contact with the divine, immortal nature in Christ. God "not only conferred benefit on the lost one [that is, man], but on him, too, who had wrought our ruin," since the devil's nature as well as that of humanity was purged by the divine power of Christ like a fire, thus "freeing both man from evil, and healing even the introducer of evil himself," that is, the devil (*GC* 26).

Interestingly, Gregory seems to ascribe little significance to Jesus' ministry and teaching in his doctrine of salvation. In fact, he writes that "the method of our salvation was made effectual not so much by his precepts in the way of teaching as by the deeds of him who has realized an actual fellowship with man, and has effected life as a living fact, so that by means of the flesh which he has assumed, and at the same time deified, everything kindred and related may be saved along with it" (*GC* 35). This implies that the way Christ saves is not by enabling others to lead a new life through his teaching and example but by uniting the divine to the human so that the human may become divine.

Is Salvation Automatic and Universal?

Gregory's understanding of Christ's work raises a number of difficulties and questions. First, salvation seems to be automatic, brought about merely by the union of divine and human natures, as if these were two substances. Gregory's repeated use of material examples (air and water, fire and wood, honey, cement, and so forth) led the noted nineteenth-century German scholar Adolf von Harnack to claim that "Gregory made of the whole system a rigorous physico-pharmacological process."[8] In other words, the incarnation, death, and resurrection of God's Son "work" to produce certain salvific effects in humanity or human nature like chemicals or medicines "work" to bring about desired effects.

Gregory's teaching that human nature as a whole has been transformed through the coming of God's Son also implies that *all* human beings have been saved, since all share in the one human nature assumed and transformed by Christ. If all are saved, however, then it is not clear why it should be necessary for people to come to faith in Christ and live according to God's will as members of Christ's body the church. In fact, Gregory teaches that baptism is necessary for salvation: "Without the laver of regeneration it is impossible for a person to be in the resurrection" (*GC* 35). The Eucharist also communicates immortality to human beings; employing once more the same type of material examples criticized by Harnack, Gregory argues that Christ's immortal body received in the Eucharist serves as a type of antidote or leaven:

> For, in the manner that, as the Apostle says, a little leaven assimilates to itself the whole lump, so in like manner that body to which immortality has been given it by God, when it is in ours, translates and transmutes the whole into itself. For as by the admixture of a poisonous liquid with a wholesome one the whole draught is deprived of its deadly effect, so too the immortal body, by being within that which receives it, changes the whole to its own nature. Yet in no other way can anything enter within the body but by being transfused through the vitals by eating and drinking. (*GC* 37)

Of course, this raises the question of why it is necessary for the immortal divine nature to be imparted to people through the Eucharist if it was already imparted to all persons when God's Son joined the divine nature to the human nature common to all at the incarnation. This would mean that the human nature shared by all is not yet fully transformed by the divine. Gregory sees this as a process that takes place gradually, similar to leaven fermenting dough. Just as when a serpent receives a mortal blow to the head the tail continues to move on its own for a while, so "in like manner we may see sin strike its deadly blow and yet in its remainders still vexing the life of man" (*GC* 30). Thus the union of the divine nature to the human in Christ has *begun* the transformation of humanity, but this process must still be completed.

For Gregory, this process advances as believers begin to live a new life, growing in their union and friendship with God as God's adopted children.[9] This takes place primarily through the work of the Holy Spirit; whereas Christ's saving work lies primarily in the past, in uniting the divine nature to the human and liberating the latter from sin and the devil, the work of the Spirit continues in the life of each believer.[10] This is where the example and teaching given by Christ during his life come into play, since this also enables believers to lead a new life.

The Spirit is given "sacramentally" in baptism in the context of the church, and believers then are able to resist the temptations of the devil and to change their sinful habits (*OBC*). In fact, Gregory even says that if this change of life does not take place in those baptized, in reality the Holy Spirit was not communicated to them in the water of baptism: "In these cases the water is but water, for the gift of the Holy Spirit in no ways appears in the person who is thus baptismally born" (*GC* 40).

Yet, while the process of purification is made possible in believers through the Spirit's presence in the church and the sacraments, according to Gregory, eventually *all people* will be purified. Those who are not purified from sin in the present life will undergo a purification process after they die, "in order that, the vice which has been mixed up in them being melted away after long succeeding ages, their nature may be restored pure again to God. Since, then, there is a cleansing virtue in fire and water, they who by the mystic water have washed away the defilement of their sin have no further need of the other form of purification, while they who have not been admitted to that form of purgation must needs be purified by fire" (*GC* 35).

Thus, while Gregory does at times speak of the fires of hell as eternal, he seems to maintain that, ultimately, all people will be purified from their sins and thereby be saved.[11] He affirms that "the complete whole of our race shall have been perfected from the first human being to the last,—some having at once in this life been cleansed from evil, others having afterwards in the necessary periods been healed by the fire." How long the period of purification lasts will depend on how sinful the person was: "According to the amount of ingrained wickedness of each will be computed the duration of that person's cure," which "consists in the cleansing of that person's soul"; this "cannot be achieved without an excruciating condition." In this way, all will ultimately be restored to the divine image: "When such, then, have been purged from it and utterly removed from the healing processes worked out by the fire, then every one of the things which make up our conception of the good will come to take their place, incorruption, that is, and life, and honor, and grace, and glory, and everything else that we conjecture is to be seen in God, and in his image, man as he was made" (*OSR*). Following the general resurrection and the final purification of the entire race, humanity will return to a paradisaical existence contemplating God's goodness and beauty, as Adam and Eve were originally to do in the Garden of Eden. As noted above, it seems that even the devil is ultimately to be healed and redeemed. For Gregory, evil cannot be eternal and thus must come to an end.[12]

Evaluation

Since the time of Gregory, the idea that Christ's work consists of purifying fallen human nature by uniting it to the divine nature has remained popular. While this is particularly true with regard to Eastern Christianity, where discussions regarding sin and salvation continue to revolve around the concept of nature, the idea of human nature or "humanity" being transformed by Christ is widely found in the West as well.[13] Nevertheless, as we have seen, this idea is problematic on several accounts. Christ's saving work is directed immediately at some*thing*, the human nature or humanity to be transformed, rather than at some*one*, human beings, who in this way are affected by Christ not *directly* but *indirectly* through their nature.

This process also appears to be automatic, magical, or "mechanical," in that what takes place in Christ "works" to transform humanity through some type of "cause-and-effect" mechanism: human nature seems to be healed and restored merely by entering into contact with the divine nature so as to be joined to it, and each of these natures appears to be some kind of substance containing energies or powers, such as sin or death (in the case of the fallen human nature) or life and immortality (in the case of the divine). When this union of natures with the consequent divinization of the human nature is said to take place at the incarnation of God's Son, it remains unclear what role Christ's life, death, resurrection, and exaltation play. It is equally unclear why people still need to become attached to this divine nature through faith, the sacraments, and the church if they were *already* attached to it when God's Son assumed the one human nature common to all.

Of course, like Gregory himself, adherents to this understanding of salvation tend to be aware of many of these difficulties and attempt to resolve them. Such efforts, however, seem inevitably to lead to elaborate, complex systems of thought that are often plagued with apparent contradictions. Human nature is wholly healed and made immortal by Christ, yet it is *not yet* wholly healed and made immortal; we all came to share in the immortal divine nature when God's Son became human, yet that new nature must still be communicated to us through the sacraments. Similarly, it is often argued that this understanding of Christ's work is not automatic or magical, usually on the grounds that something else, such as faith or repentance, is necessary;[14] yet this seems merely to make faith or repentance part of a "magic formula," so that when it is present, the desired "effects" of Christ's work are inevitably and automatically produced.

In light of what we considered in the first three chapters, it should also be evident that this understanding of salvation is far removed from what we find in the Scriptures. The story of salvation told by Gregory is no longer a story about Israel and its redemption by a Messiah descended from King David. The Jew/Gentile distinction, which is so important for understanding the New Testament, has disappeared, and the story now revolves around the universal human nature in which all persons share. Undoubtedly, Gregory makes frequent use of the Scriptures and even claims to "make the Holy Scriptures the rule and the measure of every tenet" (*OSR*). Instead of being understood in their original context, however, numerous biblical passages are essentially reduced to "proof texts" for Gregory's system, particularly those that are sufficiently ambiguous to lend themselves to having later ideas read back into them. In addition, Gregory's theological system is built just as much on Greek (and especially Platonic) philosophy, cosmology, and anthropology as it is on the teaching of the New Testament. For example, without the ontological link uniting all human beings to one another that Gregory's understanding of the universal human nature provides, the whole system falls to the ground, since what took place in Christ's *particular* life, flesh, or body can no longer be said to have an immediate effect on the life, flesh, or body of the rest of humanity.

In spite of all of this, there is much in Gregory's thought that no doubt appeals to many. Often, Gregory attempts to address issues and resolve questions that are entirely valid yet are simply not dealt with in Scripture. Thus, at times, there does seem to be a need to go beyond Scripture in some sense, as Gregory does. Similarly, many would consider the fact that Gregory tells a universal story about human salvation rather than a story revolving around a particular people, such as Israel, a positive rather than a negative. Above all, Gregory's belief that, ultimately, all human beings will be saved, although a period of "purification through fire" will be necessary in many cases, seems attractive in that it reconciles God's love with God's justice: all people are justly rewarded or punished for their behavior in the present life, yet in the end God's love triumphs when salvation is shared in by all without exception.

CHAPTER 6

Anselm and the Satisfaction of Divine Justice

In Western Christianity, no treatise on Christ's saving work has been more influential or polemical than Anselm's *Why God Became Man*, better known by its Latin name, *Cur Deus Homo*, completed in 1098. The context in which Anselm (1033–1109) wrote differed in important ways from that of Irenaeus and Gregory of Nyssa.[1] Whereas the Hellenistic culture in which the Eastern Fathers had been educated was noted particularly for its developments in the area of philosophy and abstract thought, since the rise of the Roman Empire the Latin-speaking West had been characterized by its strong interest and expertise in administrative and legal matters. It is therefore not surprising that Anselm, like other Western theologians both before and after him, made much greater use of juristic or legal categories and terminology to speak of salvation. Of these Western theologians, the greatest was undoubtedly St. Augustine (354–430). It is rightly said that "no writer, other than those of scripture, has exercised so great an influence over the development of western Christian thought as Augustine of Hippo"; in fact, Anselm himself not only drew heavily on Augustine's thought but equated orthodoxy with conformity to what Augustine had written.[2]

Following the fall of Rome at the beginning of the fifth century and the subsequent disintegration of its vast empire, the political and economic situation of the West had also changed. Europe had become a collection of smaller feudal kingdoms and lordships, which were often in competition with one another and tended to resist the type of centralized authority that the church represented with its pope in Rome. As bishop in the city of Canterbury in England, Anselm (himself an Italian) was often caught in the middle of the conflicts between the English crown and Roman pope; precisely for this reason, he had to finish *Cur Deus Homo* while in exile in the Italian province of Capua. The feudal world in which Anselm lived is evident throughout this work, where God is consistently viewed as a feudal lord to whom his subjects owe absolute obedience.

The rise and expansion of Islam to the south also presented a challenge to the church. In fact, the first crusade to the Holy Land took place during Anselm's lifetime. Like other Christian theologians, Anselm felt the need to respond to questions and criticisms raised by the unbelievers, or "infidels," of his day, including not only Muslims but the influential Jewish population in Europe. Perhaps the strongest objection raised by Muslim and Jewish thinkers to Christianity involved the claim that, in Jesus Christ, God had become human and had died a shameful death on a cross. In the preface of *Cur Deus Homo*, Anselm refers to "the objections of unbelievers (*infideles*) who repudiate the Christian faith because they regard it as incompatible with reason" and then states as his objective "to prove by rational necessity" that no one can possibly be saved without Christ and that human salvation required that God become human.

Anselm's appeal to reason alone was necessary because neither Muslims nor Jews accepted the authority of the Christian Scriptures. Thus, even though he repeatedly alludes to the New Testament, Anselm sought to present a convincing argument on the basis of philosophical rather than biblical considerations. In *Cur Deus Homo*, Anselm was not attempting to present a full, systematic treatment of the Christian doctrine of salvation. Nevertheless, this treatise provides us with all of the basic elements needed to reconstruct an overall story of redemption that eventually came to exert a tremendous amount of influence on Western Christian thought.

Another of Anselm's objectives in *Cur Deus Homo* was to offer an alternative to the stories of redemption that had come to predominate in the Christian tradition that spoke of Jesus' death as a ransom paid to the devil. By means of Boso, the student with whom Anselm is presented as carrying on a dialogue throughout the work, Anselm rejects this understanding of Jesus' work, claiming that God did not owe the devil anything and was under no obligation to treat the devil justly, since the devil had deceived human beings and come to torment them unjustly: "There was in the devil no reason why God ought not to use his power against him in order to liberate humankind" (1.7).[3] Anselm thus sought to provide a different answer to the question of why God's Son had to become human and die on the cross in order for humanity to be saved.

Creation and Its Purpose

From the outset of *Cur Deus Homo*, Anselm states his understanding of the purpose of creation: "Human nature was created in order that the whole man (i.e., with a body and soul) would some day enjoy a happy immortality" (Preface). While Anselm does not claim that human nature was created before human beings themselves, as Gregory did, he does understand the creation of the first human being as the creation of the human race in general, since all human beings were somehow included in Adam. This human nature was created "rational," in that it was able to distinguish between good and evil, just and unjust; in this way it might fulfill its "purpose of loving and choosing the Supreme Good above all other things" (2.1). This means that human beings had a free will. Originally, human beings were created "just" or "righteous," in that they would "hate and shun evil, and love and choose good" (2.1). In paradise, however, Adam and Eve were not yet immortal but had the capacity to be "transformed into immortal immortality" if they continued to choose good rather than evil: "In Paradise human beings had a kind of immortality—viz., an ability not to die. But this ability was not 'immortal' because it was able to 'die'" (1.18). In other words, strictly speaking, Adam and Eve were neither mortal nor immortal when they were created but would become one or the other depending on whether they sinned or not.

Among the rational beings created by God, however, were not only human beings but the angels. Like human beings, the angels were created with a free will, which meant that they too could fall into sin, as in fact some did (2.10). According to Anselm, God intended for a "calculable and perfect number" of angels and human beings to exist in what he terms the "heavenly city," which will be constituted in its fullness at the end (1.16). Because God foresaw that some of the angels would fall into sin, he intended from the start to replace them with human beings to make up this perfect number, although he also intended for the number of elect human beings to be greater than the number of fallen angels. Once the number of elect human beings has been completed, "the human reproduction which occurs in the present life will cease" (1.18). In Anselm's eschatology, this will be followed by the perfection of everything: "We believe that the physical mass of the world is to be transformed for the better and that this will not occur until the number of elect men and women is filled up and the Blessed City completed" (1.18).

The Fall

Anselm follows the ancient patristic tradition in speaking of the "fall" of "man," which took place in paradise when Adam and Eve were tempted by Satan in the form of a serpent: man "freely permitted himself—merely because of the temptation and without being compelled by any force—to be conquered according to the devil's will and contrary to the will and honor of God" (1.22). Here and elsewhere, Anselm uses the word *man* in the same abstract sense that Irenaeus and Gregory of Nyssa do: the "man" of whom Anselm constantly speaks is not merely Adam, but *all* human beings collectively, as if they were a single person. Because "man" voluntarily placed himself in subjection to the devil, ultimately, it is not the devil who is to be held responsible for the sin of "man" but "man" himself. Of course, the fact that the devil was already present in paradise tempting Adam and Eve presupposes the previous fall of Satan and the angels who followed him in sinning against God. In a sense, the devil's sin was worse than that of "man," since he was stronger than "man" but "had sinned in heaven untempted by anyone" (1.22); in contrast, "man" had fallen only when tempted by someone more powerful. In fact, God had allowed the devil to tempt "man," apparently to test him (1.19).

As a result of this sin, "man" was cast out of paradise (1.19) and became subject to the devil and the powers of sin and death, so that he is now "not able by himself to avoid either sin or the penalty of sin" (1.19) and is "now weak and mortal" (1.22). As John McIntyre notes: "Anselm accepts the view that man's disobedience to God is the cause of man's death, and there is no doubt that the death he intends is physical as well as spiritual or moral death, and it is eternal."[4] When Anselm speaks of death and "eternal torments" as the *penalty* for sin, it is important to observe that he is establishing an *extrinsic* relationship between sin and its consequences: death and eternal suffering are the punishment for sin because God has decreed this to be so (1.7, 9), not because they are the natural and inevitable consequence of sin (though, by virtue of God's decree, they have now become so).

Because Anselm follows most of the other church fathers in using the word *man* to refer to all particular women and men and to human nature as a whole, he maintains that when Adam and Eve sinned, so did all human beings.[5] "Now, since human nature was present as a whole in our first parents, it *was conquered* as a whole in them, with the result that it sinned" (1.18); "by man's defeat the whole of human nature became corrupted and leavened, as it were, with sin" (1.23). Anselm calls this "original sin" and claims that "from our first parents it is imparted unto the whole human race" (2.17); the human race "was completely contaminated with sin" (2.16). Following other Latin fathers, Anselm looks to Rom 5:12 to assert that all people sinned in Adam (2.16); thus all are equally guilty, since all share in the one "man" or human nature.[6]

The sin of "man," as well as that of the evil angels, consists primarily of disobeying God by practicing injustice and not giving God the honor due to him. To speak of the duty of "man" in relation to God, Anselm uses the Latin verb *debere*; this term "carries both the sense of 'owe' and the sense of 'ought,' so that he is able to see this obligation in terms of a debt to God."[7] Thus "man" "ought" to obey God and pay God the honor, respect, and justice that he "owes" to God. This is, in fact, what God demands of "man"; when "man" does not fulfill this obligation, he steals or takes away from God what belongs to God (1.11). In fact, the sin of "man" has stolen "man" himself away from God, since instead of belonging to God as God had originally intended, "man" is now under the power of the devil (1.23).

Throughout *Cur Deus Homo*, Anselm speaks of God as if God were a feudal ruler, "a supreme overlord, holding the universe and all estates of men under his control, establishing an order within which everyone is obligated to offer appropriate service to his superior in the social scale."[8] While this service is defined primarily in terms of paying God the honor that is due to him, as R. W. Southern notes, when Anselm spoke of honor, "he meant something different from the word in modern usage. He spoke not of that personal thing associated with a man's good opinion of himself and the good opinion of others, but of something objective, social in nature, and the guarantee of social stability."[9] Because the stability of society depended on the submission of all to the feudal lord, who was responsible for maintaining order and providing for the needs of his subjects, when they failed to honor him and submit to him obediently, the result was disorder and instability.

Thus, while many have criticized Anselm for presenting God as a tyrant concerned only for his own honor, in reality Anselm claims that God's concern for his honor is ultimately a concern for his creation. When "man" sins by not submitting willingly to God's governance and will, he "disturbs the order and beauty of the universe," even though he does no real harm to God (1.15).[10] Thus God demands that human beings honor him and do his will, not for *his* sake but for *theirs*, since only in that way can the world be the orderly, beautiful place God intended.

Punishment or Satisfaction

For Anselm, the sin of "man" places God in a dilemma. It would not be fitting for God simply to punish and destroy "man," since if his "very precious work" had "utterly perished," then God's plan for "man" would be "completely thwarted" (1.4). If Adam's race is not "fully restored" to "the dignity that would have been its possession had Adam not sinned," then "God's plan would seem to be a failure," and this would be "unfitting" for God (2.8). It would also appear that God either was "unable to complete what he had planned or else he regretted his good plan" (1.19).

At the same time, however, it was not proper for God merely to cancel the debt that "man" had incurred (1.12). "Man" had been "stained by the mire of

Bronze detail of the Crucifixion (Cathedral St. Mary, Hildesheim, Germany). According to Anselm, God's Son became human for the purpose of dying, so he might thereby make satisfaction to God for the sins of the whole world.
Photo © Foto Marburg / Art Resource, NY.

sin" and could not be accepted back into paradise under that condition (1.19); "it is not fitting that God should forgive something that is disordered within his kingdom" (1.12). In addition, if God allowed sin to go unpunished, "God would be dealing with the sinner and the nonsinner in the same way—something which is unsuitable for him [to do]," since injustice would be more at liberty than justice and God would appear to be unjust (1.12). "Therefore, if it is not fitting that God do something unjustly or inordinately, it does not pertain to his freedom, or kindness, or willingness that he forgive—without punishing her or him—a sinner who does not repay to him what she or he has stolen" (1.12). Because of the gravity of sin (1.21), it would be a mockery for God simply to be merciful and freely forgive sin, "for this kind of divine mercy is utterly contrary to God's justice, which allows only for punishment to be requited for sin. Therefore, as it is impossible for God to be at odds with himself, so it is impossible for him to be merciful in this way" (1.24).

Because God cannot freely forgive sins and remain just, the only alternative is for him to demand satisfaction, which involves a restoration of what was taken away from him: "man" must "repay to God the honor which he has stolen" (1.11). But it is "not enough for him merely to repay what has been stolen," since justice requires that "man" also give extra compensation or restitution for dishonoring God, just as those who steal from other human beings must not only give back what they stole but pay some further price or penalty (1.11). The problem of "man," however, is that he cannot pay this debt and make satisfaction. Even if he becomes completely obedient, paying to God the honor he owes through things such as penitence, a contrite heart, fasting, and almsgiving, he still cannot offer sufficient satisfaction and make up for what he has stolen in the past (1.20). "Man" is thus "inexcusable," since "he voluntarily became obligated to that debt which he is unable to pay, and through his own doing he lapsed into his inability, so that he is unable to pay either what he owed before sinning—viz., that he keep from sinning—or what he owes because he has sinned. . . . [H]e is blameworthy for having the inability by which he is unable either to retain justice and avoid sin or to pay what he owes for his sin" (1.24).

The Necessity of the Incarnation

Because God could not let his plan for "man" go to ruin but also could not forgive the sin of "man" without receiving adequate satisfaction, and because sinful "man" was unable to pay the debt he owed so as to make such satisfaction, it was necessary for God's Son to become "man"; "it was impossible for the world to be saved in any other way" (1.10). This was because only God himself, through his Son, was able to pay the debt owed by "man"; yet since "man" was the guilty party, the payment had to be made by one who was himself "man." Thus someone "fully divine and fully human" was needed to make satisfaction, namely, God's Son (2.6–7).

The satisfaction that God's Son was to make was the giving up of his life: "No

Henry II, German king and Holy Roman Emperor from 1014–1024 (Bamberg Cathedral, Germany). Anselm conceived of God as a feudal ruler like those of medieval times; harmony and order could be maintained only when human beings submitted to God as Lord, paying God the honor and obedience they owed to him.
Photo © Erich Lessing / Art Resource, NY.

one can willingly and out of no obligation suffer anything more harsh and difficult than death; and one cannot at all give oneself to God to any greater extent than when one hands oneself over to death for the honor of God" (2.11). Christ's death would thus outweigh "the number and the magnitude of *all* sins" (2.14). The incarnation was totally oriented toward this objective: "He became human for the purpose of dying" (2.16). Yet, if God's Son were to die "out of no obligation," the human nature he assumed could not be mortal, subject to death, since in that case he would already be obliged to die. Thus he had to become incarnate in sinless human nature (2.11). This stands in contrast to Eastern thought, such as that of Gregory of Nyssa, in which Christ had to take diseased, sinful, mortal human nature to heal it from within. According to Anselm, however, while Christ would no doubt be sinless according to his divine nature, if he took human flesh from the Virgin Mary, that flesh would be subject to death, as hers was because it belonged to fallen human nature and was affected by original sin. To resolve this problem, Anselm argues that the flesh of Mary herself was pure by virtue of the satisfaction that Christ would make on behalf of all, including her; thus the flesh he took from her was also pure (2.16).

While the incarnation and the death of God's Son were necessary for human salvation, Anselm attempts to avoid the idea that God demanded that his Son become human and die the cruel death of the cross. In fact, he asks, what justice might there be "in delivering up unto death, in place of a sinner, the most just of all people? What person would not be adjudged worthy of condemnation if he or she were to condemn an innocent party in order to free a guilty one?" (1.8). Anselm responds to this problem by insisting that the Son voluntarily offered himself up on behalf of humankind, and not because God demanded it of him: "The Father did not force the Son to die against his will; nor did he permit him to be put to death against his will. Instead, that man willingly underwent death in order to save women and men" (1.8; cf. 1.9). Thus, for Anselm, God cannot be regarded as the one who put his own Son to death; this was the act of sinful human beings.

The Satisfaction Made by Christ

By offering up his life to God on the cross, Christ paid the debt to God's honor that sinful human beings were unable to pay: "The life of this man was so sublime and so precious that it can suffice to make payment for what is owed for the sins of the whole world—and even for infinitely more [sins than these]" (2.18). It is important to note that, for Anselm, it is not Christ's death itself that satisfies God, as if the mere shedding of his blood or his physical sufferings merited human salvation; in fact, Anselm scarcely alludes to these ideas. Nor does he develop to any extent the idea that Christ's death placated or appeased God's wrath; nowhere does he imply that Christ experienced God's wrath or judgment in his death. Rather, what satisfied God was that his Son remained fully obedient to his will to the end and "persevered so steadfastly in justice that he incurred death as a result" (1.9; cf. 2.18). Thus it was the honor Christ rendered to God in his death that made satisfaction for human sin, not Christ's death itself.

According to Anselm, the payment of honor and obedience made to God by his Son is salvific in that it was deserving of a reward on God's part; God had to pay the Son what he owed him for what he had done. However, since everything that is the Father's belongs to the Son as well, and because the Son was in no need of any reward, the Son determined to "give the fruit and the recompense of his death" to "those for whose salvation he became a man" (2.19). In this way, not only God's justice but also God's mercy was demonstrated: God's justice was upheld in that sin was not unjustly forgiven, and God's mercy was shown in the fact that God took it upon himself to satisfy his own justice. "Indeed, what can be more merciful than for God the Father to say to a sinner, condemned to eternal torments and having no way to redeem himself: 'Receive my only begotten Son and render him in place of yourself,' and for the Son to say, 'Take me and redeem yourself'?" (2.20). In this way, "man" is now "free from sins," and thus "free from God's wrath and from hell and from the power of the devil" (1.6).

This satisfaction rendered by God's Son is valid for human beings of all times and places. To make this point, Anselm tells a parable about a king, an innocent servant, and a people who have offended the king. He affirms that once the servant has rendered satisfaction to the king, the king

> grants absolution from all past guilt to all those who either before or after that day acknowledge their desire both to obtain pardon on the basis of the work done on that day and to assent to the agreement then contracted. And [the king grants that] if they sin again after this pardon, they will be pardoned anew through the efficacy of this agreement, provided they are willing to make an acceptable satisfaction and thereafter to mend their ways. Nevertheless, [all of this occurs] in such way that no one may enter his palace until after the execution of the service on the basis of which his guilt is pardoned. (2.16)

This raises a problem similar to one we have noted in the previous two chapters. If the guilt of all people was remitted by virtue of the satisfaction made by Christ, and "man" in general has been restored, then are not *all* human beings saved, independently of whether or not they come to faith and repentance? And if they are not, then are not those who are ultimately condemned to eternal death being required to pay a debt that was already paid for them by Christ? In fact, when in this parable Anselm says that people will be pardoned anew "provided they are willing to make an acceptable satisfaction and thereafter to mend their ways," it appears that *further* satisfaction is required when people sin and thus that Christ did not actually "make recompense for *all* the debts of *all women and men*" or "make payment for what is owed for the sins of the *whole world*" (2.18). While Anselm's idea appears to be that the satisfactions made by sinners are accepted only by virtue of the satisfaction rendered by Christ, the fact that they must still make satisfaction and amend their ways means that, if they do not do so, they will not actually be pardoned. Thus, while there is an objective redemption on their behalf, it is not effective unless there is a proper subjective response on their part; and if this is so, then their redemption and pardon ultimately end up depending not on what Christ did but on their response to it. Christ has merely made it *possible* for them to attain salvation on their own through their faith, repentance, and acts of satisfaction. Prior to Christ's death, they could not be saved by these things, but now they can.

Anselm does not reduce Christ's work merely to making satisfaction for sins; he also insists that Christ "gave men and women an example, in order that they would not, on account of any detriments they can experience, turn aside from the justice they owe to God" (2.18; cf. 2.19). Yet this raises the same problem just mentioned: if the satisfaction made by Christ on their behalf is sufficient for their salvation, it is not clear why they should still need to follow the example of justice laid down by Christ in order to be saved. Apparently, they were saved only "potentially" or "in principle," but their "actual" salvation depends on what they do. Similarly, Anselm affirms that, by making satisfaction, Christ has restored human nature (1.3) and overcome the devil (1.23; 2.19).[11] In this way, Anselm seems to equate deliverance from the *guilt* of sin with deliverance from the *power* of sin, as if having one's sins pardoned leads automatically to a new way of life in which one is no longer dominated by the impulses of fallen human nature or the devil. In reality, it seems problematic to affirm that being delivered from punishment in and of itself results in a restored human nature or freedom from bondage to Satan.

Thus, in spite of Anselm's language regarding the restoration of human nature and the defeat of the devil, it seems that ultimately he *equates salvation with forgiveness* or, rather, with being spared punishment (1.12). This stands in contrast to the understanding of salvation considered in the previous two chapters, in which forgiveness plays little role and is no real problem for God; for Irenaeus and Gregory of Nyssa, salvation has to do instead with the transformation of humanity. In their view, salvation involves a change *in human beings*, whereas in Anselm's thought, the change appears to be *in God* or in the way God relates to sinful human beings. When salvation is equated with forgiveness, and this forgiveness is said to depend entirely on what God does in Christ rather than on anything human beings do, then human beings are saved without any change taking place in them. Just as in the *Christus Victor* explanation (see chapter 4), human beings seem to stand by idly while God (or Christ) and the devil carry out some type of transaction or struggle to get possession of them, in Anselm's view they assume a totally passive role as God acts to satisfy his own justice through his Son's incarnation and death. In fact, in Christ, God seems to be saving human beings *from himself* by means of a transaction between himself and his Son; God's mercy must save humanity from his justice, so that God constitutes both the problem and the solution.

Of course, some proponents of ideas like Anselm's consider the fact that human beings play no role in their salvation a virtue: precisely because God does it all, salvation is in no way dependent on what sinful, frail human beings can or must do. This means that they can have certainty with regard to their salvation, since it is a work of God alone. However, once it is said that human beings must come to faith and repent in order to actually be saved, then their salvation once more does depend on some change in them, namely, the change from unbelief and impenitence to belief and repentance.

Evaluation

The interpretation of Christ's work given by Anselm in *Cur Deus Homo* has faced heavy criticism almost from the start. Abelard (1079–1142), writing shortly after Anselm, was one of the first to argue that a God who required the bloody death of his innocent Son as the price for human redemption was cruel and wicked.[12] Since then, many others have leveled the same basic criticism, including some feminist theologians who have argued that Anselm's understanding of Christ's work represents a type of "divine child abuse."[13]

While such criticisms can rightly be leveled against many of those who followed Anselm, Anselm himself made a conscious effort to avoid such ideas. As noted above, Anselm insists that God did not want his Son to die but that this was necessary for human salvation. He also stresses that it was not his Son's death or blood itself that pleased and satisfied God but, rather, his Son's total commitment to practicing justice and righteousness. Ultimately, Anselm follows Scripture in claiming that it was sinful human beings who put Christ to death, not God. Furthermore, for Anselm, God's ultimate concern was not for himself or his honor but for the "order and beauty of the universe." However problematic this claim may be, at least Anselm attempts to argue that satisfaction was necessary not for God's sake but for the sake of humanity and creation.

Although Anselm's view of God undoubtedly merits criticism, this is not because he presents God as a cruel and vindictive tyrant but because, in spite of his protests to the contrary (2.17), he ultimately subjects God to a necessity that is greater than God. Paul Fiddes rightly notes that "theories of legal satisfaction set a law above the character of God"; "even when the law is said to be God's own law, the theory still requires God to act in a way which is confined by legal restraints," and the law becomes "a supreme principle."[14] If the law requiring that justice be satisfied by the punishment of sin is said to be part of the natural created order, then it appears that God is now subject to the order God has created and cannot or will not transcend it. If, instead, it is argued that God's perfectly holy and righteous nature itself demands that sin must be punished, then God is subject to some law inherent to the divine nature; in that case, it is divine nature that defines and limits God, determining what God can and cannot do, rather than God who defines God's own nature. To say that "it is impossible for God to be at odds with himself" (1.24), as Anselm does, involves defining God in human terms and then subjecting God to that definition. All of this is true of any understanding of salvation based on the idea that God cannot save humanity and the world simply through a sheer act of will or power, by *fiat*; the only way around this idea is to claim that God is under some obligation or necessity, even if this be defined in terms of the need to act in a way that is "fitting," "proper," or "suitable" for God, as in Anselm's thought.[15]

The understanding of justice that lies at the heart of Anselm's argument also merits criticism. Anselm works with a *retributive* view of justice, which involves giving each person what he or she deserves; for Anselm, because all are sinners, all deserve punishment. Besides the fact that it could be argued that God is unjust for treating all people alike or for not rewarding human beings when they do good rather than only punishing them when they sin, the retributive understanding of justice is also problematic in that it claims that justice is satisfied merely when sin is punished. As was noted in chapter 1 with regard to Isaiah's thought, Scripture understands justice more in terms of establishing well-being for *all* people; justice exists when all have what they need, so that divine justice and mercy go hand in hand rather than being opposed to each other. Similarly, the understanding of justice found in Gregory of Nyssa's thought (chapter 5) has to do not with meting out punishment but with correcting sinners and eventually perfecting them; God and God's justice are "satisfied" only when human beings are made righteous as God originally intended. If it is argued that God punishes sin to preserve the "order and beauty of the universe," then it can hardly be claimed that Christ's death alone accomplishes this; the order and beauty of the universe are preserved or restored not when one representative man (or God-man) does what is right but when *all* people come to do so.

Numerous other problems and inconsistencies with Anselm's argument have been pointed out. His argument that Christ's death was in some sense equivalent to or greater in value than the deaths of all other human beings combined seems quite weak and has been questioned since ancient times.[16] Anselm's use of the word *forgiveness* or *pardon* is also questionable, since in reality God forgives nothing; every human sin is paid for by Christ rather than pardoned. Although it is important to recognize that *Cur Deus Homo* was not intended as an exhaustive treatment of how human beings are saved through Christ, it has often been noted that Christ's earthly life and ministry, as well as his resurrection, have little if any significance for this understanding of his work; neither do the church, the Holy Spirit, and the sacraments seem to be of great importance, unless the need for a subjective response of faith, obedience, and further satisfaction for sin on the part of believers is stressed.

In light of what we have seen in the previous chapters, other questions and problems should be evident as well. In spite of the claim that "whatever is in the Old and in the New Testament has been proved" (2.22), it is clear that in much of his argument in *Cur Deus Homo*, Anselm has gone far beyond anything found in Scripture. In speaking of "satisfaction," Anselm has placed at the center of his understanding of Christ's work a notion that is not found explicitly (and probably not even *implicitly*) in the New Testament. His understanding of salvation as an eternal, blessed existence in a heavenly city seems far removed from what Isaiah, Luke, and Paul affirm regarding redemption, and many other aspects of his argument are clearly grounded more in his own philosophical system than in Scripture. Finally, it is evident that, in many regards, Anselm is in discontinuity not only with the New Testament but also with the Eastern patristic tradition. This means that, to the extent that it followed Anselm, the understanding of salvation and Christ's work in Western Christianity increasingly distanced itself from that found in the East.

Christ as Redeemer from Sin, Death, and the Devil in the Thought of Martin Luther

The theology of Martin Luther (1483–1546) was born out of struggle. During Luther's early years as an Augustinian monk, this struggle was an internal one: Luther incessantly sought peace with God, whom he believed to be a stern judge full of wrath at human sin. For years, Luther wrestled with deep-seated feelings of guilt and with his enemy the devil, convinced that he needed to overcome the powers of sin and Satan in himself in order to achieve the standard of righteousness demanded by God for salvation. Yet no matter how hard he tried and how harshly he disciplined himself, he felt that his efforts were in vain and that he remained under God's wrath. Finally, however, through his study of the Scriptures, most notably Paul's epistles, Luther encountered another God, a God who forgave sins and accepted sinners out of pure grace and mercy through his Son, Jesus Christ. To find peace, joy, and freedom from all fear and anxiety, all one needed to do was cling to Christ in faith, receiving through him both the forgiveness of sins and a new life of righteousness. For Luther, despair turned to gladness.

The resolution of this struggle within Luther led to a new struggle—this time an external one with the authorities of the church. Luther became convinced that, rather than proclaiming the gospel of God's grace and mercy to liberate people in the way that he himself had been liberated, the church was burdening and oppressing the faithful through corrupt practices and teachings that obliged them to seek salvation through their own efforts and resources, as he had attempted for so long. When he protested in 1517 against the sale of indulgences, which promised remission of sins and deliverance from the torments of purgatory for those on whose behalf they were purchased, Luther sparked a controversy that would lead not only to his being excommunicated and branded a heretic by the pope in

Rome but to the breakup of the Western church. Many sided with Luther in his call for a profound renewal of the church's doctrines and practices and a return to the gospel as Luther had come to understand it; as a result, the Reformation movement spread throughout much of Europe.

In the midst of all of these struggles, what sustained Luther was his unshakable faith in God and God's Son, Jesus Christ. In Luther's theological thought, this faith is the center around which all else revolves and on which all else depends. His understanding of God's saving work in Christ, therefore, is deeply personal and intimate; rather than speaking in general terms about creation and redemption, for example, he consistently speaks on an individual level, instructing others to confess together with him: "*I* believe that God has created *me*," and, "*I* believe that Jesus Christ . . . is *my* Lord. He has redeemed *me*, a lost and condemned human being. He has purchased and freed *me* from all sins, from death, and from the power of the devil . . . , in order that *I* may belong to him" (*SC*).[1]

Largely because Luther's theology was greatly shaped by his own intense experiences, it is impossible to reduce his teaching to a neat, orderly system. In Henri Rondet's words: "The father of the Reformation is not a systematizer. He [thinks] intuitively, he is a 'prophet,' a tumultuous torrent, he loves crude images, he works his thought into paradoxes, and one commits a serious error by taking what he writes always literally."[2] Luther's belief that Holy Scripture was to be the sole authority for doctrine and practice also contributed to this lack of a clear system, particularly concerning his understanding of Christ's saving work. In this regard, Marc Lienhard rightly notes that it is "necessary to avoid talking of a 'system' or of a 'theory' of atonement with Luther. He is content to follow the different ways by which the biblical witnesses attempted to translate the fall of human beings and the saving work of Jesus Christ, variations which must not be arbitrarily harmonized and which can have very different emphases."[3]

The Divine Law and the Human Plight

Although Luther believed that human salvation was foreseen and foreordained by God even before creation, and thus that a divine plan existed from eternity, that belief is not the place to begin when considering the story of redemption he tells. Similarly, even though Luther maintained that, in God's love, God had created the world and graciously continued to preserve it along with all of its inhabitants, the starting point of Luther's theology was not so much the doctrine of creation per se but his understanding of God's law. It is no coincidence, for example, that he begins his *Catechisms* with a discussion of the Ten Commandments rather than the First Article of the Apostles' Creed, which speaks of God's work of creation. Thus, when he affirms that God created the world out of "solicitude and benevolence toward us, because he provided such an attractive dwelling place for the future human being before the human being was created," he immediately adds that "all this generosity is intended to make humankind recognize the goodness of God and live in the fear of God" (*LW* 1:39). The objective, therefore, was that humanity might enjoy a life of blessings in communion with God by doing God's will as expressed in God's law.

According to Luther, everything that God's law prescribes is summarized in the first of the Ten Commandments, "You shall have no other gods before me." Of all the commandments, this is "the very first of all" and "the highest and the best, [the one] from which all others proceed" (*LW* 44:30). It requires "that one's whole heart and confidence be placed in God alone, and in no one else. . . . [Y]ou lay hold of God when your heart grasps him and clings to him. To cling to him with your heart is nothing else than to entrust yourself to him completely" (*LC*). Naturally, when one loves and trusts God in this way, one will also practice love toward one's neighbor, which is also commanded in God's law. This is what God intended and desired from the start: Adam was created in the image of God in the sense that he had "a most sincere desire to love God and his neighbor" and "lived in a life that was wholly godly," characterized by "supreme pleasure . . . in obedience to God and submission to his will"; "he obeyed God with the utmost joy" (*LW* 1:63, 65, 113). In this original state, Adam and Eve were truly free; they had a free will and lived free from any type of fear, trusting fully in God for everything.

This changed, however, when Satan, in the form of a serpent, induced Adam and Eve to fall into sin. From that point on, they lost their capacity to love, obey, and trust in God. While they maintained a certain degree of freedom in their life on earth, they were no longer free to relate to God in the way they had previously. Luther refers to this condition as *original* or *inherited sin*. In this condition, human beings live in bondage to sin and Satan. They are beset with evil desires ("concupiscence") and are constantly assailed and tempted by the devil: "When God is not present and at work in us everything we do is evil" (*LW* 33:64). The fallen human will is "immutably the captive and slave of evil, since it cannot of itself turn to the good" (*LW* 33:67). The fact that human nature has become "curved in upon itself because of the viciousness of original sin" (*LW* 25:291) makes it impossible to obey God's law.

In this fallen condition, sinful human beings are under God's wrath and condemnation. God's wrath is manifested in various types of afflictions endured by human beings in their life on earth but, more particularly, in the sentence of eternal death and damnation God pronounces on them. God's law becomes a heavy burden to them, constantly accusing them of sin and setting their guilt before their eyes: "The law brings the wrath of God, kills, reviles, accuses, judges, and condemns everything that is not in Christ" (*LW* 31:54). Luther even speaks of God's employing the devil and the law as his instruments to afflict human beings and incite them to sin, as well as of God's abandoning them in his wrath.[4]

While much of this no doubt sounds harsh and perhaps even repulsive, as if God desires that human beings sin and die, in Luther's thought God's purpose is to drive fallen human beings to the same type of despair that Luther himself had experienced. In a sense, by "attacking" human beings on all fronts—making them shudder under his wrath, abandoning them, threatening them with death and hell through his law, setting loose the devil upon them, and even inciting

Martin Luther, woodcut by Lucas Cranach the Elder.
Photo courtesy of the Brauer Museum of Art (87.02), Valparaiso University. Used by permission.

them to fall deeper and deeper into sin—God is seeking not to *destroy* or *harm* them but to *save* them. Because, for Luther, salvation depends on human beings' placing their trust entirely in God and not in themselves or their own efforts and strength, it is necessary for them to despair fully of everything else in order to look to God alone; only when they have reached the depths of absolute despair will they realize their need to cling in faith to God's mercy and grace in Christ, as Luther himself discovered in the monastery.

In particular, this is the role of God's law: "The foremost office or power of the law is that it reveals inherited sin and its fruits. It shows human beings into what utter depths their nature has fallen and how completely corrupt it is. . . . Thus they are terrified, humbled, despondent, and despairing. They anxiously desire help but do not know where to find it" (*SA*). Gerhard Forde rightly makes the comparison to the idea of an alcoholic "bottoming out," that is, "reaching the absolute bottom where one can no longer escape the need for help."[5] Ultimately, then, for Luther, God is love, not wrath; Luther repeatedly insists that anyone who regards God "as angry is not seeing him correctly" (*LW* 21:37):

> For you do not know the Father if you regard him as an angry Judge and
> flee from him. He is not at all inclined to enjoy anger and condemnation;
> nor does it please him if we flee from him. He did not institute the
> law—though it is intended to work knowledge of sin and to terrify the
> impenitent—to perpetuate the fear of those who recognize their sins and
> are frightened. No, his real purpose and will is that you be rescued from
> all this misery, from sin, death, and damnation. For this purpose he sent
> you his Son Christ. (*LW* 24:61; cf. 12:322)

This understanding of salvation and the human plight results in a rather negative view of unredeemed humanity and human nature on Luther's part. Fallen
human beings are wholly and completely "sin," precisely because they were created to depend entirely on God; when they fail to do so, nothing that they do is
able to please God. When, on the basis of their own reason, strength, actions,
or abilities, they attempt to win God's favor or approval, they can only remain
under God's wrath and condemnation, because they are still looking to themselves rather than to God alone, as God desires and commands. For Luther, the
real problem is not the external actions performed by sinful human beings—that
is, "sins"—but what human beings have become on the inside, namely, "sin."
William Lazareth notes: "For Luther, it is crucial to profess that one is a sinner
before one commits sins. . . . Unbelief (*Unglaube*) in God and doubt of God's
Word are therefore the original or primal sin."[6]

The solution, therefore, is not to demand that sinners attempt to mend their
ways, calling on them to change their lives and do good works, as Luther believed
that the church of his time was mistakenly teaching. In their fallen state, this is
impossible for sinful human beings and will only drive them more deeply into
despair, since it lays the burden of their salvation on their own shoulders. Rather,
the only solution is to point them to the gospel of God's grace and mercy in
Christ, calling and inviting them to have faith and trust fully in God. In contrast
to the law, which "shows nothing but our sin, makes us guilty, and thus produces
an anguished conscience," the gospel "supplies a longed for remedy to people in
anguish of this kind. . . . [T]he law announces wrath, but the gospel peace" (*LW*
25:416; cf. 31:364). Whereas the law "makes demands on us" and "grieves and
frightens" those who do not keep it, the gospel is a "blessed word" that "demands
nothing of us, but announces everything that is good, namely, that God has given
us poor sinners his only Son" to "give his life for us, to redeem us from sin, from
eternal death, and from the power of the devil" (*LW* 12:164–65).

The Work of Christ

By the time of Luther, several different understandings of Christ's work had
become widespread in the West.[7] The *Christus Victor* idea (see chapter 4) continued to be taught but had declined considerably in popularity. In contrast,
Anselm's understanding of Christ's work (chapter 6) had become widely accepted,
although many continued to raise the same objections to it that Abelard had and

preferred to follow Abelard in teaching that Christ's death was salvific because it revealed God's love to human beings to move them to repentance and new life. In some circles, a more mystical understanding of Christ's work became common, according to which believers might be joined or united to Christ and his death in some way. This idea, though somewhat similar to what we find in Eastern Christian thought, stresses the union of human *persons* to Christ's own person through faith, rather than the union of human beings to Christ through the human nature they share with him.

Despite the apparent contradictions among many of these different views, Luther took up virtually all of them. While this has created many difficulties for Luther's interpreters, especially when they have attempted to reconcile these different ideas with one another or systematize his teaching, it appears that Luther himself did not see any problem in adopting them all, precisely because for him what ultimately saves human beings is clinging to Christ in faith. Thus any understanding of Christ's work that points human beings to trust in Christ alone for salvation seems to have been useful for Luther. In fact, the understanding of the human plight outlined in the previous section might even be seen as demanding a variety of explanations of the way in which Christ saves human beings, and Luther combines them all freely. As Philip Watson has observed, Luther speaks of five forces hostile to human beings, from which they need to be saved: sin, death, the devil, the law, and the wrath of God.[8] Thus, for Luther, all of these forces needed to be overcome by Christ, and this is accomplished in different ways.

One of Luther's favorite ideas was that Christ had triumphed over Satan through his death and resurrection. Luther adapts the imagery employed by Gregory of Nyssa (see chapter 5) so as to speak of Satan being deceived, like a fish caught by a baited hook: "For the hook, which is the divinity of Christ, was concealed under the earthworm. The devil swallowed it with his jaws when Christ died and was buried. But it ripped his belly so that he could not retain it but had to disgorge it. He ate death for himself. This affords us the greatest solace; for just as the devil could not hold Christ in death, so he cannot hold us who believe in Christ" (*LW* 22:24; cf. 26:267). For Luther, Christ triumphs over Satan by overpowering him through his divinity. This triumph took place when Christ descended into hell after his death and then rose victorious.

Luther uses similar imagery to describe Christ's victory over God's law, which he also speaks of as if it were a real person:

> Here Christ says: "Lady Law, you empress, you cruel and powerful tyrant over the whole human race, what did I commit that you accused, intimidated, and condemned me in my innocence?" Here the law, which once condemned and killed all men, has nothing with which to defend or cleanse itself. Therefore it is condemned and killed in turn, so that it loses its jurisdiction not only over Christ—whom it attacked and killed without any right anyway—but also over all who believe in him. Here Christ says (Matt. 11:28): "Come to me, all who labor under the yoke of

the law. I could have overcome the law by my supreme authority, without any injury to me; for I am the Lord of the law, and therefore it has no jurisdiction over me. But for the sake of you, who were under the law, I assumed your flesh and subjected myself to the law. That is, beyond the call of duty I went down into the same imprisonment, tyranny, and slavery of the law under which you were serving as captives. I permitted the law to lord it over me, its Lord, to terrify me, to subject me to sin, death, and the wrath of God—none of which it had any right to do."
(*LW* 26:370)

Luther similarly spoke of sin and death as if they were actual persons, though it is doubtful that he intended such imagery to be taken literally (unless sin and death are understood as personifications of the devil). He writes, for example, that sin "is a very powerful and cruel tyrant, dominating and ruling over the whole world, capturing and enslaving all women and men. In short, sin is a great and powerful god who devours the whole human race. . . . He, I say, attacks Christ and wants to devour him as he has devoured all the rest. But he does not see that he is a person of invincible and eternal righteousness. In this duel, therefore, it is necessary for sin to be conquered and killed, and for righteousness to prevail and live. Thus in Christ all sin is conquered, killed, and buried" (*LW* 26:281; cf. 26:33).

In these passages, we encounter the same ideas associated with the *Christus Victor* view found in patristic thought (see chapters 4 and 5). In this case, however, it is not the devil who overstepped his rights by inflicting death on God's innocent Son or who failed to realize that the human being he had devoured was also God but, rather, sin and the law personified. Luther describes Christ's victory over death in the same terms:

For when death overcame him and slew him, without however having any claim or cause against him, and he willingly and innocently permitted himself to be slain, death became indebted to him, having done him wrong and having sinned against him and having handled all things inattentively, so that Christ has an honest claim against it. The wrong which death perpetrated against him, is so great that death is unable to pay or to atone for it. And so death must be under Christ and in his power forever. Thus death is overcome in Christ and strangled. (*LW* 52:156)

Luther generally alluded to Christ's victory over sin, death, the devil, and the law in the same contexts in which he spoke of Christ rendering satisfaction to God's justice and appeasing God's wrath by suffering the penalty for human sin. Adopting a version of Anselm's argument for the necessity of the incarnation and death of God's Son, Luther maintained that because "God cannot and will not regard sin with favor, but his wrath abides upon it eternally and irrevocably," the redemption of sinners "was not possible without a ransom of such precious worth as to atone for sin, to assume its guilt, pay the price of the wrath and thus abolish sin"; the only remedy was for God's Son to "step into our distress and himself become human, to take upon himself the load of awful and eternal wrath and make his own body and blood a sacrifice for sin."[9] Luther also argues that Christ had to be God because only God was able to overpower the forces hostile to human beings: "For to conquer the sin of the world, death, the curse, and the wrath of God in himself—this is the work, not of any creature but of the divine power. Therefore it was necessary that he who was to conquer these in himself should be true God by nature" (*LW* 26:282).

Luther's understanding of the satisfaction made by Christ differs somewhat from that found in Anselm's *Cur Deus Homo*. Whereas Anselm had taught that Christ had made satisfaction to God by paying the debt of obedience and honor owed to God by human beings so as to deliver them from the punishment due to them, here the distinction Anselm made between satisfaction and punishment has disappeared: instead of human sin being left *unpunished* because Christ restored to God the obedience and honor God had lost by virtue of that sin, the idea is that human sin was *fully punished* when the penalty to which all were subject was endured by Christ on the cross in the stead of sinful humanity. In this case, what delivers human beings from the penalty their sins deserve is not that Christ offered God what they owed him *on their behalf* but that he suffered that penalty *in their place* as their substitute. Thus what makes atonement is not the *obedience* Christ offers up to God in death, as in Anselm, but his *sufferings* and his death *in itself*. Luther even speaks of Christ experiencing the torments of hell in the place of others: "Christ suffered damnation and desertion more than all the saints" (*LW* 25:382). He also affirms that Christ "placated the wrath of God by his own blood" (*LW* 26:355), and even follows many of the medieval scholastic theologians in claiming that Christ's blood was so precious in God's sight that "just one drop of this innocent blood would have been more than enough for the sin of the whole world" (*LW* 30:36; cf. 22:459; 26:132, 176).[10]

In developing these ideas, Luther follows a distinction later made between Christ's active and passive obedience. Christ's *active* obedience consisted of fulfilling the law's commandments in the place of human beings during his life, while his *passive* obedience involved subjecting himself to suffering and death by letting himself be mistreated and crucified: "Not only did he do works [of the law] which he was not obliged to do, but he also willingly and innocently suffered the penalty which the law threatens and decrees for those who do not keep it" (*WLS* 1:189).

Precisely how these two ideas are to be combined, however, is somewhat problematic. It appears that what ultimately delivers human beings from God's wrath is the fact that Christ endured this wrath in their place, that is, his *passive* obedience. Yet, if it is Christ's endurance of God's wrath in the place of sinful human beings that saves them, it is not clear why he also needed to fulfill the law in their place. For Anselm, Christ's obedience had been sufficient to make satisfaction to God's justice, but for Luther and other Reformers, it was not; it was also necessary for Christ to undergo the penalty for human sin.

This question was later resolved by claiming that Christ's *active* obedience qualified him to die in the place of all as their substitute, since because he lived

Christ on the Cross, woodcut by Albrecht Dürer (used in the 1524 Nuremberg edition of Luther's Old Testament). For Luther, believers can have full assurance of their salvation by looking in faith to Christ, who died in their stead in order to deliver them from God's wrath, sin, death, and the devil.

a perfect life innocent of sin, the death he endured could be said to have been due to *their* sins rather than to any of his own. Luther himself hints at this idea by emphasizing Christ's own innocence: "Thus the righteous and innocent man must shiver and shake like a poor condemned sinner and feel God's wrath and judgment against sin in his tender, innocent heart, taste eternal death and damnation for us—in short, he must suffer everything that a condemned sinner has deserved and must suffer eternally" (*LW* 12:126-27). However, Luther also speaks of Christ delivering believers from God's law by fulfilling the law in their place: he "is obedient to the Father in our stead" (*LW* 34:119). This implies a type of "double satisfaction" on Christ's part, since he satisfies in the stead of believers God's demand both that the law be obeyed perfectly *and* that those who disobey the law be punished. It is not clear why *both* of these conditions needed to be met, since one or the other would appear to have sufficed. A modern analogy would be that of a person in debt who is ordered by the court to pay the debt or else be put in jail as punishment: if the person does pay the debt, that person no longer must be punished in jail. In Luther's view, however, both payment *and* punishment are required: even though the debt that human beings owe to God (obedience to God's law) is paid by Christ in their stead, the punishment they deserve for *not* paying the debt must still be endured by Christ.

While many objections have been raised against the notion that Christ satisfied God's wrath by suffering the punishment due to human sin in the stead of others, one reason Luther found this idea attractive was no doubt that it made salvation depend entirely on what God had done in Christ rather than on anything that human beings do. The same is true of the *Christus Victor* idea: Christ defeats the devil on behalf of sinful human beings independently of any activity on their part. Precisely because our "salvation depends on him alone" (*LW* 12:59) and "depends entirely on his bearing our sin" (*LW* 22:165), rather than on human efforts, sinners who look to Christ in faith can have full confidence of their deliverance from sin, death, the devil, and God's wrath, thus receiving a "most delightful comfort" (*LW* 26:278).

Although the idea of penal substitution is undoubtedly central to Luther's understanding of Christ's work, ultimately it appears to depend on the *Christus Victor* idea, in that God's wrath and God's law, which threaten human beings, are hostile powers that are engaged and defeated by Christ. The victory over these powers, however, is consummated not on the cross but in Jesus' resurrection: "If Christ is not risen from the dead, then sin and death have devoured and killed him. Since we could not rid ourselves of our sins, Christ took them upon himself that he might tread sin, death, and hell underfoot and become their Lord. But if he did not rise, he did not overcome sin but was overcome by sin" (*WLS* 1:181).

While the incarnation, death, and resurrection of God's Son make it possible for him to defeat the forces hostile to human beings, these events also enable him to be present among believers so as to be united to them personally. This idea is also central to Luther's understanding of Christ's work: Christ saves human beings by becoming one person with them through faith. Apparently influenced by mystical thought, Luther came to conceive of the relation between Christ and believers in extremely intimate terms.[11] "But faith must be taught correctly, namely, that by it you are so cemented to Christ that he and you are as one person, which cannot be separated but remains attached to him forever and declares: 'I am as Christ.' And Christ, in turn, says: 'I am as that sinner who is attached to me, and I to him. For by faith we are joined together into one flesh and one bone'" (*LW* 26:168). Faith "unites the soul with Christ as a bride is united with her bridegroom," so that "everything they have they hold in common" (*LW* 31:351).

By becoming one with believers through faith, all that Christ did *independently* of them becomes theirs personally. To express this idea, Luther speaks of a "joyous exchange" that takes place between Christ and believers, in which his righteousness is communicated to them while, in turn, their sin is communicated to Christ: "By this fortunate exchange with us he took upon himself our sinful person and granted us his innocent and victorious Person" (*LW* 26:284).

> Is not this a beautiful, glorious exchange, by which Christ, who is wholly innocent and holy, not only takes upon himself another's sin, that is, my sin and guilt, but also clothes and adorns me, who am nothing but sin, with his own innocence and purity? And then besides dies the shameful death of the Cross for the sake of my sins, through which I have deserved death and condemnation, and grants to me his righteousness, in order that I may live with him eternally in glorious and unspeakable joy. Through this blessed exchange, in which Christ changes places with us (something the heart can grasp only in faith), and through nothing else, are we freed from sin and death and given his righteousness and life as our own. (*LW* 51:316; cf. 26:166–67, 278; 31:298, 351–52)

Luther's thought in this regard is also somewhat problematic in that it appears that the sins human beings now commit long after Christ died were somehow assumed by Christ on the cross. At times, in fact, Luther implies that those sins are transferred to Christ only *in the present*, by virtue of the union believers have with the risen, glorified Christ, who "absorbs" them into himself (*LW* 12:239) through the exchange taking place between Christ and believers. Furthermore, both the human sins transferred to Christ in this exchange as well as the righteousness communicated by Christ to believers seem to be some type of objective reality, entity, or substance that can be passed from one person to another. The idea thus appears to be somewhat mechanical, as if the mere exchange of sins and righteousness between believers and Christ automatically effected some change in the being of believers.

For Luther, Christ's death on the cross not only serves as the means by which sin, death, the devil, and God's wrath are overcome but also reveals that "God can be found only in suffering and the cross" (*LW* 31:53), thus condemning human wisdom and works as means to attain to God. This is Luther's "theology of the cross," which stands in contrast to the "theology of glory"; the theologian of glory "prefers works to suffering, glory to the cross, strength to weakness, wisdom to folly, and, in general, good to evil" (*LW* 31:53). The knowledge provided by the cross moves believers to seek their salvation not in themselves but in the cross of Christ alone, where God is to be found. Christ's lowly birth in Bethlehem reveals the same truth: that God is to be found only in humility and weakness, as God's Son appeared in the stable.

Justification by Grace through Faith

At the heart and core of Luther's understanding of salvation is the doctrine of justification. This doctrine later came to be called the "article by which the church stands or falls" in Lutheran thought. Following St. Paul, who deals with the subject of justification in his letters to the Romans and to the Galatians, Luther stresses that justification is by grace alone (*sola gratia*) and by faith alone (*sola fide*). Luther's understanding of grace differed from that found in much of the Roman Catholic theology of his day, where grace was often understood in terms of a power or energy infused into human hearts. As Alister McGrath notes, Luther abandoned that notion by interpreting grace "as the absolute favor of God towards an individual, rather than a quality, or series of qualities, at work within man's soul."[12] In other words, for Luther, God's grace is God's undeserved love and mercy toward sinful human beings in Christ.

In general, justification for Luther was, thus, synonymous with forgiveness: God accepts as righteous those sinners who have faith in Christ. Luther speaks of Christ's righteousness as something *outside* of believers or "alien" to them that is reckoned to them and accepted as their own. This is commonly spoken of as "forensic justification," since it has to do with being pronounced righteous by a judge (in this case, God), as in a court of law. Believers receive the righteousness of Christ by being united to him through faith: "Faith justifies because it takes hold of and possesses this treasure, the present Christ" (*LW* 26:130). "Therefore the Christ who is grasped by faith and who lives in the heart is the true Christian righteousness, on account of which God counts us righteous and grants us eternal life"; this involves "the imputation of righteousness" (*LW* 26:130, 235).

Yet, because believers are united to Christ through faith, those who are justified or accepted by God as righteous also *become* righteous as Christ lives and works in them. As Simo Peura has argued, Luther speaks of justification both in terms of God's gracious favor, by which "a sinner is forensically declared righteous," as well as a gift, through which the sinner "is made effectively righteous."[13] By faith, "we receive a different, new, clean heart"; even though "sin in the flesh is still not completely gone or dead, God will nevertheless not count it or consider it" (*SA*) on account of Christ.

Thus, by virtue of the change brought about in them by Christ dwelling in their heart, believers begin to do what is good in God's eyes and to fulfill God's law. "Good works follow such faith, renewal, and forgiveness of sin" (*SA*). "The righteous person herself does not live, but Christ lives in her, because through faith Christ dwells in her and pours his grace into her, through which it comes about that a person is governed not by her own spirit, but by Christ's" (*LW* 27:238; cf. 25:19). "Faith, however, is a divine work in us which changes us and makes us to be born anew of God. . . . It kills the old Adam and makes us altogether different women and men, in heart and spirit and mind and powers; and it brings with it the Holy Spirit. O it is a living, busy, active, mighty thing, this faith. It is impossible for it not to be doing good works incessantly" (*LW* 35:370). Thus, just as for Luther one is already a sinner before one sins, so also must one become righteous before one actually does what is just and right. Luther often compared this to a tree and its fruits:

> Consequently it is always necessary that the substance or person himself be good before there can be any good works, and that good works follow

and proceed from the good person, as Christ also says, "A good tree cannot bear evil fruit, nor can a bad tree bear good fruit.". . . "Let whoever wishes to have good fruit begin by planting a good tree." So let whoever wishes to do good works begin not with the doing of works, but with believing, which makes the person good, for nothing makes a person good except faith. (*LW* 31:361–62)

Of course, while believers begin to actually *become* righteous in this life after graciously being *declared* righteous by God, their justification does not depend on the actual righteousness they attain. In that case, their salvation would once again depend on *them* and what *they* do, rather than on God and Christ alone. In fact, no matter what degree of righteousness they attain in this life, or how well they come to fulfill God's law by loving God and their neighbor, they remain sinners. Luther repeatedly stressed that believers are simultaneously righteous and sinful: "The saints at the same time as they are righteous are also sinners; righteous because they believe in Christ, whose righteousness covers them and is imputed to them, but sinners because they do not fulfill the law, are not without concupiscence, and are like sick persons under the care of a physician; they are sick in fact but healthy in hope and in the fact that they are beginning to be healthy, that is, they are 'being healed' " (*LW* 25:336).

Just as Luther tended to focus particularly on the individual in presenting his doctrines of creation, redemption, and justification, so also in his eschatology he looked forward to the perfection not only of the world but of each Christian. In the end, every believer will be restored fully to the image of God as it is found in Christ: "So long as we live here on earth, believing in his word, we are a work that God has begun, but not yet completed; but after death we shall be perfect, a divine work without sin or fault" (*LW* 32:24). "We have indeed begun to be justified by faith, by which we have also received the first fruits of the Spirit; and the mortification of our flesh has begun. But we are not yet perfectly righteous. Our being justified perfectly still remains to be seen, and this is what we hope for. . . . Thus both things are true: that I am righteous here with an incipient righteousness; and that in this hope I am strengthened against sin and look for the consummation of perfect righteousness in heaven" (*LW* 27:21–22).

The renowned Luther scholar Karl Holl pointed out that this idea is intimately related to Luther's understanding of justification.[14] Luther often claimed that God accepts believers as righteous in the present because of what they will some day become in the future through Christ: "God does not hold against us whatever sin is still to be driven out, because of the beginning that we have made in godliness and because of our steady battle against sin which we continue to expel. He chooses not to charge this sin against us, though, until we become perfectly pure, he might justly do so. For this reason, he has given us a bishop, namely Christ, who is without sin and who is to be our representative until we too become entirely pure like him" (*LW* 32:28; cf. 27:227; 34:153). In this case, the basis for their justification is not so much what Christ did *for* believers in the past but what he will do *in* them in the future. God's acceptance of Christ's righteousness instead of their own is therefore only something temporary; some day they will actually *become* fully righteous, thanks to Christ's activity in them, and on that basis God accepts them as righteous now. In the present, Christ intercedes to God for them, asking God to tolerate them in their sinful condition until he can actually *make* them fully righteous in the end.

Church, Spirit, Word, and Sacraments

As Luther stresses in his explanation of the Third Article of the Apostle's Creed in the *Small Catechism*, faith in Christ is the work of God through the Holy Spirit: "I believe that by my own understanding or strength I cannot believe in Jesus Christ my Lord or come to him, but instead the Holy Spirit has called me through the gospel, enlightened me with his gifts, made me holy and kept me in the true faith, just as he calls, gathers, enlightens, and makes holy the whole Christian church on earth and keeps it with Jesus Christ in the one common, true faith." Similarly, he affirms in the *Large Catechism*: "Neither you nor I could ever know anything about Christ, or believe in him and receive him as Lord, unless these were offered to us and bestowed on our hearts through the preaching of the gospel by the Holy Spirit." As is evident from these passages, for Luther, the Holy Spirit is active primarily in the context of the church through the proclamation of the word of the gospel. The Spirit not only creates faith but preserves it, as well as producing its fruits in the lives of believers so that they grow in holiness or sanctification.

Because, for Luther, everything revolves around faith, and faith in turn is dependent on the hearing of the word of the gospel, both the church and the sacraments are seen as having the purpose of communicating the gospel to people to awaken and strengthen their faith. Baptism and the Lord's Supper are thus indissolubly tied to God's Word: in his *Small Catechism*, Luther defines baptism as "water enclosed in God's command and connected with God's Word" and says that, in Holy Communion, Christ's words "given for you" and "shed for you for the forgiveness of sins" are the "essential thing in the sacrament" when accompanied by eating and drinking, so that "whoever believes these very words has what they declare and state, namely, 'forgiveness of sins.'"

While, for Luther, forgiveness of sins is received through baptism and the Lord's Supper, his belief in the indwelling of Christ in the believer is also reflected in his understanding of the sacraments. Baptism "promises and brings . . . victory over death and the devil, forgiveness of sin, God's grace, *the entire Christ*, and the Holy Spirit with his gifts" (*LC*). Regarding Holy Communion, he repeatedly stresses that the body and blood of Christ are truly present in the bread and wine. This ensures believers that they actually receive the gift of Christ there:

> Christ appointed these two forms of bread and wine, rather than any other, as a further indication of the very union and fellowship which is in this sacrament. For there is no more intimate, deep, and indivisible union than the union of the food with the person who is fed. For the food enters into

and is assimilated by that person's very nature, and becomes one substance with the person who is fed. Other unions, achieved by such things as nails, glue, cords, and the like, do not make one indivisible substance of the objects joined together. Thus in the sacrament we too become united with Christ, and are made one body with all the saints. (*LW* 35:59)

Evaluation

Luther's presentation of Christ's work has faced many of the same criticisms as Anselm's teaching. God seems to be portrayed as a wrathful tyrant who is not "satisfied" until punishment has been exacted on human sin. Even when it is said that God himself acts in love to satisfy his own justice by sending Christ to die in the place of human beings, it appears that God must save us from himself, and thus that there are two Gods struggling against each other, one of strict justice and another of love and mercy.

Other criticisms have been leveled against Luther's understanding of the atonement as well. For example, it is said that he is "too literalistic in his interpretations and too extreme in his expressions" and that he makes use of "grotesque imagery" in "portraying Christ's victory over the devil" and representing Christ as "the greatest of sinners."[15] While this may be true, particularly if such language is taken literally rather than figuratively, there can be no doubt that it grew out of Luther's own intense experiences of struggle, as well as the intimate, personal relationship with Christ in faith through which the fear and terror he felt in his heart were replaced by unspeakable joy and peace.

CHAPTER 8

Christ Our Righteousness in John Calvin's *Institutes*

The early years of the Protestant Reformation were a time of great uncertainty. Those who sided with the Reformation movement, including both the religious and secular authorities, were under constant threat of aggression by the powers allied with Roman Catholicism. Violence, war, and bloodshed became commonplace. In Roman Catholic areas, Protestants were persecuted, imprisoned, tortured, and even massacred. Of course, in Protestant territories, there was also persecution against Roman Catholics, and both Protestants and Roman Catholics used violent means to repress other groups that sought a more radical reformation of the church, such as the Anabaptists. For many, the world had become a place of chaos and confusion, where nothing was certain any longer.

The same type of uncertainty existed on a religious level. For centuries, the Roman Catholic Church had been seen as the guarantor and mediator of salvation. The Reformers, however, not only criticized Roman Catholicism for making salvation dependent on human works, thus seemingly leaving believers in a state of perpetual uncertainty regarding their eternal fate, but called into question the Roman Catholic Church's authority to mediate forgiveness and salvation. Instead, like Luther, the Reformers pointed to Scripture as the sole authority for Christians and made salvation dependent on faith in Christ alone. Precisely what one needed to be saved, therefore, was no longer clear for many who were caught in the middle of this debate. Who spoke for God? Where and how was one to find assurance of salvation?

Among those seeking to bring certainty and order into this context of confusion was John Calvin (1509–1564), who stands alongside Luther as the most prominent of the sixteenth-century Reformers. After embracing the Reformation as a young lawyer and academic in Paris in his native France, thereby exposing himself to possible persecution, in 1533 Calvin fled to Switzerland, where he became a leader in the Swiss Reformation. Calvin spent most of the rest of his life in Geneva, where he led the efforts to turn that city-state into a model Christian community and dedicated himself to teaching, preaching, and writing. In the face of the many uncertainties of the day, Calvin particularly stressed the idea of God as the all-powerful and sovereign Lord, who is in full control of the course of human history. In Calvin's mind, such an understanding of God provided a firm foundation for assuring believers of their future salvation as well as enabling them to trust that the cause of the Reformation they had embraced would ultimately prevail, as a project not of human beings but of God.

Although Calvin composed thousands of sermons and wrote biblical commentaries on most of the books of the Bible, his most important and comprehensive work was his *Institutio Christianae Religionis*, or *Institutes of the Christian Religion*, which he revised and expanded throughout his life after the publication of its first edition in 1536; the definitive edition of the *Institutes* appeared in 1559. Calvin's primary purpose in the *Institutes* was to provide instruction in the basics of the Christian faith to those who were to lead the Reformation movement as theologians and pastors (hence the title *Institutio*, meaning "instruction"). For this reason, it was originally written in Latin, the language in which theology was still taught in the schools, although French versions were also prepared by Calvin and others. In many respects, the *Institutes* appears to be a work of systematic theology. However, Calvin regarded himself primarily as a biblical scholar and always strove to be faithful to the Scriptures.[1] While a more detailed and comprehensive analysis of Calvin's thought would require examining his commentaries and sermons in addition to the *Institutes*, the latter work is all we need here to present in broad terms the story of redemption told by Calvin.[2]

Humanity, Creation, and the Fall

The question of whether Calvin's thought has a central doctrine around which all else revolves has long been debated among scholars but without any consensus being attained; the most common proposals have included the doctrines of divine sovereignty, predestination, and union with Christ.[3] While all of these ideas are no doubt important for Calvin, it is significant that he begins the *Institutes* with a discussion regarding the knowledge of God. According to Calvin, "all men and women are born and live to the end that they may know God" (1.3.3). In his discussion of creation, Calvin focuses primarily on the idea that we attain knowledge of God's glory, wisdom, and power by contemplating the created order. This knowledge enables us to know ourselves as well and moves us to seek God and worship God as the greatest good (1.1.1—1.4.4); only in this way can we attain "true and complete happiness" (1.5.6, 10). Because such knowledge leads believers to trust fully in God, it gives them certainty in life.

Yet, while it is possible to know God through creation to a certain extent, full knowledge can come only through God's revelation in Scripture: "The human mind because of its feebleness can in no way attain to God unless it be aided and assisted by his Sacred Word" (1.6.4). For Calvin, this "feebleness" is the result of humanity's fall into sin. As originally created, the first man had "full possession of right understanding," and his will and affections were "kept within the bounds of reason" (1.15.3; cf. 1.15.8); he was to be conformed to the "perfect image of God" that we can now see in Christ (1.15.4). However, as the Genesis account narrates, Adam disobeyed God together with Eve, falling into apostasy through his unfaithfulness to God and his desire to attain equality with God: "Contemptuous of truth, he turned aside to falsehood" (2.1.4). In this way, not only Adam but his posterity lost the divine image: "After the heavenly image was obliterated in him, he was not the only one to suffer this punishment—that, in place of wisdom, virtue, holiness, truth, and justice, with which adornments he had been clad, there came forth the most filthy plagues, blindness, impotence, impurity, vanity, and injustice—but he also entangled and immersed his offspring in the same miseries" (2.1.5).

For Calvin, this is original sin: an "inherited corruption" involving the "depravation of a nature previously good and pure" (2.1.5). Fallen human beings are "infected with the disease of sin" (21.6). This condition affects both the human intellect and the human will (2.1.9; 2.2.24).[4] Human beings live in blindness and darkness (2.2.21) and have lost the freedom to choose what is good (2.2.26). The human will "is so deeply vitiated and corrupted in its every part that it can beget nothing but evil" (2.2.26); only damnable things come forth from human nature (2.3.1).

Because human nature is "a seed of sin" and "the whole of man is of himself nothing but concupiscence," "man" stands under God's judgment and curse: "We are so vitiated and perverted in every part of our nature that by this great corruption we stand justly condemned and convicted before God, to whom nothing is acceptable but righteousness, innocence, and purity" (2.1.8). Following Augustine, Calvin insists not only that we inherit a corrupt nature from Adam but that Adam's act has "made us guilty" (2.1.8). In this way, he defines humanity's plight in terms of being subject both to the *guilt* and the *power* of sin: "Not only has punishment fallen upon us from Adam, but a contagion imparted by him resides in us, which justly deserves punishment" (2.1.8).

Calvin's teaching on this point appears problematic, however, in that it is not clear how the descendants of Adam can be held guilty for sinning if, through no choice or fault of their own, they have inherited a totally corrupted nature that makes it impossible for them to do otherwise. The question of human responsibility for sin is further complicated when the sin of human beings is also attributed to the devil, who is the "author, leader, and architect of all malice and iniquity" (1.14.15) and to whom human beings have been subjected by God himself (1.14.18). Is not the devil, then, to be blamed for the fact that all now sin, or even God himself, who created human beings in such a way that they would inevitably fall under the power of sin and the devil? In any case, salvation ultimately must involve being delivered not only from the *guilt* of sin and the *power* of sin that has inhered in human nature but from the devil as well; and the only one who could bring about such a salvation is God.

Divine Sovereignty and Election

Seeking to be faithful to Scripture, Calvin continually stresses the sovereignty and omnipotence of God, who "so regulates all things that nothing takes place without his deliberation" (1.16.3). God is "the ruler and governor of all things, who in accordance with his wisdom has from the farthest limit of eternity decreed what he was going to do, and now by his might carries out what he has decreed"; thus "no place remains in human affairs for fortune or chance" (1.16.8). For Calvin God does not merely *permit* things to happen but is the *cause* behind all that takes place: "Nothing is more absurd than that anything should happen without God's ordaining it, because it would then happen without any cause" (1.16.8). Calvin even affirms that "it is often by means of Satan's intervention that God acts in the wicked, but in such a way that Satan performs his part by God's impulsion and advances as far as he is allowed"; thus "God's will is said to be the cause of all things" (1.18.2; cf. 1.17.1).

In ordaining all that takes place, God does not act without reason but, rather, has a plan that he is carrying out: "All events are governed by God's secret plan" (1.16.2). This secret plan, which existed before creation, involved the election of some human beings to salvation, but the rejection of others, who were instead predestined to eternal damnation:

> God by his secret plan freely chooses whom he pleases, rejecting others. . . . As Scripture, then, clearly shows, we say that God once established by his eternal and unchangeable plan those whom he long before determined once for all to receive into salvation, and those whom, on the other hand, he would devote to destruction. We assert that, with respect to the elect, this plan was founded upon his freely given mercy, without regard to human worth; but by his just and irreprehensible but incomprehensible judgment he has barred the door of life to those whom he has given over to damnation. (3.21.7)

Thus, according to Calvin, "no one can deny that God foreknew what end humanity was to have before he created it, and consequently foreknew because he so ordained by his decree. . . . God not only foresaw the fall of the first man, and in him the ruin of his descendants, but also meted it out in accordance with his own decision. For as it pertains to his wisdom to foreknow everything that is to happen, so it pertains to his might to rule and control everything by his hand" (3.23.7).

Calvin is well aware of the problems raised by these affirmations.[5] It appears as if human beings have no free will, since God determines everything ahead of time; and if they have no free will, how can they be held responsible for what they do (2.5.1–3, 13–14)? What sense does it make to exhort others to obedience (2.5.4–5; 3.23.13), or pray for others (3.20.3), if all that is to take place was already determined by God before creation, so that nothing we now do can change it? The Scriptures themselves seem to contradict the idea that everything is determined ahead of time, since they speak of God "repenting" or changing his mind regarding things he had intended to do (1.17.13). God appears to be an unjust tyrant, arbitrarily choosing some for salvation and others for eternal damnation, through no merit or fault of their own, since his election or rejection of human beings is not based on any foreknowledge of what they would do (3.22.1—3.23.3, 10). If the fall into sin was predetermined by God, prior to any human decision, then God appears ultimately to be the cause of the fall (3.23.3–9). Furthermore, the idea that God predestined only some to salvation seems to run counter to certain biblical passages, such as 1 Tim 2:3-4, where it is said that God desires that *all people* be saved (3.24.15–16).

Calvin employs a variety of arguments to respond to these problems. Above all, he insists that, although the doctrine of predestination appears problematic to us, we must accept it because it is clearly taught in Scripture. In fact, the purpose of this doctrine is to enable believers to be "clearly persuaded, as we ought to be, that our salvation flows from the wellspring of God's free mercy" rather than from any efforts or merit of our own (3.21.1), and that "the Lord wills that in election we contemplate nothing but his mere goodness" (3.22.9). Thus the knowledge that all is in God's hands rather than our own provides us with assurance (3.24.5–6). Precisely because those who criticize the doctrine of election undermine the certainty of salvation, Calvin has very harsh words for them. He laments that "there are many swine that pollute the doctrine of predestination with their foul blasphemies," and argues that Scripture requires that we "consider this great mystery" with much "reverence and piety": "For Scripture does not speak of predestination with intent to rouse us to boldness that we may try with impious rashness to search out God's unattainable secrets. Rather, its intent is that, humbled and cast down, we may learn to tremble at his judgment and esteem his mercy" (3.23.12).

Ultimately, in response to the problems raised by the doctrine of election, Calvin simply asserts that the only explanation as to why God shows mercy to some but rejects others is "that it so pleases him"; "when it is said that God hardens or shows mercy to whom he wills, women and men are warned by this to seek no cause outside his will" (3.22.11). Thus we must merely accept what God has revealed and not attempt to go beyond it: "For it is not right for human beings unrestrainedly to search out things that the Lord has willed to be hid in himself, and to unfold from eternity itself the sublimest wisdom, which he would have us revere but not understand that through this also he should fill us with wonder. He has set forth by his Word the secrets of his will that he has decided to reveal to us. These he decided to reveal in so far as he foresaw that they would concern us and benefit us" (3.21.1).

Christ's Sacrificial Death

Because sinful humanity was "subject to the curse of eternal death, excluded from all hope of salvation, beyond every blessing of God, the slave of Satan, captive under the yoke of sin, destined finally for a dreadful destruction and already involved in it," human beings could only be saved by an act of God (2.16.2).

However, because "there is a perpetual and irreconcilable disagreement between righteousness and unrighteousness" (2.16.3), God could not simply accept human beings in their fallen state. Because of God's righteousness, therefore, sin had to be punished. "God's wrath and curse always lie upon sinners until they are absolved of guilt. Since he is a righteous Judge, he does not allow his law to be broken without punishment, but is equipped to avenge it" (2.16.1).

Following Anselm and Luther, Calvin argues that the only way for human beings to be saved from this punishment was for God's Son to become human and die on the cross; he alone could "satisfy God's judgment, and pay the penalties for sin" as well as conquer sin and death by uniting divinity to our human nature (2.12.2–3). While Calvin insists that it was "necessary" that Christ be "both true God and true man," he attempts to avoid the idea that there was something above God, such as God's law, justice, or holiness, that made it impossible for God to save human beings in any other way; it was not an "absolute necessity," but, rather, "stemmed from a heavenly decree" (2.12.1). Thus Christ's coming was necessary only because from eternity God willed it to take place.[6] In fact, the same seems to be true regarding the cross: Calvin appears to follow the medieval scholastic theologian Duns Scotus in affirming that Jesus' death only merited forgiveness because God had graciously determined to accept it as sufficient satisfaction for human sin, and not because it was impossible for God to forgive sins in any other way or because Jesus' sacrificial death had some inherent value of its own that put God under obligation to remit human sins once Jesus had died (2.17.1).[7]

According to Calvin, Christ came as the advocate of fallen human beings and "took upon himself and suffered the punishment that, from God's righteous judgment, threatened all sinners" and "purged with his blood those evils which had rendered sinners hateful to God" (2.16.2). This involved penal substitution, in that Christ endured in the stead of sinners the penalty to which they were subject: "This is our acquittal: the guilt that held us liable for punishment has been transferred to the head of the Son of God. . . . We must, above all, remember this substitution, lest we tremble and remain anxious throughout life—as if God's righteous vengeance, which the Son of God has taken upon himself, still hung over us" (2.16.5). This was the goal of the incarnation: "The only reason given in Scripture that the Son of God willed to take our flesh, and accepted this commandment from the Father, is that he would be a sacrifice to appease the Father on our behalf" (2.12.4).

Calvin repeatedly reads the penal substitution idea back into the New Testament texts that speak of Jesus' death, claiming, for example, that Pilate's declaration of Jesus' innocence in the Gospels demonstrates that in his death Jesus was "burdened with another's sin rather than his own" (2.16.5). For Calvin, no other type of death would have sufficed to satisfy God's justice, since "a form of death had to be chosen in which he might free us both by transferring our condemnation to himself and by taking our guilt upon himself" (2.16.5). Similarly, Christ's descent into hell is interpreted as having as its objective not only Christ's victory over death and the devil but also his undergoing "the severity of God's

Engraving of John Calvin in his study (Bibliotheque Nationale, Paris).
Photo © Snark / Art Resource, NY.

vengeance" by enduring the "terrible torments" of hell that were the penalty for human sin (2.16.10).

While, at times, Calvin follows the New Testament in speaking of sinners being reconciled to God through Christ's death (2.16.3–4), he also affirms that God was reconciled to human beings, an idea not found explicitly in the New Testament. According to this idea, because of God's righteous wrath at human sin, God hated sinners as his enemies: God was "our enemy until he was reconciled to us through Christ. . . . [A]part from Christ, God is, so to speak, hostile to us, and his hand is armed for our destruction. . . . For God, who is the highest righteousness, cannot love the unrighteousness that he sees in us all. All of us, therefore, have in ourselves something deserving of God's hatred" (2.16.2–3). God's wrath and enmity toward sinners came to an end, however, when the sentence to which we were subject was executed upon Christ in his death: "God is appeased by that one atonement in which Christ endured his wrath" (3.13.4); "he was reconciled to us by Christ's blood" (2.17.2). "God, to whom we were hateful because of sin, was appeased by the death of his Son to become favorable to us" (2.17.3).

As this last quote makes clear, for Calvin, Christ's death effects a *change in God*, in that God's wrath is put away and he becomes favorable and gracious to human beings. Christ's sacrificial death served to "obtain God's favor for us" (2.15.6), and in this way he "truly acquired and merited grace for us with his Father" (2.17.3).

Calvin's thought here is problematic in that he affirms that Christ *obtained* God's grace and favor toward human beings yet at the same time maintains that God was *already* gracious and favorable toward human beings *prior* to Christ's death. Once again, Calvin is aware of the problem and addresses it, stating that God "loved us even when he hated us" (2.16.4) and that, "in some ineffable way, God loved us and yet was angry toward us at the same time, until he became reconciled to us in Christ" (2.17.2). As Bruce McCormack has argued, however, Calvin seems to "introduce a contradiction into the being of God between God's mercy and his righteousness," in that God's righteous wrath toward sinners is pitted against his mercy; this makes "God's mercy the prisoner, so to speak, of his righteousness, until such time as righteousness has been fully satisfied."[8]

Calvin's understanding of Christ's death is problematic in other regards as well. At times, he views Christ's death in mechanical fashion, as if Christ's death or blood in itself satisfied the condition necessary for human sins to be remitted. Thus he affirms that "the *effect* of his shedding of blood is that our sins are not imputed to us" (2.17.4) and that "his death has everlasting *efficacy*" (3.14.11). This implies that Jesus' death "worked" to "effect" reconciliation with God and forgiveness, as if all that were required for God's wrath to be put away were the "bare death" of his Son, the shedding of his blood, or his enduring a certain amount of physical and spiritual torments. At other times, however, Calvin combines this idea with the claim that Christ's *obedience* satisfies God's justice and reconciles God to human beings: Christ came "to take Adam's place in obeying the Father, to present our flesh as the price of satisfaction to God's righteous judgment, and, in the same flesh, to pay the penalty that we had deserved" (2.12.3).[9] This raises the same difficulty we noted in chapter 7 when considering Luther's thought, namely, that God seems to be demanding both that the obedience owed to him be paid to him *and* that the penalty for disobedience be exacted. Whereas, for Anselm, only *one* of these conditions had to be satisfied, for Luther and Calvin it was necessary for *both* to be fulfilled.

Calvin's claim that both the Old Testament sacrifices and the sacrificial death of Christ involved penal substitution has also been criticized for confusing cultic acts of worship with legal sanctions.[10] His understanding of divine justice appears to be at odds as well with what we find in the Old Testament. There, God's punishment of sins has as its objectives the destruction of evil, the purification of his people's hearts, and their deliverance from their oppressors. Ultimately, God punishes sin and evil for the sake of human beings rather than for his own sake, and God's wrath is put away only when his people themselves (rather than some substitute) return to him in love and obedience; this alone can "satisfy" God.

For Calvin, however, punishment seems to be an end in itself, so that what actually satisfies God is the execution of his sentence of condemnation, which took place when Christ suffered the dreadful judgment deserved by sinners in their stead. This implies that God demands that human sins be punished for *his own* sake, to satisfy some inner need related to his holy and righteous nature, rather than for the sake of human beings. Thus, for Calvin, it is not the return of sinners to God in repentance and obedience that satisfies God, as the Scriptures teach, but Christ's death alone; if people must still satisfy God and merit forgiveness on their own by repenting and obeying God's commandments, then Christ's death was *not* sufficient for human salvation.

Perhaps the greatest difficulty in Calvin's teaching regarding Jesus' death, however, becomes evident when considering his understanding of the atonement in combination with his doctrine of election. If God elected only *some* to salvation, predestining others to eternal damnation, the question then arises as to whether the atonement effected by Christ is *unlimited* or *limited*, that is, whether Christ's death atoned for the sins of *all* people or only for those of the *elect*. To claim that Christ died for all is problematic in that he appears to have died in vain for those rejected by God. Furthermore, if the punishment for their sins was endured by Christ on the cross in their place, then when they are condemned to damnation, their sins are being punished a second time. However, to claim that Christ died only for *some* seems to limit God's grace, as well as contradict certain passages from Scripture, such as 1 Tim 2:5-6, which says that Christ gave himself as a "ransom *for all*." Calvin interpreted this passage to mean that Christ died for all *classes* of people, rather than all people universally.

Scholars of Calvin have debated extensively whether Calvin taught limited or unlimited atonement.[11] This question, however, makes sense only when it is assumed that Christ's death in itself "effects" atonement, fulfilling some condition for divine forgiveness without which such forgiveness was impossible; the problem then arises as to whether this condition was fulfilled for *all* people or only for *some*. Once it is recognized that such an idea is foreign to the thought of the New Testament, however, this problem disappears. As was argued in chapters 2 and 3, the New Testament idea is that Christ offered up his life to God seeking the salvation of all who would come to form part of the community under him, that is, his body the church. According to this idea, Christ's hope was that all people attain salvation, yet it is not his death per se that constitutes the condition for this salvation, but the faith and repentance that God himself graciously gives through Christ and the Holy Spirit.

Christ's Ongoing Saving Activity

According to Calvin, Christ's saving work did not end when he died; it continues into the present, as Christ remains active from heaven. Following some of the church fathers, Calvin speaks of three offices of Christ: prophet, king, and priest. Christ began to exercise all three of these offices during his earthly ministry. As prophet, he was "herald and witness of the Father's grace" and brought a "perfect doctrine" (2.15.2). He was also acclaimed king during his lifetime (2.15.1) and acted as priest when he offered himself up as a sacrifice to "obtain God's favor for us and appease his wrath" (2.15.6). Nevertheless, these three offices are particularly exercised by Christ in the present. Through the "continuing preaching of the gospel" in the church, Christ exercises his "prophetic dignity" by leading believers to know that perfect wisdom is contained in his doctrine (2.15.2). As "heavenly king," Christ "shares with us all that he has received from the Father," "arms and equips us with his power, adorns us with his beauty and magnificence," and "enriches us with his wealth" (2.15.4). His ongoing priestly activity involves serving as an "everlasting intercessor"; he "obtains for us that grace from which the uncleanness of our transgressions and vices debars us" (2.15.6). This last idea appears problematic in that, if Christ must still intercede for sinners to "restore us to the Father's favor," as "an everlasting propitiation by which sins may be expiated" (3.4.26), it would seem that his past work did not fully attain these things. Even though Calvin affirms that the basis for Christ's ongoing intercession is his death, it is not clear why he should have to continue to turn away God's wrath and restore sinners to God's favor through his intercession if his death did so once and for all.

For Calvin, Christ's ongoing work involves not only acting *on behalf of* believers in various ways but being active *in* them by virtue of his union with them.[12] Christ ascended into heaven so that he might be present for all the members of his body the church: "Christ left us in such a way that his presence might be more useful to us—a presence that had been confined in a humble abode of flesh so long as he sojourned on earth" (2.16.14). What Christ did in the past is only redemptive for those who come to live in union with him: "As long as Christ remains outside of us, and we are separated from him, all that he has suffered and done for the salvation of the human race remains useless and of no value for us. . . . [A]ll that he possesses is nothing to us until we grow into one body with him" (3.1.1).

Although Calvin speaks of the ongoing presence of Christ in the church and the union of believers to him, at the same time he stresses that Christ remains bodily in heaven. For this reason, believers can be united to him only through the Holy Spirit, who is "the bond by which Christ effectually unites us to himself" (3.1.1). When Calvin speaks of Christ's real presence in the Lord's Supper, he stresses the same idea: those who commune are "made one in body, spirit, and soul with him," yet the "bond of this connection" with Christ is the Spirit, "with whom we are joined in unity," and who "is like a channel through which all that Christ himself is and has is conveyed to us"; "the Spirit alone causes us to possess Christ completely and have him dwelling in us" (4.17.12).[13] In fact, according to Calvin, just as Christ remains in heaven now rather than being corporally present among us, so also he remained in heaven during his time on earth: "The Son of God descended from heaven in such a way that, without leaving heaven, he willed to be born in the virgin's womb, to go about the earth, and to hang upon the cross; yet he continuously filled the world even as he had done from the beginning!" (2.13.4; cf. 4.17.30).

Faithful to Scripture, Calvin sees Christ's saving activity as continuing throughout the present age until he comes again in glory (2.15.5; 2.16.17). Calvin also looks to Scripture for his eschatology, affirming that "there will be no end to the blessedness of the elect or the punishment of the wicked" when Christ has separated the two groups from each other at the final judgment (3.25.5). The elect will attain "spiritual blessedness" in heaven, experiencing eternally the glory, joy, and splendor of God's kingdom, and a "happiness of whose excellence the minutest part would scarce be told if all were said that the tongues of all women and men can say" (3.25.10). In contrast, however, "no description can deal adequately with the gravity of God's vengeance against the wicked" and the "torments and tortures" they will endure; their "unhappy consciences" will "find no rest from being troubled and tossed by a terrible whirlwind, from feeling that they are being torn asunder by a hostile Deity, pierced and lanced by deadly darts . . . so that it would be more bearable to go down into any bottomless depth and chasms than to stand for a moment in these terrors" (3.25.12).

Faith, Justification, and Sanctification

For Calvin, salvation and reconciliation with God are brought about objectively both by what Christ did in the past and what he continues to do in the present in union with believers, and they revolve around the concepts of both substitution and participation in Christ.[14] Yet this objective salvation must be subjectively appropriated by faith, which is "the principal work of the Holy Spirit" (3.1.4) and "embraces Christ," who is offered to believers "not only for righteousness, forgiveness of sins, and peace, but also for sanctification" (3.2.8). As Christ is "grasped and possessed by us in faith," both the *guilt* and the *power* of sin are dealt with: "By partaking of him, we principally receive a double grace: namely, that being reconciled to God through Christ's blamelessness, we may have in heaven instead of a Judge a gracious Father; and secondly, that sanctified by Christ's spirit we may cultivate blamelessness and purity of life" (3.11.1). Through faith in Christ, then, believers are both *justified* and *sanctified*.

Like Luther, Calvin equates justification with the forgiveness of sins and bases it on the righteousness of Christ, which God reckons or imputes to sinners: "One is not righteous in oneself but because the righteousness of Christ is communicated to one by imputation" (3.11.23).[15] Yet this is true only of those who have faith: "Faith is said to justify because it receives and embraces the righteousness offered in the gospel" (3.11.17). Because the justification of believers is based entirely on the perfect righteousness of Christ, which avails in their stead, rather than on anything they do, they can have full assurance of their salvation and live free from doubt and uncertainty (3.13.4).

While Calvin speaks of righteousness as something "acquired for us by Christ's obedience and sacrificial death" (3.11.5), he also affirms that "Christ transfuses into us the power of his righteousness" (2.1.6). In this way, believers are not only justified and *accepted* as righteous but also sanctified so as actually to *become* righteous. Calvin repeatedly stresses that justification in no way depends on the degree of sanctification attained by believers or the good works they do. They remain sinners, since sin continues to dwell in them as a power (3.3.10–11). Like their justification, their sanctification depends entirely on Christ; the good works believers do that are pleasing to God are bestowed on them by Christ himself, who "works in them through his Spirit" (3.17.5). For Calvin, because Christ *makes* righteous those to whom his righteousness is imputed, the justification and sanctification of believers are inseparable from each other; they form a "living unity" in Christ and are "two aspects of the same process in our lives."[16]

Because believers "need outward helps to beget and increase faith within us, and advance it to its goal," God has instituted the church, which proclaims the gospel and teaches believers what they should know for their salvation (4.1.1). God has also "instituted sacraments" as "highly useful aids to foster and strengthen faith" (4.1.1). Baptism is a "token and proof" of the cleansing of believers, confirming to them that their sins are "abolished, remitted and effaced" (4.15.1). It also serves as a "sure testimony to us that we are not only engrafted into the death and life of Christ, but so united to Christ himself that we become sharers in all his blessings" (4.15.6). The Lord's Supper communicates the same ideas, confirming to believers that Christ was sacrificed on their behalf and that they are united to him (4.17.1–2). Both the church and the sacraments, therefore, are means by which the faith of believers is established and strengthened; this occurs both as they recall what Christ did in the past to attain God's forgiveness and favor for them, and as they live in union with the risen and ascended Christ in the present.

The Protestant Church in Lyon, built after King Henri IV promulgated the Edict of Nantes, granting the Protestants freedom of cult (Bibliotheque Publique et Universitaire, Geneva). For Calvin, the church is the community of those who were elected by God for salvation from eternity, and gather together to hear the gospel of salvation and grow in holiness of life.
Photo © Erich Lessing / Art Resource, NY.

For Calvin, of course, it is the elect alone who obtain justification and salvation from God through Christ and the Holy Spirit: "Only those predestined to salvation receive the light of faith" (3.2.11). If this is the case, however, then it appears that the ultimate cause of the justification and salvation of believers is their election by God, rather than anything done *for* them, *in* them, or *by* them. In reality, they were saved not so much when Christ died for them or when they were united to Christ through the Holy Spirit in faith but when they were elected by God for salvation. As Graham Redding notes, such an understanding of election implies that "at its deepest level it is grounded in a divine decree that has been made apart from Christ and prior to grace."[17] Whatever else God has done and continues to do in history seems to be reduced to a mere formality, including Christ's expiatory sacrifice and his union with believers through the Holy Spirit, who creates faith and good works in them. These things are necessary only in that, in his sovereignty, God determined that they would be the means for bringing about the salvation he had decreed for the elect from eternity.

Evaluation

Undoubtedly, the greatest strength of Calvin's teaching concerning God's sovereignty, predestination, the work of Christ, salvation, and justification is that it directs believers to look not to themselves or their own strength but to God and Christ alone for assurance of salvation. Once salvation is made to depend on human beings, who are inevitably frail and sinful, any such certainty is undermined.

Nevertheless, in order to provide this assurance and certainty, Calvin seems to go further than is necessary. While it might have been sufficient merely to point believers to God's loving providence, encouraging them to entrust themselves to God so as to find the assurance and confidence they need, Calvin also found it necessary to sustain a view of the world and history in which everything is ordained by God ahead of time, in essence leaving no room for any type of human decision or freedom. This assumes that assurance of salvation can be attained only through a doctrine of absolute determinism, in which God has not only the *last* word regarding what happens with regard to humanity and the world but the *only* word.

Of course, in developing his doctrine, Calvin consistently sought to be faithful to Scripture. While in itself this may be regarded as commendable, Calvin's interpretation of Scripture is problematic in that he uses parts of it to construct a theological system that he in turn reads back into the biblical text as a whole. This is particularly evident in his doctrine of predestination and his understanding of Christ's work, which has faced many of the same criticisms leveled at Anselm's and Luther's teachings. Many today would agree that Scripture cannot be reduced to a neat, orderly system in which all apparent tensions and contradictions can be explained away or simply labeled as "mysteries," in the way Calvin attempted to do. Instead, we find a variety of different theologies in Scripture that cannot be fully harmonized with one another. For this reason, an approach to Scripture is required that recognizes and affirms the diversity of thought found there.

CHAPTER 9

Albrecht Ritschl and the Kingdom of God

The many changes and developments in Europe during the eighteenth and nineteenth centuries had a profound impact on Western theology. The advances in scientific knowledge, as well as the writings of Enlightenment thinkers such as David Hume (1711–1776) and Immanuel Kant (1724–1804), presented serious challenges to the Christian faith, which increasingly came to be seen by many as irrational and outdated; in particular, the claims of Scripture regarding miracles and Jesus' resurrection were called into question. The political expansion of the European powers and their establishment of colonies throughout the world not only brought the West into greater contact with the competing truth claims of other religions, such as Islam, Buddhism, and Hinduism, but required ideological justification. Such justification was found in ideas such as those of Charles Darwin (1809–1882), who argued that nature in general and humanity in particular evolved through a process of natural selection, in which the strong prevailed over the weak. History was interpreted along the same lines as a gradual growth toward perfection, led by the West, which had shown itself to be culturally, socially, politically, and technologically superior to all other cultures and peoples; this justified its domination throughout the world.

All of these changes led to a great deal of diversity and controversy among Christians. Many in the churches held fast to the old orthodoxies, with their traditional dogmas, refusing to accommodate their understanding of the faith to the new ways of thinking. Others, however, believed that, in light of the increasing number of people abandoning the church and the challenges to religious belief presented by the Enlightenment worldview, it was necessary to rethink the Christian faith. The latter approach was taken by perhaps the most influential theologian of the period, Friedrich Schleiermacher (1768–1834), who in 1799 addressed a book on the Christian religion to "its cultured despisers." In response to the attacks on the rationality of the Christian faith and the reliability of the Christian Scriptures, Schleiermacher attempted to ground the truth of Christianity in

Albrecht Ritschl

human experience, claiming that human beings possess a common conscious-ness or feeling of absolute dependence on God. This "God-consciousness" was reflected most perfectly in Jesus, whose saving work consisted primarily in inspir-ing and enabling others to become like him.

Following Schleiermacher, other Christian theologians rejected much of the orthodox dogmatic theology of the time and sought to reformulate the Chris-tian faith in terms that were more in accordance with the spirit of the times. In particular, attempts were made to base the Christian religion on reconstructions of the "historical Jesus": because, for many, it was no longer possible to believe the claims appearing in the Gospels regarding such things as Jesus' miracles, his bodily resurrection, and his divinity, Jesus came to be reinterpreted as a historical figure who revealed divine universal truths to human beings as a great teacher and who founded Christianity as the loftiest and most superior form of reli-gion known to humankind. Even many who made use of the historical-critical method to study the Bible as a book of human origin like any other book main-tained that, in some sense, it was still divinely inspired and that eternal truths and principles for human existence could therefore be discerned from it. Those who sought to rethink the Christian faith in these ways were labeled "theological liberals." Although, in conservative church circles, these thinkers were accused of attempting to undermine and destroy the faith, in their own minds they were seeking the exact opposite, namely, to rescue Christianity by convincing those who had rejected it and adopted the modern worldview that the Christian faith was compatible with that worldview and thus was not irrational.

Among the most prominent of the nineteenth-century liberal theologians was Albrecht Ritschl (1822–1889), a Lutheran who served as professor of theology at the University of Göttingen for twenty-five years.[1] During his time there, he composed his most important work, a three-volume treatise titled *The Christian Doctrine of Justification and Reconciliation*.[2] Although, in his preface to the third volume of this work, which he considered an "almost complete outline of Systematic Theology," Ritschl insisted that his theology "has no place in the ordinary classification of theological parties" (vii), he is generally classified as a liberal theologian because his thought reflects most of the basic characteristics associated with liberal Protestantism. As Stanley Grenz and Roger Olson indicate, among these characteristics are a commitment to the "task of reconstructing Christian belief in the light of modern knowledge," an "emphasis on the freedom of the individual Christian thinkers to criticize and reconstruct traditional beliefs" entailing "the rejection of the authority of tradition or church hierarchy to control theology," a focus on "the practical or ethical dimension of Christianity," and an effort to "base theology on some foundation other than the absolute authority of the Bible."[3]

Like other theologians and biblical scholars of his day, Ritschl followed a historical method in expounding his understanding of the Christian faith. He also sought to address perhaps the most difficult problem raised by Enlightenment thinkers: the basis on which we can ground human knowledge (epistemology). Kant had argued that realities lying beyond space and time cannot be known by scientific means; among these realities, of course, is God. Influenced by Kant's ideas, Ritschl believed that Christian theology must be based on what can be observed in history and the reality around us, rather than on any type of metaphysical speculation concerning realities beyond space and time. Thus we can know God only through the effects God has had on human beings in history, not as God is in himself.

The Kingdom of God as the Objective of Creation

The starting point and central focus of the Christian story of redemption told by Albrecht Ritschl is the kingdom of God proclaimed by Jesus. Ritschl understands the kingdom of God as the "organisation of humanity through action inspired as love" (12) and repeatedly stresses this kingdom as the aim or objective of God from the beginning: "A universal ethical kingdom of God is the supreme end of God himself in the world" (451). While this kingdom depends on God's grace, it also depends on human beings practicing "the universal principle of brotherly and sisterly love" (414) in obedience to God: "The kingdom of God is the *summum bonum* which God realises in men and women; and at the same time it is their common task, for it is only through the rendering of obedience on the part of human beings that God's sovereignty possesses continuous existence" (30).

It is important to note that, for Ritschl, this kingdom is to be realized primarily *in history*, rather than outside of history in some eternal or heavenly realm. He criticizes "the projection of the idea of eternal life entirely into the next world" (496), particularly because this involves speculation about realities lying beyond our historical realm: "If the idea of eternal life be applied merely to our state in the next life, then its content, too, lies beyond all experience, and cannot form the basis of knowledge of a scientific kind," since it "cannot be verified in such experience as is possible now" (499–500). Thus, while Ritschl does not do away entirely with the idea of eternal life in a future heavenly realm, as some of his critics have argued,[4] his emphasis lies on the here and now: "The elements of the future life are to be found in our present experience of joy, blessedness, and the feeling of elevation" (500). Eternal life includes "not only the perfecting of fellowship with God, but also, the specific attitude of the individual to the world" (497), and "is present in our experiences of freedom or lordship over the world" (534).

In continuity with the spirit of his day, Ritschl also posits a gradual progression toward perfection in history, guided by God, who actively educates the human race, "guiding them to the Christian ideal of morality" (306). In fact, the establishment of the kingdom of God among human beings has been preceded by other "graduated forms" of human fellowship that developed over time, such as the family, the state, and the world-empire (308–9), and Christ is at present "working towards the gradual subjection of the world to this its true end," namely, "the union of humankind through love, or, in other words, the realisation of the kingdom of God" (414).

The Kingdom of Sin

As David Mueller has shown in his study on Ritschl's theology, Ritschl refused to follow the approach of much Protestant orthodoxy in addressing the questions of sin and the fall prior to defining the nature of salvation in Christ. Instead, he reverses the order, first looking to Jesus and the revelation given through him in order then to define what human sin is. Ritschl's "criticism of the traditional doctrine of sin is that the first Adam rather than the Second Adam, Jesus Christ, serves as the ideal of humanity. Such an idealization of the original state is unfounded." In Ritschl's thought, "we must look to Jesus Christ—not to Adam—for illumination and understanding both about the nature and extent of man's sin and his reconciliation."[5] This means that we must grasp the meaning of salvation as the coming of God's kingdom before we can understand what sin is.

Therefore, if salvation is understood in terms of the establishment of the kingdom of God, which is God's "final end" in the world (521), then sin must be "active opposition to God's final end" and "an obstacle to its realisation" (320). And since the kingdom consists of "fellowship with God," sin must be defined as its opposite, namely, *the separation of sinners from God*, the suspension of humanity's proper fellowship with him" (42). In fact, Ritschl goes so far as to speak in

The Twelve-Year-Old Jesus in the Temple (1879, Max Liebermann,
Hamburger Kunsthalle, Germany). For Ritschl and other nineteenth-century
liberal Protestants, Christ saves human beings by the knowledge, wisdom,
and revelation he brings to them from God.
Photo © Bildarchiv Preussischer Kulturbesitz / Art Resource, NY.

terms of a "kingdom of sin," which stands in opposition to the "kingdom of
God." This kingdom of sin exists wherever the brotherly and sisterly love characteristic of the kingdom of God is lacking:

> Sin is, rather, in all its instances, opposition to the good, that conception
> being defined in the ethical sense. . . . [I]gnorance is the essential condition of
> the conflicts which arise between the will and the order of society regarded
> as the standard of the good. . . . Sin, which alike as a mode of action and as a
> habitual propensity extends over the whole human race, is, in the Christian
> view of the world, estimated as the opposite of the Kingdom of God—in
> the latter respect forming the kingdom of sin. (379, 383–84)

Two ideas from this passage are particularly significant. First, for Ritschl,
although sin is a matter of the human will opposing the good, its cause is primarily *ignorance*. The problem is, therefore, one of a *lack of knowledge* on the part of
human beings, and the solution must consist of *teaching* or *revealing* to human
beings what they need to know, so as to *educate* them.

Second, Ritschl's idea of the "kingdom of sin" is intended as an alternative to the doctrine of original sin: it is "a substitute for the hypothesis of original sin which gives due prominence to everything that the notion of original sin was rightly enough meant to embrace" (344). As A. Durwood Foster notes, Ritschl refuses to trace human sinfulness back to the fall of Adam, as Augustine and his successors had done, since "by referring subsequent sins back to the first, it obscures present responsibility for them."[6] In other words, human beings must be held responsible and must accept guilt for their own sins, rather than blaming Adam for the sinful actions they now commit or attributing their sin to some type of corruption of human nature that resulted from Adam's sin. Ritschl thus insists that sin "is not inherited at all" and that "inherited sin and personal guilt cannot be combined in thought without inaccuracy" (340).

Of course, for Ritschl, there is a sense in which the sin that each individual inevitably commits is a result of what took place previously in human history. Human beings sin because they have learned to do so from one another through "the association of individuals in common evil" and a "sinful federation with others" (335, 338). According to this line of thought, each of us inevitably falls into sin because we live in a world where all have become accustomed to sinning.

Closely related to this understanding of sin is Ritschl's rejection of the idea that human sin leads God to react in wrath by punishing sinners, both in this life by sending various kinds of evils upon them and in the next life by condemning them to eternal torments. In contrast to Calvin, Ritschl insists that "it is impossible to conceive sinners, at the same time and in the same respect, as objects both of God's love and God's wrath" (264).[7] The evils that people endure in the present life are not to be attributed to God's wrath; rather, they have an educative purpose: "It is an error to think of evil in its entirety as the equivalent of divine punishment. . . . God is educating us in patience and humility" (354, 357). To return to a distinction made previously, Ritschl thus sees the relationship between sin and suffering as an *intrinsic* rather than an *extrinsic* one: "Evil is always a natural event" (351). God is to be understood not as sending evils upon people to punish them for their sins but, rather, as letting them suffer the natural consequences of their own actions. In this way, they learn that those actions must be avoided.

Ritschl follows the same line of thought in considering death, insisting that "the theory is excluded that death is a consequence of our own sin" (360). Rather than being divine punishment, death is merely "our most painful experience of the instability of all the elements of this world" (457). Ritschl seems to leave open the question of whether something like eternal condemnation exists for those who refuse to repent of their sin, in part once more because we cannot speculate on what exists outside of the history and the world to which we belong. However, he does appear to recognize that people can become so entrenched in their ignorance and opposition to God's will that they cannot overcome their resulting separation from God. In this case, the reason they can no longer experience God's love is that they, rather than God, make such an experience impossible through their "active opposition to God's final end" and their "persistence in such a course" (320). Only in this sense can we speak of God's wrath, which "signifies his determination to destroy those who definitively set themselves against redemption and the final end of the kingdom of God" (323).

Although Ritschl follows traditional Christian thought in seeing guilt as the consequence of sin, he understands this differently. For Ritschl, the problem posed by human guilt is on the side not of God but of human beings: it is not that God holds us guilty but that we ourselves do so, experiencing alienation and separation from God by virtue of our consciousness of having sinned. What is necessary, then, is not that God no longer reckon us guilty but that we cease to let our feelings of guilt alienate us from God; it is "the consciousness of guilt which separates women and men from God" (320).

Justification and Reconciliation

Faithful to the Lutheran tradition to which he belonged, Ritschl placed the doctrine of justification at the heart of his theology, yet he set alongside it the idea of reconciliation: "justification or reconciliation is the fundamental principle of Christianity as a religion" (120). Ritschl also followed Lutheran orthodoxy in equating justification with the forgiveness of sins, affirming that justification is by faith alone, and speaking of God imputing Christ's righteousness to believers: "Justification is God's forgiveness or pardon, reconciliation with him, adoption into the position of children; and, in God's revelation of grace through Christ, it operates as the imputation of Christ's righteousness in such a way that the position, given to him and maintained by him, as Son of God and original object of God's love, is also imputed to those sinners who belong to the community of Christ by faith" (167). For Ritschl, as for Luther, justifying faith appropriates the promise of forgiveness attached to Christ's work and "is to be understood as trust in God and Christ, characterized by peace of mind, inward satisfaction, and comfort" (142).

At the same time, however, Ritschl's understanding of God and the work of Christ produced an understanding of justification that differed fundamentally from that found in Protestant orthodoxy, which based justification on the doctrine that, in his death, Christ had suffered the penalty for sin in the place of sinful human beings. Because Ritschl rejects the notion that sinners need to be saved from God's wrath, he also rejects the idea that Jesus endured and exhausted God's wrath by dying as humanity's substitute: "It is impossible to accept an interpretation of Christ's sacrificial death which, under the head of satisfaction, combines in a superficial manner his death and his active life, while at bottom it ascribes to the death of Christ quite a different meaning, namely, that of substitutionary punishment. . . . [T]he asserted necessity of a penal satisfaction to God as a condition of the exercise of his grace has no foundation in the biblical conception of God" (477–78). This means that, for Ritschl, Christ's death is not the basis on which believers are justified, nor does his sacrifice attain forgiveness for them; rather, the basis on which they are justified is simply God's love for all people:

The ground of justification, or the forgiveness of sins, is the benevolent, gracious, merciful purpose of God to vouchsafe to sinful men and women the privilege of access to himself. The form in which sinners appropriate this gift is faith, that is, the emotional trust in God, accompanied by the conviction of the value of this gift for one's blessedness, which, called forth by God's grace, takes the place of the former mistrust which was bound up with the feeling of guilt. Through trust in God's grace the alienation of sinners from God, which was essentially connected with the unrelieved feeling of guilt, is removed. (108)

As is evident in this passage, for Ritschl, justification involves a change not in the way God views sinful human beings but in the way *they* view *God*. God is always willing to forgive and accept those who sin, in spite of their guilt; what is necessary is that human beings become conscious of this and thus lay aside their feelings of guilt and mistrust in relation to God so as to draw near to God in faith and trust. This makes it possible for the alienation that characterized their relation to God to be overcome: "Justification, then, signifies the bringing back of the sinner into nearness with God, the removal of the alienating effect of the existent opposition to God and the accompanying consciousness of guilt" (100). In this way, the separation from God and lack of fellowship that are the "punishment" of sin, imposed not by God on sinners but by sinners on themselves, are brought to an end. For the relationship to be healed, what must be removed is not the guilt itself but the feeling of guilt that sinners have.

Although Ritschl often speaks of justification and reconciliation with God as if they were virtual synonyms, in reality he distinguishes slightly between the two. As Alister McGrath notes, for Ritschl, justification or forgiveness is an objective reality, embracing all, whereas reconciliation occurs when one subjectively appropriates that forgiveness: reconciliation "expresses as an actual result the effect which is intended" in justification, namely, "that the individual who is justified actually enters into the intended relationship."[8] As most liberal theologians liked to stress, there is no need for God to be reconciled to human beings, since there is no enmity or wrath on God's part toward sinners; rather, it is sinners who need to be reconciled to God, changing their attitude and relationship toward God.

The Work of Christ

If Christ's saving work does not involve obtaining divine forgiveness for human beings by dying in their stead, then of what does it consist? Ritschl rejected not only the penal substitution interpretation of Christ's death but the *Christus Victor* idea, which he considered mythical and nonethical.[9] Instead, following most other liberal theologians of his day, he preferred the understanding of Christ's death generally associated with Abelard, according to which Christ gave up his life so as to lay down an example for others to follow and to move them to greater love of God (371, 473).[10] Nevertheless, Ritschl's understanding of Christ's work is considerably more complex than Abelard's. As Rolf Schäfer notes, it revolves around two central ideas: Christ's revelation of God and Christ's lordship over the community and the world as God's representative.[11] Closely related to these ideas is Ritschl's adaptation of the doctrine regarding Christ's three offices of prophet, priest, and king that we considered in chapter 8 when examining Calvin's thought.

Of these three offices, Ritschl assigns priority to that of Christ's kingship, which he exercised throughout his earthly life, thereby making manifest his divine origin.[12] According to Ritschl, this is evident in the Gospels, where by "describing himself at one time as a mere ambassador who has seen and executes [God's] commands, and at another time as the Son of God who pursues God's work and in his own person exercises God's lordship over men and women for the ends of the kingdom of God, Jesus attributes to his life as a whole, in the unity which for his own consciousness it possesses, the worth of being the instrument of the *complete self-revelation of God*" (436). In other words, precisely because, as God's Son, Christ is king, he can fulfill the other two offices, being a prophet by revealing and representing God to human beings, and serving as a priest by representing human beings before God (431–33). He is thus a "royal prophet" and a "royal priest," dedicated to establishing God's kingdom by exercising his lordship over the world as king and founding the community of believers under him: "His kingship must be shown to consist in these very same priestly and prophetic activities in so far as both are inspired by his purpose to found and maintain a community of believers. Only the prophetic and priestly activities refuse to coalesce, because they run in exactly opposite directions. . . . [T]he former moves in the direction from humanity to God, and the latter in exactly the opposite direction, from God to humanity" (433, 429).

Yet, while in one sense Ritschl gives priority to Christ's kingly office, in another sense he appears to give priority to Christ's *prophetic* work of revealing and teaching to human beings what they need to know in order for the kingdom of God to be established. As noted above, if sin is primarily due to human ignorance, then this ignorance must be overcome through knowledge. Because Christ is the one who "brings the perfect revelation of God, so that beyond what he brings no further revelation is conceivable or to be looked for," Christ is "the bearer of the final revelation of God" (388; cf. 452). What Christ reveals to human beings is primarily "his Father's love, grace, and truth" (546), as well as the need for them to practice love toward one another: "If Christ is thus the personal revelation of the will of God as essentially love, then certainly, from the point of view of degree, the love of God finds its perfect revelation in the fact, that the members of the kingdom of God fulfil the law of sisterly and brotherly love" (466). In this way, Christ is the founder of a religion superior to all others (414–15).

Ritschl's idea that it is *human beings* rather than God who must change would seem to make any priestly activity "from humanity to God" on the part of Christ unnecessary, since in that case Christ does not need to implore God to accept sinful human beings, appease God's wrath at their sin, obtain forgiveness on their behalf, or reconcile God to them. Ritschl resolves this difficulty by seeing Christ's *Godward* activity as having the objective of making a change possible, not in God but in *human beings*. Christ does this by fulfilling first in himself what is to be fulfilled in others: "What Jesus actually was and accomplished, that he is in the first place for himself" (442). Thus *"Christ is first of all a priest in his own behalf* before he is a priest for others," in that "he is the subject of that true and perfect religion, compared with which no other has been able to bring women and men to the desired goal of nearness to God. For since Christ was the first to possess complete and exhaustive knowledge of God, he is therefore also the first who was qualified in the true and final manner to exercise that fellowship with God which was the aim of every religion, and to experience in himself in its fulness the reciprocal and saving influence of God" (474–75). In other words, when Christ drew near to God through prayer and obedience, he was practicing the true religion as well as manifesting it to others so that they too might come to practice it. In this way, Christ brings about their justification and reconciliation with God.

Thus, by living in fellowship with God throughout his life, Christ enabled others to do the same, revealing God's nearness to them so that they might also draw near to God and be received "into the same communion with God in which he stands" (537). His priestly activity in relation to God does not exercise "a determining influence upon God to be gracious to men and women" but is "subordinated to his displaying, as the revealer of God, the grace and truth—the love of God to sinners" (551). As God's Son, Christ himself "stands to God as Father in a relation of incomparable fellowship, which is realised in his knowledge of God"; and he consequently "lives in the intention of transmitting to his disciples his own fellowship with God" (476), so that they may also be assured of God's love and nearness. In this way, Christ serves as the representative of others before God, yet this representation is "inclusive" rather than "exclusive": "The meaning of the idea is not that what Christ does as a priest, the community does not require to do; but rather that what Christ as a priest does first in the place and as the representative of the community, there the community itself has accordingly to take up its position" (546).

Just as believers are enabled to enter into a new relationship with God through Christ's priestly activity, so also are they brought into a new relationship with the world through Christ's exercise of lordship over the world. This is made possible as well by the revelation Christ brings, which gives human beings a knowledge they previously lacked: "Through him we know ourselves raised to kingship or dominion over the world, and to priesthood or undisturbed communion with God. . . . [T]he aim of Christ's activity as King and Priest is to secure for us freedom with regard to the world and with regard to sin, and freedom in our intercourse with God" (418). For this lordship to be accomplished in others, it first had to be accomplished in Christ himself, just as he needed to be a priest on his own behalf before he might be a priest for others. In Christ as king, human beings encounter the lordship of God himself so that they submit to that lordship and in that way gain freedom and dominion over the world: "Christ presents himself as the bearer of God's moral lordship over men and women, through whose unique speech and conduct men and women are impelled to submit themselves to the power which proceeds from him" (446). He is thus the "source of strength for all imitation of him, because he himself made God's supreme purpose of the union of women and men in the kingdom of God the aim of his own personal life; and thereby realised in his own experience that independence toward the world which through him has become the experience of the members of his community" (387).

Jesus' Life and Death

What role, then, does Jesus' death play in human salvation? In contrast to many other understandings of Jesus' work, Ritschl stresses the continuity between Jesus' life and death so that Jesus' death is not an end in itself but merely the consequence of the life he lived: "We do not conceive the purpose of Christ's death under any principle which would be opposed to the purpose of his life" (543). Ritschl speaks of the purpose of Jesus' life in terms of his "vocation," that is, his total dedication to the task of establishing the kingdom of God, which he manifested throughout his ministry. "The business of his vocation was the establishment of the universal ethical fellowship of humankind. . . . Christ's supreme aim, namely, the kingdom of God, is identical with the supreme end of the Father" (449, 454).

Jesus' efforts to establish this kingdom were met with the "opposition of the leaders and rulers of his nation" (448), and this eventually led to his death. However, Jesus remained faithful to his vocation in the midst of the suffering he endured; in this way, by "overcoming the seductive opposition of the world" (462), he established his lordship over the world. As "a consequence of his loyalty to his vocation," Christ's patience in suffering demonstrated "his unique power over the world," in that in him "the individual impulses of self-preservation, avoidance of pain, and the keeping inviolate of personal honor" were "subordinated to the consciousness of his vocation" (460–61). Once again, this enables others to enter into the same relation to the world: "Christ's position of supremacy toward the world finds application also to other men and women, who, within his community and in accordance with the view of the world which he proclaimed, enter into that relation to God which was his aim for them, and which has been made possible to them through him" (456–57). For Ritschl, then, Christ died for the same objective for which he had lived: the establishment of the kingdom of God through the founding of a community of believers who learn from him to relate to God and the world as he did.

Christ's sufferings, therefore, which he endured not only in death but throughout his public ministry (430), are not salvific in themselves and do not obtain divine forgiveness. For Ritschl, what was necessary was not that Christ move God to love and forgive human beings but that he reveal that God *already* loves and forgives sinful human beings. Ritschl stresses that the fact that throughout his ministry Jesus "repeatedly gave the assurance of forgiveness of his spoken word" demonstrates that "this effect is not necessarily and exclusively bound up with his death"; this "refutes all those theories which are designed to show that Christ, by his death as a satisfaction for human sins, succeeded in making God willing to forgive" (537). Once more, what was necessary was not that God be enabled to forgive but that human beings repent and come to practice righteousness. This is what Christ's death helps to accomplish, "moving them to repentance. . . . In particular, the death of Christ serves to beget in us the new life, through the power which this event exercises upon the heart, inasmuch as by it sin is broken at the very heart of the life of this world" (565, 580–81). By being restored to a relation of "trust in God, humility, and patience" through the knowledge they receive from Christ and the cross, believers come to "occupy that position of supremacy over the world which constitutes eternal life" (535). As Christ did in his death, each believer comes to "set himself above the world, which is no longer for him his ultimate source of impulse" (529).

While Jesus' life and death are important for Ritschl's doctrine of salvation, the same cannot be said of Jesus' resurrection and exaltation. For Ritschl, the only Jesus we can really know is the historical one who existed in our spatiotemporal realm. Thus there is no sense in speculating on anything outside of that realm, whether it be Christ's divine preexistence as God's Son before creation or his present exalted condition. The conception of Christ's present lordship "receives its content from the definite characteristics of his historical activity" (406), and his present activity must be "conceived as the expression of the abiding influence of his historical manifestation" (432). In other words, while Christ may be spoken of as exalted in heaven at present, the only influence he can exert upon us now is through what he did in the past during his life on earth.

The Community of Believers

As should be evident from the preceding discussion, the Christian community lies at the center of Ritschl's thought: "The Christian community is God's supreme end in the world" (464). As Philip Hefner notes, through his doctrine of the church, Ritschl expressly sought to avoid the "perversely individualistic" understanding of salvation he associated with traditional orthodoxy.[13] He insists that the community exists before the individuals who make it up, since they come to know Christ only in the context of the community: "A person always finds the community already existing when she arrives at faith" and does not "attain this end without the action of the community upon her" (549). In fact, Ritschl even speaks of "the community's eternal election" as "the divine final end" (301), although he rejects the idea that God elected particular individuals for salvation (121, 295); only the establishment of the community as a whole was foreordained from eternity.

Ritschl understands Christ's preexistence in similar terms: "Christ precedes his community" in that from eternity God intended to found the community through Christ (469). While Ritschl insists that the church must not be equated with the kingdom of God (286), he does establish a direct relationship between the coming of the kingdom and the existence of the community: it was Christ's "manifest purpose by deed and word to establish the community of the kingdom of God and to lead it to its goal. . . . For by the kingdom of God which Christ establishes is meant a community resting, not on legal rights, but on loving conduct" (430, 433).

This implies that salvation comes only through the community of believers. It is through the community alone that the gospel is proclaimed and that forgiveness and salvation are known and appropriated by human beings (110–11). Forgiveness of sins or reconciliation with God "is not recognisable and operative outside the community founded by Jesus Christ" (607); "our assurance of forgiveness, *i.e.* of a communion with God which is possible in spite of our sin—and our belonging to the community of those who believe in Christ, are identical" (550–51). Thus the Christian community is necessary for the kingdom to be established throughout the world, and for God's purposes for humanity to be achieved, which can happen fully only if all people become Christian: "The nations fulfil their destined end, namely, their development into one whole supernatural humanity, through their reception into the religious community of Christianity" (138); "humanity, entering into the community of Christ, is brought to the goal of the kingdom of God, which is God's own most personal end" (551).

Ritschl devotes very little attention to the role of the Holy Spirit in salvation. He insists that the Spirit's working is not "mechanical like that of a supernatural physical force," instead affirming that "his action on the individual can be shown to exist only when the individual is a member of the community of believers" (176–77). Above all, the Holy Spirit gives knowledge and freedom over the world (533–34; 605–6). The sacraments of baptism and Holy Communion also seem to be of secondary importance for Ritschl, playing no significant role in his discussion of justification and reconciliation.

Evaluation

As will become evident in the following chapters, in many ways the work of Albrecht Ritschl marks an important stage in the development of Christian thought regarding the work of Christ. The idea that Christ saves human beings primarily through the *divine revelation* they receive through his life and death came to be central to the understanding of Christ's work held by many of the theologians who followed Ritschl. Likewise, his view that salvation and God's kingdom have to do primarily with the *present world* rather than a future heavenly realm inspired numerous Christians to struggle for a more just and equitable world and to proclaim a "social gospel," rather than an individualistic gospel aimed at "saving souls."

Ritschl's work also makes manifest the rift between the conservative "orthodox" and the "liberal" positions that arose in the nineteenth century and has continued to this day. This makes it somewhat difficult to evaluate many of Ritschl's ideas, since what some would consider the strengths of his thought are considered by others to be grave defects.[14] Thus, for example, while many Christians who are more "liberal" would agree in principle with Ritschl's view of a loving, nonwrathful God and his rejection of a penal substitutionary understanding of Christ's death, those of more conservative tendencies regard such ideas as a betrayal of the message of the Scriptures and the teachings of the Reformers, which they claim faithfully represent those Scriptures.

Aside from certain aspects of Ritschl's understanding of God and the work of Christ, perhaps the idea that many today would consider most objectionable in Ritschl's work is that Christianity—particularly the form of Western Christianity espoused by Ritschl himself—is superior to all other religions as the perfect revelation of God and therefore must eventually prevail among the nations of the world, like the kingdom of God that Ritschl associates with the Christian community. Implicit in this view of history is that the Christian West is superior to all other cultures and thus is to establish its "lordship over the world," not only in the spiritual sense mentioned by Ritschl but in a political sense as well. Like many other ideologies of the nineteenth century, Ritschl's theology ultimately provides a ground for justifying the domination of "superior" Western Christians over the other "inferior" cultures and religions of the world, a domination that unfortunately did not come to an end with the close of the age of Western colonialism but, rather, continues in many other forms today. Such an understanding of the "kingdom of God" can hardly be regarded as standing in continuity with that proclaimed by Jesus some two thousand years ago.

CHAPTER 10

Karl Barth's Doctrine of Reconciliation

The outbreak of the First World War in 1914 and the immense sufferings and hardships that came in its wake put an end to the mood of optimism with regard to the future that had prevailed in many circles over the previous century. Rather than solving the world's problems and bringing progress and improvement, the advances made in areas such as science and technology had led to war, bloodshed, and mass destruction. Whatever hopes had been placed in the essential goodness of human nature and the "brotherhood of man" had been dashed; no longer was it possible to believe in the gradual advancement of humanity toward a "kingdom of God" on earth such as that which many of the liberal theologians had proclaimed.

The most powerful theological response to this situation came from the Swiss Reformed theologian Karl Barth (1886–1968), who argued in his commentary on Paul's Epistle to the Romans following the First World War that the gospel "proclaims a God utterly distinct from human beings," thus stressing that humanity, with its historical projects and constructions, was not to be identified with God but instead stood under God's judgment.[1] For Barth, whose theology was in large part a reaction to the political events surrounding the two World Wars that took place during his life, sinful humanity had to be humbled and destroyed before it might be saved. Salvation, therefore, could not originate in human beings or result from human activity; it could only be the work of a sovereign, almighty God who transcends human history as the "wholly other." For Barth, there is an infinite qualitative difference between God, who exists in eternity, and mortal human beings, who exist in time.

Precisely because of his doctrine of divine transcendence, Barth believed that human language is incapable of grasping or representing God adequately. God can be spoken of only through "dialectic," that is, paradoxical language that does not attempt to arrive at syntheses but lets apparently contradictory affirmations stand alongside one another, claiming that only in this way can truth be expressed. Barth is thus known as a "dialectical theologian," as well as a "neo-orthodox" thinker, in that he rejected liberal theology in order to return to certain orthodox positions that were nevertheless quite different from those of traditional Protestant orthodoxy.[2]

While Barth was extremely productive theologically for over half a century during his teaching career in Germany (which he left in 1934 due to his opposition to the Hitler regime) and then in Switzerland, his greatest and most comprehensive work was his *Church Dogmatics*, composed from 1932 to the end of his life and consisting of four volumes that, when subdivided, actually total twelve, averaging some six hundred pages each. Naturally, it is not possible to deal with all the intricacies of Barth's understanding of the story of salvation in Christ in just a few pages; at most, we can hope to sketch that story here only broadly. Our primary focus will be the fourth volume, which deals with the doctrine of reconciliation.[3]

God, Christ, and "Man" in Eternity

Reflecting his Calvinist roots, Barth assigns a central role to the doctrine of election in the story of redemption he tells.[4] Nevertheless, he distances himself from Calvin's teaching that, from eternity, God had elected some individuals for salvation but had rejected others, and instead speaks of Jesus Christ as the "elected man" who "does not stand alongside the rest of the elect, but before and above them as the One who is originally and properly the Elect" (2/2:116). However, since Jesus Christ is also God, existing from eternity together with the Father and the Holy Spirit, he is not only the "elected man" but also "the electing God" (2/2:103, 116).

According to Barth, the election of Jesus Christ had as its goal the election and salvation of "all men and women" in him; "his election is the original and all-inclusive election" (2/2:116–17).[5] The election of all others follows from Jesus' election because, as true God and true man, Jesus Christ stands between God and "man," "mediating between the two" (2/2:94). Barth defines God's plan or purpose in creation as that of establishing a covenant with humanity in Christ; "the covenant is the goal of creation and creation the way to the covenant" (3/1:97). This covenant is understood primarily in terms of fellowship between God and human beings. God has created "man" "in fellowship with himself in order that in this natural fellowship he may further speak and act with him" (3/1:185); "man" is thus created to be God's "covenant partner."

To make this covenant fellowship a reality, God intended from eternity that his Son should become "man" (2/2:101). However, God also determined that his Son would be crucified: the election of Jesus Christ was an "election to suffering" (2/2:120); "the elected man Jesus was foreordained to suffer and to die" (2/2:122). To speak in these terms implies that the fall of human beings into sin and the breaking of the covenant were also foreseen by God before creation, as was God's response to human sin: "The election of the man Jesus means, then, that a wrath is kindled, a sentence pronounced and finally executed, a rejection actualised. It has been determined thus from all eternity. From all eternity judgment has been foreseen" (2/2:122).

While the judgment of human sin and the rejection of sinful humanity were therefore predestined, it was also determined from before history that Jesus Christ would endure this judgment and rejection in the place of sinful human beings: "The rejection which all men and women incurred, the wrath of God under which all men and women lie, the death which all men and women must die, God in his love for men and women transfers from all eternity to him in whom he loves and elects them, and whom he elects at their head and in their place. God from all eternity ordains this obedient One in order that he might bear the suffering which the disobedient have deserved and which for the sake of God's righteousness must necessarily be borne" (2/2:123). This final phrase makes clear that Barth follows the tradition according to which God's righteousness or justice made the incarnation and death of his Son necessary for the salvation of sinful, fallen humanity.

In revising the doctrine of election in this way, Barth avoids the problem raised by the Calvinist understanding of election, namely, why a just and loving God would elect only some for salvation while rejecting others. For Barth, *all* people are elected in the election of Christ, who is also the elector as well as the one elected to be rejected. However, Barth's view remains problematic in that he regards the fall of humanity into sin as something not only *foreseen* but *fore-ordained* or *predetermined* by God, like Christ's death. This implies that the fall into sin in some sense took place *in eternity*, perhaps in the mind of God, before it actually took place in human history, and thus that humanity was created flawed. It is not clear why God should create humanity in a way that would require that it first be rejected, judged, and destroyed, standing under God's wrath, in order then to be saved and exalted in Christ. If humanity is capable of being exalted to fellowship with God, why were we not created that way from the outset?

Jesus Christ and "Man"

Barth teaches that, before creation, God's Son Jesus Christ not only was foreordained to *become* man but already *was* man: "the man Jesus already was even before he was" (3/2:464); "man exists in this One at the beginning of all God's ways and works, and therefore at the beginning of all things with God himself, in the primal basis of all reality" (4/2:34). No doubt, it seems quite strange to speak of Jesus Christ as being "man" even before the incarnation, and of "man" existing in him from the beginning. Yet this idea lies at the very heart of Barth's doctrine of reconciliation and is key to understanding it. In reality, like Irenaeus and many of the other church fathers, Barth draws on the Platonic doctrine of ideas or forms to affirm that "man" in general has been assumed by Christ and redeemed by him through his death and resurrection; and because all human beings share in this "man," what occurred in Christ affects all.[6]

Yet, while Irenaeus and many of the fathers conceived of God's Son being

Karl Barth in Safenwil, Switzerland, 1916.
Photo courtesy of Special Collections, Princeton Theological Seminary
Libraries on behalf of the Karl Barth Stiftung, Basel, Switzerland.

joined to the universal "man" only from the moment of his incarnation, Barth
identifies Jesus Christ with this "man" from before creation. For Plato, the universal idea of man was eternal and perfect, existing in an ideal, heavenly realm,
while all the particular women and men who participate in the universal idea
exist only in our empirical earthly realm and are, in some sense, imperfect "copies" of that idea. Yet this idea or form of "man," like all of the eternal forms, was
in some sense *real*; in fact, Plato regards the ideas or forms as more real than all of
the particular copies that participate in them. This is because the universals exist
in the realm of "being," where they are permanent and unchanging, whereas the
particulars are found in the realm of "becoming," where everything is temporal,
constantly coming and going; unlike the universal and eternal idea of "man,"
particular men and women are born and eventually die. It is also important to
note that, while the particulars or copies *participate* in the universal idea so that
they are *one* with it and *included* in it, at the same time there is a sense in which
they are *distinct* and *independent* from the universal.

Undoubtedly, important differences exist between Plato's understanding of
"man" and that of Barth. Nevertheless, the Platonic influence in Barth's thought is
evident when he identifies Jesus Christ with "man" from eternity: "He alone is the
archetypal man" (3/2:144). "He is not only *a* true man, but *the* true man," "the *One*,

whose existence necessarily touches that of all other men and women" and "who was the Head before the foundation of the world" (4/2:27, 36). For Barth, this "idea of man" is equivalent to human nature or human being. Thus he speaks of Jesus as the "prototype," insisting that we "derive wholly from Jesus . . . our human nature"; human nature is "actualised in him as the original and in us only as the copy. Jesus is man as God willed and created him. . . . We are partakers of human nature as and because Jesus is first partaker of it. . . . [I]n him human nature is not concealed but revealed in its original and most basic form" (3/2:50, 52). "[T]he fact of this one man is prior to the existence of all other men and women. It is thus through their relationship to him that they are what they are" (3/2:161).

This understanding of the relation between Christ and all human beings stands in contrast to the idea of the church fathers, who see *Adam*, rather than Christ, as the original man, in whom human nature first existed and from whom all subsequent human beings derive their humanity. Reflecting an idea similar to that which we noted in Ritschl's thought (chapter 9), Barth insists that we must look to Jesus Christ, rather than to Adam, to understand what humanity is ideally to be.

Sin and Fallen "Man"

If God created "man" out of love to be his covenant partner, then the sin of "man" will be understood in terms of rejecting that love and failing to live under the covenant. Just as Barth looks to Christ to define "man," so also he looks to Christ to define sin as "the negation, the opposite of what God did in Jesus Christ" (4/1:142).[7] In contrast to Jesus Christ's "humbling himself" and "becoming a servant," "man" sins through his pride by acting in defiance, through his sloth and disorder, and through his falsehood; all of this is "the sin of Adam," which is "repeated in many forms" as "the sin of Israel, and of the world and of all forgetful Christians" (4/1:142–44). Sin is "the arrogance in which man wants to be his own and his neighbour's judge" (4/1:231). Under these conditions, there can be no fellowship between "man" and God: "By sin man puts himself in the wrong in relation to God. He makes himself impossible as the creature and covenant-partner of God" (4/1:528).

In this fallen state, "man" is under God's judgment, his "No," and thus must be set aside and destroyed. Barth writes that "this judgment involves the destruction of wrong and of the man who does wrong"; man "as a wrongdoer had to be negated by God and die" (4/1:550). The destruction of "man" is necessary because, in this fallen condition, he cannot be reformed: "Man cannot convert himself. He cannot make himself the friend of God instead of the enemy of God. He cannot save himself from the destruction which must inevitably follow his enmity against God. He cannot do anything to escape the wrath of God which threatens him in the position in which he has placed himself" (4/1:251).

Nevertheless, this destruction ultimately has a positive purpose, namely, the salvation of "man." The objective is to set aside sinful "man" so that another "man" may take his place. God's "No" to "man" is pronounced so that the "Yes" may follow: "The life of the new and righteous man acquires a place only with the passing and death of the old man of unrighteousness. The one has to perish in order that the other may begin. There is no place for the new man alongside the old. He can only crowd him out and replace him" (4/1:557). "The man who sets himself in the wrong against it must die as a wrongdoer, but he must rise again as the recipient of the right of the elect, of the covenant-partner of God, which is granted to him. The one man must go, the other come" (4/1:563).

But who is this "man" who must be destroyed and replaced? Here again, Barth's language must be understood against the background of the Platonic doctrine of ideas. Obviously, Barth is not referring merely to a single, individual man or person. At the same time, however, in passages such as these he uses the singular "man" rather than the plural "men." That this "man" does not simply refer to an impersonal human nature is evident in that Barth ascribes personal characteristics to "him": "He" thinks, believes, acts, obeys, knows, learns, hopes, and even has his own will (e.g., 4/1:251, 258, 534–44, 568–69, 593–99).[8] Thus this man is not some-*thing* but some*one*, a "who" rather than a "what." The idea must therefore be that this man, to whom Barth refers as "fallen man," the "man of sin," the "old man," and the "false and perverted man," is the equivalent of the universal "idea of man" in which all particular human beings participate.[9] *All people* are this "man."

Jesus Christ as the Savior of "Man"

To bring about the destruction of the old "man" of sin and bring a new "man" into existence, Jesus Christ "became and is man" (4/2:45). According to Barth, in the incarnation, God's Son "accepts and assumes man—human being—into unity with his own divine being" and "descends so deep to man in order to lift him up so high" (4/2:43). It is important to note that this "man" assumed by Christ is "man" in his sinful, fallen condition, who lies under God's judgment (4/1:258). This involves "accepting unity and solidarity with sinful man" (4/1:213).

In continuity with what we have already seen, this "man" assumed by Christ in the incarnation must be understood in terms of the universal "idea of man," who *embraces* or *includes* all particular men and women yet is distinct from them. God's Son assumed into himself "not merely 'a man' but the *humanum*, the being and essence, the nature and kind, which is that of all men and women" (4/2:48). Since all women and men share in the same "man," they are one with Christ: "In his being as man God has implicitly assumed the human being of all men and women. In him not only we as *homines*, but our *humanitas* as such—for it is both his and ours—exist in and with God himself" (4/2:59). The incarnation creates an "ontological connexion" between Christ and all women and men (4/2:275); that is, they share the same *being*. The incarnation thus does not merely involve Christ's assuming *human nature*, since when God's Son "became man" he did not become *human nature* per se; rather, it involves "God's participation in man" (4/1:551–52), that is, in the universal idea of "man" in which all human beings share.

Likewise, it is not just our human nature that exists in and with God, but "we

Descent from the Cross (1968-76, Marc Chagall © ARS, NY). In Barth's thought,
humanity as a whole was judged and put to death when Christ died, in order that all
might consequently rise and be exalted to God together with him.
Photo © Scala / Art Resource, NY.

as *homines*" or men and women. All human beings are therefore included in this
"man" assumed by Christ yet must still be distinguished from him, since Christ
did not assume all men and women in the incarnation. Thus, while "the history
of Jesus Christ embraces that of the world and all women and men" (4/3:214),
so that what takes place "in the history of Jesus Christ" also takes place "in the
history of all other men and women" (4/1:298; cf. 548; 3/2:161–62), nevertheless
his history is his alone, and not ours (4/1:230–31; 4/2:600). "We are in him and
comprehended in him, but we are still not he himself. Therefore it is all true and
actual in this Other first and not in us" (4/1:549; cf. 229, 317; 4/2:514).

By assuming "man" in his fallen state, Christ assumed the sins of "man" as
well as his punishment, which he endured when he suffered and died on the
cross; in this way, he put an end to this fallen "man." Christ "actually took away
sinful man, causing him to disappear" (4/1:295–96). "The man of sin was put to
death in him" (4/1:566–67). Barth employs the idea of "substitution" to affirm
that Christ became the "one great sinner" who "stands in our place" (4/1:243)
and "takes the place of sinful man" (4/1:555). Yet he complements this idea with
that of representation, since not only does Christ die *in the stead* of others but all
people die *with* him, because the "man" assumed by Christ includes them all.
"What took place is that the Son of God fulfilled the righteous judgment on us
women and men by himself taking our place as man and in our place undergoing
the judgment under which we had passed" (4/1:222). In this way, he is both judge

and judged, since he judges sin by enduring its judgment as our substitute and representative so as to do away with it (4/1:211–83). As G. C. Berkouwer notes, for Barth, the idea "that Christ died for us does not mean that we no longer have to die but that we ourselves have died *in and with* Christ. . . . The substitutionary work of Christ is not a work that takes place outside of us and which is *subsequently applied* to us."[10]

Precisely because the "man" assumed by Christ embraces and includes all women and men, it was not only Christ who died but humanity as a whole. "For then and there, in the person of Christ taking our place, we were present, being crucified and dying with him. We died. This has to be understood quite concretely and literally. . . . We died: the totality of all sinful men and women. . . . His death was the death of all" (4/1:295). Because of the ontological union between Christ and all women and men,

> in the suffering and death of Jesus Christ it has come to pass that in his own person he has made an end of us as sinners and therefore of sin itself by going to death as the One who took our place as sinners. In his person he has delivered up us sinners and sin itself to destruction. He has removed us sinners and sin, negated us, cancelled us out: ourselves, our sin, and the accusation, condemnation and perdition which had overtaken us. (4/1:253–54)

Nevertheless, this "judgment of God on all men and women" was a "redemptive" one (4/1:247), since its objective was to bring a new "man" into place. This occurred in Christ's resurrection and exaltation. Once more, because all women and men are joined to Christ by virtue of "that existence of his which embraces ours" (4/1:285), when he was raised and exalted to heaven, "man" as a whole was raised and exalted with him: "In the history in which he became and is man, and suffers and acts as man, there took place an exaltation of the humanity which as his and ours is the same" (4/2:28); "man himself is exalted, not as God or like God, but to God, being placed at his side, not in identity, but in true fellowship with him, and becoming a new man in this exaltation and fellowship" (4/2:6; cf. 29–30). Barth uses a variety of designations to refer to this "new man," such as "justified man," "obedient man," "true man," and "future man," among many others. Because all men and women are "in and with this Son who became man and died as man and was raised as man," all of this involves the "alteration of the situation of the men and women of all times" and "the conversion of all men and women to God" (4/1:316–17). Therefore, "the reconciliation of the world with God as it has taken place in him . . . consists in the fact that there took place in him the existence of a new and true man, and that human essence, as God lent it his own existence and made it his own, was exalted, and is once for all exalted, to him" (4/2:69–70).[11]

As Frank Hasel observes, in understanding Christ's work of reconciliation in this way, Barth departs from traditional orthodoxy by positing a change not in *God* but in *human beings*: Christ's death "did not alter anything in the relationship of God to human beings, but only in the relationship of the latter to God.

According to Barth, God does not need to be reconciled, inasmuch as God is already favorable toward human beings from the beginning and has irrevocably decided to save them."[12]

The fact that for Barth this "man" exists *independently* of both Christ and particular men and women, while at times being interchangeable with either Christ or men and women in general, is evident throughout Barth's discussion of the doctrine of reconciliation. Christ *is* "the man who is reconciled with God, the true man, and in relation to all the rest the new man" (4/2:30), yet at the same time the "new and true man" is *not* Christ, since "he" exists and is present *in* Christ (4/2:29, 69, 117). Christ "is the righteous man" and "has acted for us as this new and obedient and therefore free man," yet at the same time "he has brought in the man who is the child of this God, this new and obedient and free man" (4/1:257–58; cf. 4/2:382-84); and if this "new man" is someone "brought in" by Christ, "he" is not Christ himself.

Similarly, each of us *is* this "man" yet is *distinct* from him. "In Jesus Christ, the very man who as such is the eternal Son of the eternal Father, this future man, the new and righteous man, lives in an unassailable reality. In him I am already the one who will be this righteous man and live as such" (4/1:555). "We are all the old man himself who there in Jesus Christ was overtaken by the wrath of God and condemned and executed. Jesus Christ suffered and died in our place, in solidarity with this old man and therefore with us" (4/1:390–91). "The sentence which was executed as the divine judgment in the death of Jesus Christ is that we are these proud creatures, that I am the man of sin, and that this man of sin and therefore I myself am nailed to the cross and crucified (in the power of the sacrifice and obedience of Jesus Christ in my place), that I am therefore destroyed and replaced, that as the one who has turned to nothingness I am done away in the death of Jesus Christ" (4/1:515).

Salvation and Faith

As is clear from the preceding discussion, Barth's understanding of God's work in Christ is heavily objective, in that *all human beings* are affected by it. Christ's death was the death of all "quite independently of their attitude or response to this event" (4/1:295), and therefore reconciliation is not merely a possibility that must still come to individuals but an objective reality for all (4/1:285). This is because all participate ontologically in this one "man" who was put to death and then exalted to God in Jesus Christ.

Nevertheless, even though "the conversion of all women and men to God" has "taken place in him," not all are aware of the alteration of their situation. They must still come to "recognise and acknowledge that they are altered" by this event, "drawing out the consequences of this alteration, bowing before the divine verdict, repenting in face of the judgment of God which has come upon them . . . , accepting that they are the children of God, accepting that which is old as old, and that which is new as new" (4/1:317; cf. 4/3:269, 279–80). While all people have been justified and sanctified by virtue of their participation in the justification and sanctification of "man" accomplished in Christ, they must still *become* what they *are*: "The sanctification of man, his conversion to God, is, like his justification, a transformation, a new determination, which has taken place *de jure* for the world and therefore for all men and women. *De facto*, however, it is not known by all men and women, just as justification has not *de facto* been grasped and acknowledged and known and confessed by all men and women, but only by those who are awakened to faith" (4/2:511).

For Barth, therefore, the salvation, reconciliation, justification, and sanctification of "man" have to do not only with *ontology*, a change in the *being* of "man," but *revelation*: we must come to *know* and *acknowledge* the change effected in our situation through Christ. Barth's understanding of faith, the work of the Holy Spirit, and the church and sacraments revolves around this idea. Through the Holy Spirit, Christ "brings us to the light of the Gospel, giving us eyes to see, causing us to grasp the heavenly wisdom, and thus giving us the faith in which . . . our justification and sanctification become a concrete event" (4/2:522). As we come to faith and receive direction through the Holy Spirit, we begin to live holy and obedient lives as saints and to follow Jesus as his disciples, doing good works and taking up our cross, even though we remain sinners. By being joined to Christ and participating in him, each believer already "is the new man; the man who is impelled by the Spirit of God," even though he or she "is still the old" (4/2:570–71).

The Holy Spirit also gathers believers into the Christian community, "building up them and their work into the true Church" (4/2:617). The church exists not as an end in itself but to make known to all people what has happened to them in Christ: "The goal in the direction of which the true Church proceeds and moves is the revelation of the sanctification of all humanity and human life as it has already taken place *de iure* in Jesus Christ" (4/2:620). Just as the church's mission is thus understood in terms of proclaiming to others that in Christ they have *already* been saved, rather than offering salvation to them now,[13] so also baptism and the Lord's Supper serve primarily to remind believers that they have already been justified, sanctified, and made new through participation in Christ and his death and resurrection; they thus involve the recognition and actualization of what has already taken place (4/2:55; cf. 3/2:606, 621).[14]

Barth's view of salvation and reconciliation as something already accomplished raises the question of the sense in which salvation is still to be awaited as a future reality. At times, it appears that salvation has to do merely with living in fellowship with God in Christ as God's covenant partner in *this* world. However, Barth does speak of "the new and obedient humanity," which is "provisionally and very imperfectly but genuinely actualised" in the present in the Christian community, and sees the kingdom of God as something existing in the person of Christ, "which will be directly and universally and definitively revealed and known at the end and goal of all history" (4/2:656). Thus, as Helmut Gollwitzer has noted, Barth does not understand the kingdom of God "simply as a perfection of the individual's life or as the eternal life of the individual in communion with

God."[15] He views the kingdom not as something to be established gradually over time in human history but as something that will attain "its final revelation in the return of Jesus Christ" only "at the end of all history" (4/2:656). Barth's insistence that, in Christ, all people have been justified and converted and reconciled to God seems to lead to the conclusion that ultimately all people will be saved. Yet, as George Hunsinger notes, "Barth stops short, as widely noted, of unequivocally proclaiming universal salvation," thus "leaving the question open." However, instead of phrasing the question in terms of why God might not will to save all, Barth asks why "not all human beings will to accept God's salvation," considering this rejection on their part "inexplicable" and even "impossible."[16]

Evaluation

Undoubtedly, Barth's doctrine of reconciliation raises a number of problems, many of which have already been alluded to above. Perhaps the most serious of these is that human salvation and reconciliation with God appear to be automatic and mechanical: merely by becoming "man," dying, and then being exalted to God, Christ effects the conversion and reconciliation of all people to God by virtue of the fact that all are joined to him. It is difficult to see how people can be said to have been converted to God without necessarily being aware of it. If reconciliation is "the restitution, the resumption of a fellowship" (4/1:22), is it possible for people to have been reconciled and restored to such a fellowship with God without knowing it, so that they "are no longer the enemies of God but his friends, his children," and "no longer turned away from him, but away from their own being in the past, and turned to him" (4/1:316)? While it is no doubt true that human language is incapable of speaking adequately of God, so that paradoxes and apparently contradictory statements such as those found in Barth's writings are necessary to express the Christian faith concerning God and God's relation to the world, Barth's teaching regarding human salvation in Christ seems to go well beyond what we find in the New Testament.

In addition, many have claimed that, by stressing so strongly the utter transcendence of God and the idea of salvation as something accomplished solely by God in Christ, Barth reduces humanity virtually to nothingness, so that human beings are totally passive in their salvation and do not even have a say in it. Considering the context in which Barth wrote, however, this is understandable: while Barth sought to avoid the optimism toward the future that was grounded in a belief in the capabilities of human beings, he did not wish to fall into the other extreme of pessimism; rather, he sought to ground that optimism in God and Christ, thus pointing people to depend totally on God rather than on their own efforts, wisdom, or strength. The world had suffered tremendously by looking to human beings rather than to God for salvation. For this reason, Barth felt it necessary to point to Jesus Christ alone as the "ideal man" at every step of the way in his theology, so that no other person or group of people might claim to represent that ideal or be identified with it. In his mind, whenever that had occurred, the consequences had been tragic.

CHAPTER 11

Rudolf Bultmann and the Proclamation of the Word of the Cross

Rudolf Bultmann (1884–1976) was a contemporary and friend of Karl Barth. The two formed part of the same theological circle in Germany in the 1920s, sharing many of the same viewpoints, but eventually their thought went in two very different directions. Bultmann's theology, like Barth's, was in many ways a response to the political events of the first half of the twentieth century (though Bultmann generally denied this). In contrast to Barth, however, Bultmann did not leave Germany during the Hitler regime and the Second World War. In spite of his opposition to Hitler's National Socialism, Bultmann remained in the position of professor of New Testament to which he had been appointed at the University of Marburg in 1921 throughout the war and until his retirement in 1951, after which he continued to write and lecture.

While many consider Barth the greatest theologian of the twentieth century, Bultmann is widely recognized as the most influential biblical scholar of his time. Yet, rather than limiting himself to reconstructing the thought of the New Testament writers in their original contexts, which is how the task of biblical theology has traditionally been understood, Bultmann was particularly interested in developing a theology that would respond to the needs of his own context; that is, his concern was with not merely what the Scriptures *meant* in their day but what they *mean* in ours.

To address this latter question, Bultmann made use of existentialist philosophy, particularly that of Martin Heidegger (1889–1976), his fellow professor at Marburg from 1923 to 1928.[1] Heidegger, like other existentialist philosophers, stressed the independence of the individual in relation to the surrounding world; authentic human existence involves making one's own choices freely to determine one's own future, rather than letting society, the past, or tradition define the direction one's life is to go. The emphasis is, therefore, on the *present*, the *here and now*; the future is *open* for each individual, who alone is responsible for making his or her own decisions. Given the adverse conditions under which Bultmann labored due to forces beyond his control, such as the destruction associated with two world wars and a despotic regime that sought to define people's lives and their future for them, his adoption of an existentialist perspective is understandable. When one finds oneself living in difficult circumstances that are beyond one's power to change, one can, at most, strive to retain control over one's own life, without allowing those circumstances to define one's present and future.

Bultmann's stated interest in discerning the meaning of the New Testament witness for the present, and not just its meaning in its original contexts, produces a tendency to "cross the boundary between biblical theology and systematic theology"; at times, it is not clear when he is presenting the thought of the New Testament authors—particularly Paul and John, for whom he has a strong preference that is "genuinely Lutheran"—and when he is presenting his own.[2] Here, we will not be overly concerned about this distinction and will thus look both to his historical reconstructions of early Christian belief as well as his discussion of theological questions to ascertain the understanding of salvation in Christ found in his work.[3] Ultimately, he maintains that there is a "single, new and unique doctrine of human existence" to be found in the New Testament (*PC* 179), and this is what he presents as the essence of the Christian faith.

History, Myth, and the Gospel

For Bultmann, any discussion of the biblical teaching regarding salvation must take into account that the understanding of the world reflected in the biblical writings differs greatly from our own. On the basis of our modern worldview, many people can no longer accept literally what the Bible says concerning the creation of the world in the way Genesis narrates it, the miraculous events in both the Old and New Testaments, the bodily resurrection of Jesus, and Jesus' second coming in glory. For Bultmann, such events belong to the category of "myth." As Morris Ashcraft observes: "Bultmann maintains that a modern man with his scientific view of the universe could not believe in the mythological world view even if he wanted to. To insist that one must accept the New Testament world view in order to accept the Christian message would be both impossible and proposterous."[4]

For Bultmann, then, if the Bible is to have meaning for us today, it must be "demythologized"—that is, we must get behind the mythological language in which the gospel message is encased so as to present that same message in a way that has meaning for us today, in accordance with our own worldview. Bultmann provides an excellent example of this when he examines Paul's affirmation in 1 Cor 8:6 that there are many "gods and lords" in the world, in contrast to the one true God. Paul understood these as personal beings, such as demons, pagan deities, and other types of spirits who influenced human beings adversely. According

Rudolf Bultmann

to Bultmann, even though our modern scientific worldview no longer allows us to believe in the actual existence of such "mythical" beings, the basic truth of what Paul says still holds, namely, that "there are many powers in the world which claim us and whose claim is accepted by many women and men as divine. . . . Wherever the ultimate reality that gives meaning to our life and demands our worship is seen to lie in these powers, the many gods and lords still hold sway" (*EF* 173–74).

Interestingly, Bultmann sees Paul and John in effect carrying out the same process of "translating" the gospel message from its original context into their own, thus reinterpreting it.[5] Because that message had originally arisen in a Jewish context, in order to make it meaningful and comprehensible in the Hellenistic world in which they worked, they found it necessary to borrow concepts and terminology from non-Jewish and pagan sources, such as Gnosticism and the mystery religions; thus early or "primitive" Christianity was a "syncretistic phenomenon" (*PC* 175–79). For Bultmann, however, it was entirely acceptable for Paul and John to make use of Hellenistic modes of thought in proclaiming the gospel, just as it is acceptable to make use of modern modes of thought (such as existentialist philosophy) to make the gospel meaningful for people in our own day and age.

Similar observations must be made regarding the concept of *history*. As a New Testament scholar, Bultmann considered historical research and reconstruction of the past an indispensable tool for understanding the gospel in its original context.

Yet, while such research and reconstruction can help us understand the meaning of the gospel proclamation in the *past*, so as to establish certain "data" or "facts of history," we must go beyond all of this if the gospel is to have meaning *for us today*. This requires a process of interpretation or "hermeneutics." Our study of history is always guided by our own interests, presuppositions, and worldviews, and this is something not to be *covered up* or *lamented* but to be *recognized* and *affirmed*. Once again, we can see the same process in the writings of Paul and John. Though they were certainly aware of many of the historical facts regarding Jesus, ultimately what was important for them was not simply recalling the past but also discerning the meaning of Jesus for their own present, as Christ and Lord: "It is not the historical Jesus, but Jesus Christ, the Christ, preached, who is the Lord" (*FU* 241).

For Bultmann, this also means that what is normative for Christian theology is not what Jesus actually did and said or what "really happened" during his life and death, but the message concerning Jesus that the early Christian church proclaimed. What transformed people then, and transforms them today, is not the knowledge of past history but the proclamation of the gospel; it is the latter rather than the former that produces faith and constitutes its basis.

Human Existence in the World

Because Bultmann's primary concern lies with meaning in the present rather than myth in the past, he shows little interest in discussing such things as an eternal divine plan of salvation, the preexistence of God's Son, the creation of the world, or the human fall into sin. Undoubtedly, faith in creation and in God as Creator is important for Bultmann, but mainly in that such faith defines who we are *at present* in relation to God and the world. Faith in creation "is not a theory about the past. It does not have its meaning by relating what took place at some earlier time and no longer concerns human beings in the present, but rather speaks precisely about humanity's *present* situation. It tells a person how she is to understand herself *now*; and the reference to the past is only for the purpose of teaching her to understand her situation in the present" (*EF* 207–8).

And what is this situation? It involves a relation to God, namely, that of recognizing that "God has called the world and humanity into being and therefore is their sovereign Lord; that humanity belongs to God and is accountable to him as Judge" (*EF* 188). It also involves a relation to the people and world around oneself: our historical existence "takes place *with others*, in relation to whom one must make concrete decisions" (*EF* 214). By means of these decisions, we define our life in the present and future: "I live in my decisions in which I myself am at stake, either to win myself or to lose it" (*EF* 214). For persons to exist "authentically," in making these decisions they must surrender themselves entirely to God: "To be God's creature means absolutely and in every present to have one's source in him" (*EF* 175).[6] "If, according to the Christian faith, God has created humanity, then this means that a person receives his selfhood from God and can only be himself by receiving it"; thus "a person ought not to be himself from himself and for himself, but rather from God and for God" (*EF* 216).

Yet this is not the way human beings actually exist in the world. Instead, "each of us, from the beginning, wants to exist only from herself and for herself" (*EF* 217). "Sin is to want to live out of one's self, out of one's power, rather than out of radical surrender to God, to what he demands, gives and sends" (*EF* 255). "The *real sin of each person* is that he takes his will and his life into his own hands, makes himself secure, and so has his self-confidence, his 'boast'" (*FU* 228). This "boasting" is the "attitude of sinful self-reliance" (*TNT* 1:242). Instead of seeking security in God alone, people look to the world and its values, striving to attain that security by their own efforts: "The ultimate sin reveals itself to be the false assumption of receiving life not as the gift of the Creator but procuring it by one's own power, of living from one's self rather than from God" (*TNT* 1:232).

Bultmann understands the doctrine of original or inherited sin against the background of these ideas: "This poisoning of our life that no one can escape and no one can remove is what is meant when the church speaks of *original sin*" (*EF* 217). "At the base of the idea of inherited sin lies the experience that every person is born into a humanity that is and always has been guided by a false striving. . . . So everyone exists in a world in which each looks out for herself, each insists upon her rights, each fights for her existence, and life becomes a struggle of all against all even when the battle is involuntarily fought" (*TNT* 1:253).

While, in a sense, each person is responsible for this state of affairs (*TNT* 1:253), at the same time all are helpless to save themselves from it. Bultmann notes that both Paul and John speak of several "powers" that hold all people captive; these include not only sin but death, the flesh, the world, and the law. When human beings are dominated by the power of sin, they also become subject to "death," that is, inauthentic existence, which is the *consequence* of sin rather than its *punishment*: "For in his care and putting confidence in worldly values and accomplishments he lets these become lord over him, and because they are all transitory (1 Cor 7:31), he himself falls under death; by understanding himself in terms of the transitory and the provisional, his being is not authentic, but rather has fallen subject to what is passing away" (*EF* 130). "The thing a person supposes she can control, whether it be pleasure or serious moral effort, becomes a power which controls her and drags her into the clutches of death. . . . Thus sin results in death, for sin is just this attempt of a person to attain life through her own efforts" (*PC* 192).

By "flesh," Paul understands "the essence of the person who understands himself in terms of himself, who wants to secure his own existence" (*EF* 81). Flesh is thus

> the sphere of visible, concrete, tangible and measurable reality. . . . When a person chooses to live entirely in and for this sphere, or, as St. Paul puts it, when she "lives after the flesh," it assumes the shape of a "power". . . . For "flesh" embraces not only the material things of life, but all human creation and achievement pursued for the sake of some tangible reward, such as for example the fulfilling of the law. . . . Since the visible and

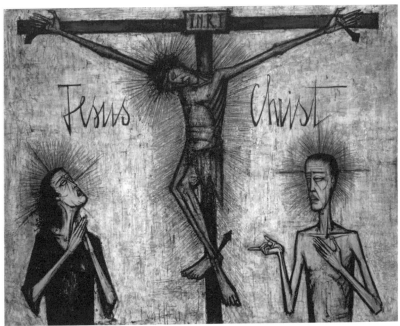

Crucifixion (1960, Bernard Buffet. Collezione d'Arte Religiosa Moderna,
Vatican Museums). For Bultmann, the event of the cross reveals to believers God's
judgment on our sinful human existence and thereby brings them
to a new understanding of themselves.
Photo © Scala / Art Resource, NY.

tangible sphere is essentially transitory, the person who bases her life on
it becomes the prisoner and slave of corruption. (*KM* 18–19)

Both Paul and John also speak of the "world" as a way of life in which men
and women "have made themselves independent of God" and thus something
that "they themselves have created by turning away from God. As such it is a
power that already encompasses each individual, encountering him and taking
him along with it, so that he cannot isolate himself from it" (*EF* 129). The term
world therefore refers to "human society, with its aspirations and judgments, its
wisdom, its joys and its sufferings. Thus every person makes her contribution to
the 'world.' It is the world in just this sense which becomes a power tyrannizing
over the individual, the fate she has created for herself" (*PC* 193).

The law conveys to human beings the claim of God on them and thus God's
demand that they submit to God obediently. In this sense, the law is holy and
good, since this obedience would bring life (*EF* 135–36). However, because no one
fulfills the law, it brings death rather than life. Paul thus includes the law among
the powers that enslave human beings, both because it "awakens a person's
desire" by prohibiting certain things, thus calling a person's attention to them

and arousing his "lustful impulses," and because it leads to a person attempting to "attain life by his own strength. . . . Thus the law, which is intrinsically holy, righteous and good, and comes from God, becomes a lethal power" (*PC* 192). In this way, the law sinks human beings even more deeply into sin, self-reliance, and boasting: "*A person's effort to achieve her salvation by keeping the Law* only leads her into sin, indeed this effort itself in the end is *already sin*" (*TNT* 1:264).

Ultimately, then, human beings are helpless to overcome the powers of flesh, the world, sin, death, and the law to attain an "authentic existence" on their own: "Each person rebels against death and knows that as one who is fallen under it he is not in his authenticity. But he does not have the possibility through his own resources of becoming lord over it" (*EF* 72). In this condition, human beings can be saved only by an act of grace on God's part.

Christ and Grace

For Bultmann, the grace necessary for human beings to be delivered from their sinful existence is given through Jesus Christ or, to be more precise, through the church's *proclamation* of the word of God, by which Jesus Christ is made present (*FU* 307–8).[7] While this proclamation (or *kerygma* in Greek) is, in certain respects, in continuity with the message proclaimed by Jesus during his earthly ministry, it also goes well beyond Jesus' own message. This is primarily because, after the events surrounding his crucifixion, Jesus went from being the *proclaimer* to the *one proclaimed*; the first Christian communities came to use a variety of different titles, such as Messiah, Lord, Son of God, Son of Man, and others, to confess their faith in him (*TNT* 1:33-53). In the Hellenistic Christian communities, the gospel message concerning Christ also underwent a transformation due to the influence of ideas from the Greek-speaking world, as is particularly evident in the writings of Paul and John. In contrast to the original community, which "kept wholly to the *proclamation of Jesus* himself" regarding the future coming of the kingdom of God, "Paul and John preach that the new age *has* already dawned, that judgment and justification, death and life are already present" (*FU* 195).

According to Bultmann, Paul placed at the center of his gospel proclamation the event of Jesus' death and resurrection, rather than Jesus' teaching or earthly life. Paul came to "acknowledge in the cross of Christ . . . the judgment of God upon a person's prior self-understanding" (*FU* 238):

> The judgment upon all humankind is consummated in the cross, and in the cross as an actual historical event. . . . The naked fact of the cross of Jesus means that a person is asked the question whether she will relinquish her secure self, her "boasting". . . . Whoever does not let herself be crucified with Christ; she for whom the world is not dead and who is not herself dead to the world; she who does not see that Christ "gave himself for me" so that I have died and "now live in faith" (Gal 2:19f.); that person does not understand the cross. That is, the cross is understood by no one who will not allow herself through this historical fact to accept resolutely a new

understanding of herself, an understanding which she can grasp only by a resolve, by a resolve which means the radical sacrifice of herself. But in such self-relinquishment, even as in the acknowledgement of God's judgment upon the "old person" as sinner, a person now understands herself as freed from herself, as risen with Christ. The *resurrection* of Christ is proclaimed simultaneously with the cross of Christ. (*FU* 239–40)

The event of the cross and resurrection, however, has this effect on human beings only when it is proclaimed and heard: it is "not a past moment in the vanishing sequence of time" but is "always contemporary wherever the preaching sounds" (*FU* 241–42). "The preaching is the saving event," in that "it is itself revelation and it brings death and life to the world, because the decision for death or for life is made when it is heard" (*FU* 242).[8] In this sense, for Paul, "*the new age has begun*," since this new age became a reality when he "submitted himself to the judgment of the cross and so learned to understand himself as a 'new creation'" (*FU* 243).

According to Bultmann, in developing this understanding of the event of Jesus' death and resurrection, Paul drew on ideas taken from both the mystery religions and Gnosticism. "Paul describes Christ's death *in analogy with the death of a divinity of the mystery religions*" practiced in the Hellenistic world in antiquity: "Participation in the fate of the mystery-divinity through baptism and sacramental communion grants the *mystes* (initiate) participation in both the dying and the reviving of the divinity; such participation, that is, by leading the *mystes* into death delivers him from death" (*TNT* 1:298).

Similarly, Paul interpreted Christ's death "*in the categories of the Gnostic myth*," which spoke of the union between a divine "Gnostic-Redeemer figure" and those who "constitute a unity" with him in the same body (*soma* in Greek): "What happens to the Redeemer, or happened while he tarried in human form on earth, happens to his whole *soma*—i.e. not to him alone but to all who belong to that *soma*. So if he suffered death, the same is true of them. . . . If he was raised from the dead, the same is true of them. . . . And just as his return to the heavenly home as the 'redeemed Redeemer' means his release from the sinister powers that rule this world below, likewise they who are bound up with him into one body share in this release or 'redemption'" (*TNT* 1:299). These ideas lie behind Paul's teaching regarding baptism and the Lord's Supper, which unite believers to the body of Christ so that they die and rise with him. In the sacraments, they participate in his death and resurrection, which are "cosmic occurrences, not incidents that took place once upon a time in the past" (*TNT* 1:299).

Bultmann regards the understanding of salvation in Christ found in John's writings as similar, although, for John, the central event is not so much the event of Jesus' death and resurrection but "*the coming of the Son of God* into the world" (*TNT* 2:33). Just as the Gnostic Redeemer figure saves human beings by coming into the world from the heavenly realm to reveal the truth to them before then departing back into that realm, so Jesus was understood as the preexistent Son of God who comes to bring salvation into the world, only then to return to God

(*TNT* 2:33–53). With Jesus' coming, which is "*the event of revelation,*" "*two possibilities* become actual for the world"—that of "*remaining* world," which is "to cling firmly to one's self," and that of choosing "not to be 'of the world'" so as "no longer to belong to it." Thus, "with the coming of the Revealer a *crisis* occurs," which "is brought about in the nature of the reaction to the revelation. . . . The two possibilities are therefore the grasping of death and of life. . . . [T]o choose God means to let the world go and to let one's security go with it" (*FU* 170–71).

Like Paul, John understood this crisis or judgment as taking place not merely when Jesus came but when the word is proclaimed: "The revelation exists only where the Word is confronting an individual. The possibility is open only when a person is addressed, not before and not after. . . . [T]he world is no longer the same as before. It can no longer be seen as it appeared formerly. . . . For now there are only two possibilities for women and men: to be in life or to be in death, in heaven or in hell. Truly—in hell. For life in the world without faith in the revelation is henceforth hell" (*FU* 175–76). Thus Jesus' word "is an authoritative word which confronts the hearer with a life-and-death decision" (*TNT* 2:62). "In the proclamation Jesus is, so to speak, duplicated. He comes again; he is always coming again. . . . Jesus himself is therefore present in his Word. . . . In so far as the Word is at any time proclaimed, the eschatological *now* stands over every present; and in every such *now*, the judgment and the giving of life is consummated" (*FU* 177–78). Unlike Paul, however, John ascribes no significant role to baptism and the Lord's Supper; his attitude toward the sacraments is "critical or at least reserved" (*TNT* 2:58–59).

According to Bultmann, both Paul and John were aware of the understanding of the cross as an expiatory sacrifice or atonement for sin found in the earliest church, and at times they repeated such ideas. However, this was not their own understanding of its significance (*TNT* 1:296–97; 2:53–55), just as it is not that of Bultmann himself: "This mythological interpretation is a mixture of sacrificial and juridical analogies, which have ceased to be tenable for us today" (*KM* 35). For Paul, Jesus' death is salvific not so much because it "cancels the guilt of sin (i.e. the punishment contracted by sinning)" but because it is "*the means of release from the powers of this age: Law, Sin, and Death*" (*TNT* 1:298). "The cross releases men and women not only from the guilt, but also from the power of sin. . . . For if we see in the cross the judgment of the world and the defeat of the rulers of this world . . . , the cross becomes the judgment of ourselves as fallen creatures enslaved to the powers of the 'world'" (*KM* 36).

For Bultmann, therefore, ultimately Jesus' death is salvific *because of what it reveals to human beings*. The revelation they receive through the proclamation of the cross enables them to be delivered from the powers that enslave them and thus come to a new understanding of themselves, so that they can live an "authentic existence." It is not God but *human beings* who are changed by the cross. However, this change does not occur in them ontologically in automatic fashion, as for Barth, but only as the word proclaimed "accosts the hearer and compels him to decide for or against it. . . . [I]n the word of proclamation Christ's death-and-resurrection becomes a possibility of existence in regard to which a decision must be made" (*TNT* 1:302).

To be sure, Bultmann associates the forgiveness of sins with Christ's death, but this forgiveness is understood primarily as deliverance from the *power* of sin: when one submits to the judgment of God proclaimed in the word of the cross so as to reach a new understanding of oneself, one is freed from one's guilt and knows that "one's entire life stands under forgiveness" (*EF* 256). Bultmann explains this in the following terms: "By accepting me, God takes me to be a different person than I am; and if I (in faith) let go of what I am in myself, if I affirm God's judgment and understand myself in terms of him, then I really *am* a different person, namely, the one that he takes me to be" (*EF* 138). Thus, "once we open our hearts to the grace of God, our sins are forgiven; we are released from the past" (*KM* 19).

Bultmann rejects as mythical not only the understanding of the cross as an atoning sacrifice but the traditional belief in Christ's bodily resurrection. "The resurrection itself is not an event of past history. All that historical criticism can establish is the fact that the first disciples came to believe in the resurrection" (*KM* 42). As Léopold Malevez notes, at most Bultmann is willing to admit that "God created the belief in the Resurrection in the minds of the disciples," who "shared the mythical views of the world of their own day."[9] Thus Jesus' resurrection must be demythologized by inquiring as to the deeper meaning it had for the first disciples. For Bultmann, this meaning is that "in everyday life the Christians participate not only in the death of Christ but also in his resurrection. In this resurrection-life they enjoy a freedom, albeit a struggling freedom, from sin" (*KM* 40). In this way, believers attain a new understanding of themselves. To believe in Jesus as the risen Lord involves the same thing: "To understand another person as Lord correspondingly means *to have a new understanding of oneself*, as standing in the service of that Lord and attaining one's own identity in such service" (*FU* 236).

Following Protestant liberalism, Bultmann also questioned the traditional teaching concerning Jesus' divinity. While Bultmann often repeats the idea that the word of God comes through Christ, and follows the New Testament in associating that word with Christ himself, so that "he is the final Word which God has spoken and is speaking" (*FU* 311), he regards the understanding of Jesus' divinity that developed in early Christianity as mythological. As Charles Waldrop observes: "Bultmann's emphasis is upon Jesus' role as the creaturely medium through whom God speaks. What is divine, in the strictest sense of the term, is not Jesus but God who is present in and through Jesus."[10] Once again, Bultmann's idea is that what matters is not what Jesus is *in himself* but, rather, what he is in relation *to us*; and in relation to us, he can be called God in the sense that "God himself encounters women and men in Jesus" (*TNT* 2:50).

Faith and Salvation

Similar to what we find in the views of Abelard and Ritschl, in Bultmann's thought, the death of Christ accomplishes salvation for all people not in an objective or universal sense but only through the effect it has on human hearts and minds. Huw Owen notes that Bultmann differs from the liberal theologians in that he does not "leave us with Jesus the teacher, prophet, and martyr" yet agrees with them in affirming that "God did not accomplish any objective reconciliation through Christ's death."[11] Undoubtedly, because reconciliation is grounded in the divine judgment made on humanity on the cross, Bultmann can affirm that "the 'reconciliation' precedes any effort—indeed any knowledge—on the part of human beings, and 'reconciliation' does not mean a subjective process within human beings but an objective factual situation brought about by God"; yet because it was not *God* who had to be reconciled but "*men and women*" who receive the reconciliation which God has conferred," only those who respond in faith are actually reconciled (*TNT* 1:286–87).

Bultmann follows Luther in affirming that salvation comes by grace through faith alone. As in Paul's thought, faith leads the believer to "a new self-understanding. It is the consciousness of standing in a new world in which she moves, free from law and sin, in obedience under God and in love for her neighbour. She is free from the past, from death, free from herself as a self who was imprisoned in a self-understanding determined by objects, by law, and by her own achievements" (*FU* 275–76). This new life is not something that human beings can bring about in themselves but is due entirely to God's gracious act in Christ: "Through this saving act the new life is offered as possible for women and men. Of themselves they do not have this possibility. . . . For they are sinners before God, imprisoned by their past, by what they have done as well as what they have left undone. They gain the new life only through the forgiveness effected in Christ" (*FU* 276).

This faith is brought about by the proclamation of God's word, through which "the hearer is summoned. He is asked whether he is willing, in the light of this fact of Christ, to understand himself as a sinner before God and to surrender himself and all that externally he is and has, to take the cross of Christ, and at the same time to understand himself as the justified one who shares the new life in the resurrection of Christ" (*FU* 277). Bultmann understands faith as obedience, in that it is "a placing of one's self at God's disposal, for the act to which God summons a person at any given moment. Thus it means being determined by the future" (*FU* 201).

It should be clear that, for Bultmann, salvation has to do with a new life in *this* world, rather than a future heavenly existence. Furthermore, even though faith leads Christians to love their neighbor, this new life is primarily an *individual* affair. Salvation occurs when "the grace of God frees the person who opens herself to it in radical self-surrender, i.e., in faith. Because a person thereby no longer belongs to herself . . . , she is free from care, free from anxiety about death, free from legal prescriptions and human conventions and standards of value" (*EF* 255). This "openness for what God demands and sends" means that the "imperative" prescribing what believers are to do follows from the "indicative," which describes what God has done in Christ: "The imperative is based on the indicative. To be crucified and risen with Christ does not mean the acquirement of a mysterious power of immortality, but rather the freedom of a life lived in the service of

God. . . . For John, the imperative is the command of brotherly and sisterly love which is a new command because it has its basis in the love of God for women and men that is bestowed in Jesus" (*EF* 255–56).[12] While all are called to live out that imperative in their individual lives, for Bultmann their objective is not the *transformation* of the world but their *independence* from it: "This absolute independence from the world, however, produces a certain detachment from all worldly interests and responsibilities. Primitive Christianity is quite uninterested in making the world a better place; it has no proposals for political or social reform. . . . In this respect, it is the Christian's duty to be indifferent to the world" (*PC* 206).

In understanding salvation in this way, Bultmann sought to offer a solution to the problem of eschatology that had been raised at the outset of the twentieth century. Whereas liberal theologians such as Ritschl had viewed the kingdom of God primarily as a new social reality to be established gradually in the present world (maintaining what is generally termed a "realized" eschatology), to many it became clear that both Jesus and the New Testament held to an *apocalyptic* eschatology, which "awaits salvation not from a miraculous change in historical (i.e. political and social) conditions, but from a cosmic catastrophe which will do away with all conditions of the present world as it is" (*TNT* 1:4). Bultmann rejected as mythological the early Christian beliefs regarding Jesus' second coming, or *parousia*, and the establishment of God's reign on earth under Jesus' lordship, insisting "that there was never a literal fulfillment of whatever kind of these expectations and that there will never be one."[13]

As an alternative, he proposed that the New Testament's eschatological language be demythologized so as to be understood *existentially* and *individually*: in a sense, every moment of our existence represents our own personal end, since the eschatological question of whether we will live according to the new understanding of ourselves given in the cross requires a decision that must be "made again and again anew" (*TNT* 1:322). As John taught, each moment of our lives "is *the eschatological now* because in it is made the decision between life and death"; because Jesus is constantly coming to us in the preaching of the word, in reality "the *parousia* has already occurred! . . . Whatever cosmic catastrophes may come, they cannot be radically different from what happens every day in the world" (*FU* 175). "The judgment, then, is no dramatic cosmic event, but takes place in the response of men and women to the word of Jesus" (*TNT* 2:38).

Because faith is necessary for salvation as Bultmann understands it, and because the proclamation of the word of the cross is necessary for faith, the church is also indispensable for salvation. Like Jesus' death and resurrection and the proclamation of the word, the church itself is a saving event. As Joseph Cahill points out, in Bultmann's thought, "The object of faith is the revelation of God in Jesus Christ which meets man as preached word in the Church."[14] For Bultmann, the church is also the eschatological community of those who are "in Christ" and live an authentic existence in faith; because its members have broken with the "flesh" and the "world," the church is "withdrawn from the world" (*TNT* 1:309) and "delimited from the world" (*TNT* 2:92).

Following the New Testament, Bultmann also assigns a salvific role to the Holy Spirit, understood as *"the power within the Church which brings forth both knowledge and the proclamation of the Word"* (*TNT* 2:88). Bultmann prefers to avoid speaking of the Holy Spirit as a divine person or some type of impersonal force working on human hearts (*TNT* 1:155–63). The Spirit should be "conceived of not as a mysterious power working with magical compulsion but as the new possibility of genuine, human life which opens up to him who has surrendered his old understanding of himself, letting himself be crucified with Christ, in order to experience the 'power of his resurrection'" (*TNT* 1:336). The Holy Spirit is thus "the eschatological existence into which the believer is placed by having appropriated the salvation deed that occurred in Christ" (*TNT* 1:335).

Evaluation

Bultmann's interpretation of the New Testament teaching regarding salvation in Christ has been highly influential in the decades following his work. Pauline scholars in particular have picked up on his idea of "participation" to understand the salvific significance of Jesus' death and resurrection primarily in terms of believers participating in this event. This idea provides an alternative to the penal substitution understanding of atonement often attributed to Paul. Particularly influential in this regard has been E. P. Sanders, who drew on much of Bultmann's work to argue that Paul saw Christ's death "as providing the means by which believers could participate in a death to the power of sin" and regarded "the *purpose* of Christ's death to be that Christians may participate in it."[15]

Despite the tremendous influence of Bultmann's work, it has faced much criticism on several accounts.[16] Perhaps the most common objection has to do with Bultmann's treatment of history: Christian faith seems to be grounded no longer in historical events but only in the meaning that we give to what was and is proclaimed regarding Christ and the cross. Salvation appears not to consist of a future life or world which we now await, but only something to be experienced in the present as we live authentically in openness to the future; if all that matters is the life of the individual in the present, it is not clear why we should attempt to change the world or work for social justice.

In addition, Bultmann's response to the question of the necessity of Christ for salvation seems rather unconvincing: Is the word of the cross in reality absolutely essential for human beings to be transformed so as to live an "authentic existence," and was the death of Christ the only way for this to become a possibility? This understanding of Jesus' death also implies that God staged the event of the crucifixion precisely to make such an existence possible; this ignores the historical reasons for Jesus' execution on a cross. Thus, while Bultmann's presentation of the story of redemption in Christ is in many ways meaningful and powerful, particularly for those who wish to reinterpret the Christian faith in terms that are in accord with the modern scientific worldview, it raises a number of questions for which there are no easy answers.

CHAPTER 12

Jon Sobrino and the Crucified People

The imposition of colonial rule in the Americas following Christopher Columbus's arrival to the region in 1492 led to tremendous suffering for the vast majority of people throughout the two American continents, including those descended not only from the indigenous peoples but also from the slaves brought in forcibly from Africa. While the Western powers who established their political, economical, and cultural domination over the region often justified this situation ideologically by arguing that in some ways it was actually beneficial for those colonized, the perspective of the peoples and nations subjected to those powers tended to be quite different; for them, colonialism meant injustice, oppression, slavery, exploitation, and widespread misery. Even after attaining their political independence, these peoples and nations have continued to be heavily dependent on the powerful countries of the world, usually through no choice of their own, and thus still today the majority of people in the region live in conditions of great poverty, deprived of many of the most basic human necessities and rights. In this regard, these peoples share a common plight with other impoverished peoples and nations throughout the world.

Throughout Latin America and much of the Caribbean, Spanish and Portuguese colonizers forced the indigenous peoples and African slaves to be baptized and live as Roman Catholic Christians. Even though a large part of the population became very attached to the Christian faith over time, the Roman Catholic Church was often seen as siding with the rich and powerful in Latin American society. Many criticized its teaching regarding God and Jesus, who was put forward as the prime example of one who willingly and patiently endured the violence and oppression of injustice, thus passively accepting God's will that he suffer a bloody death; "good" Christians were expected to do the same, resigning themselves submissively to the hardships imposed on them in this life and looking only to the next world for hope, thereby renouncing any attempt to improve their lot in the present. Thus many people felt the Roman Catholic Church contributed

Jon Sobrino
Photo © AP Images

to the oppression and exploitation of the impoverished masses, together with other Christian churches that eventually established themselves in the region, albeit in much smaller numbers.

While many in the Latin American churches had always criticized this alliance with the rich and powerful, during the late 1960s a movement of theologians within many of these churches arose that sought to develop an alternative theology, one that might foster human liberation rather than justifying oppression. According to this "theology of liberation," far from representing God's will, the reality of injustice and poverty that is the daily experience of the multitudes is diametrically opposed to that will. Thus it is necessary for Christians to take up the struggle against oppression and all those responsible for it. Liberation theologians such as Gustavo Gutiérrez insisted that, rather than putting forward a new and distinct theological *content*, they were proposing "a *new way* to do theology."[1] This involved taking the experience of the poor and oppressed as a starting point to reflect critically on that reality in the light of God's word, thereby promoting a liberating transformation of society and the construction of a new reality characterized by greater justice, equality, and well-being for all.[2]

Among the Latin American liberation theologians whose work has been widely read and studied throughout the world is the Roman Catholic scholar Jon Sobrino. Born in 1938 in Spain of Basque parents, Sobrino became a Jesuit in 1956 and was ordained into the priesthood in 1969. Since 1974 he has worked

Archbishop Oscar Romero, archbishop of San Salvador, El Salvador, celebrates
a wedding a week before his death. For Sobrino, as for Archbishop Romero, the
church is to follow Jesus in proclaiming that the kingdom of God belongs to the poor
(Luke 6:20) while seeking to overcome injustice and oppression.
Photo © Christian Poveda/Corbis

as a missionary, priest, and theologian in the Central American country of El
Salvador, where he lived through the bloody Salvadoran civil war that lasted
from 1980 to 1992, during which eighty thousand people died and hundreds of
thousands were displaced. Sobrino was a close friend and associate of Archbishop
Arnulfo Romero, whom right-wing forces had assassinated in cold blood while
he was officiating Mass in 1980, and also worked closely with the six Jesuits who
were brutally murdered by members of the United States–backed Salvadoran
military in 1989, together with two women. The body of one of the Jesuits, in
fact, was dragged into Sobrino's room and left there in a pool of blood, leaving
no doubt that had Sobrino been there, he would also have been killed. Among
the murdered Jesuits was Ignacio Ellacuría, whose work strongly influenced
Sobrino. Sobrino's firsthand experience of extreme poverty, widespread injustice,
bloodshed, and war has greatly shaped his understanding of Jesus and the cross.

The Historical Jesus as Starting Point

Sobrino's most important theological work is in the area of Christology, the doctrine of the person and work of Christ.[3] One problem traditionally associated
with Christology has been electing a starting point. Sobrino considers and rejects
a number of the different starting points often adopted, such as the dogmatic
formulations of the patristic period, the various titles ascribed to Jesus in the New

Testament, the believers' experience of Christ in worship, Christ's resurrection, the early Christian kerygma, the teaching of Jesus, and the Christian doctrine of salvation. He also subjects the work of several prominent European scholars to the same critique. According to Sobrino, such starting points can lead to an abstract Christology, divorced from history and easily manipulated according to human interests and ideologies (*CC* 1–37).

In spite of the difficulties it entails, Sobrino chooses a different starting point: the historical Jesus. He argues that this makes sense because of the "clearly noticeable resemblance between the situation here in Latin America and that in which Jesus lived" (*CC* 12), and because Latin Americans, like the first Christians, have to elaborate a Christology for their own context based on the "concrete features of Jesus' life" (*CC* 13).

However, this starting point is problematic in that New Testament scholars have demonstrated the difficulties associated with attempting to reconstruct the historical Jesus, especially on the basis of the Synoptic Gospels, which are not considered entirely historically reliable. In fact, Sobrino has been criticized for the reconstruction he proposes, primarily on the basis of the Gospel of Mark. Michael Cook, for example, argues that Sobrino's approach is weak in that "it wants to claim too much about the historical Jesus without sufficient evidence," so that Sobrino ends up saying "much more about Jesus than strictly historical judgment would allow."[4] While Sobrino is aware of these difficulties, he nevertheless regards the other starting points considered even more problematic. It is important to note that in Latin America, as in other Third World contexts, the question of the historicity of things such as Jesus' miracles and his resurrection does not raise the same difficulties that it does in places like Europe, due to the fact that the modern scientific worldview is not as deeply ingrained in the thought and culture of the people in those contexts.

The Kingdom of God and the Anti-Kingdom

Having established the historical Jesus as the starting point for his Christology, Sobrino turns to the concept that lies at the heart of his understanding of salvation, the "reign" or "kingdom of God": "The most certain historical datum about Jesus' life is that the concept which dominated his preaching, the reality which gave meaningfulness to all his activity, was 'the kingdom of God' " (*CC* 41). For Sobrino, everything is defined in terms of the kingdom, including the beginning and end of human history, sin, salvation, and liberation. Sobrino recognizes that Jesus never actually defined what the kingdom of God is (*JL* 69) and thus is somewhat hesitant to do so himself. He generally associates such things as justice, joy, and liberation with the kingdom and at several points does offer a tentative definition: "The phrase 'kingdom of God' is a utopian symbol for a wholly new and definitive way of living and being. It presupposes renewal in many areas: in the heart of the human person, in societal relationships, and in the cosmos at large" (*CC* 119). "The Reign is plural salvation from concrete needs (illness, hunger, demonic possession, the worthlessness and despair of the outcast sinner)"; "it is the utopia of the poor, the termination of their misfortunes, liberation from their slaveries, and the opportunity to live with dignity" (*ML* 367, 371).

Several points are important to note here. First, for Sobrino, the salvation associated with the kingdom is something that is to take place primarily *within* human history rather than *beyond* it: "The salvation brought by the Kingdom— though this is not all the Kingdom brings—will, then, be *being saved in history* from the evils of history" (*JL* 125). Second, this kingdom has to do with a *collective salvation*; it "impinges directly on the transformation of the whole of society, the whole of a people" (*JL* 71–72). Third, the kingdom involves a "plural salvation" in that it has to do with satisfying not only spiritual but physical and material needs. Finally, it is something *primarily for the poor*, namely, the end of their suffering and oppression: "The Kingdom is addressed directly only to the poor" (*JL* 82).

Because his main interest is in Christology, Sobrino dedicates little attention to the doctrine of creation. When he does discuss the subject, however, he sees the kingdom of God as its goal: "God's will for creation is . . . that human beings, God's creatures, should live in a particular manner, that history and human society should come to be truly after God's heart: in solidarity, peace, justice, reconciliation, openness to the Father. . . . This reality is the content of the Kingdom of God" (*JL* 108).

Obviously, what obstructs the coming of this kingdom is human sin, which involves "saying no to the kingdom of God. . . . For Jesus sin is the rejection of God's kingdom which is drawing near in grace; and the anthropological essence of sin is people's self-affirmation which leads them to assert their own power in two negative ways. On the one hand they use it to secure themselves against God; on the other hand they use it to oppress others" (*CC* 51). Sobrino understands the doctrine of original sin in terms of sin being a reality that "is already inside people in their twisted intent long before it shows up in their exterior conduct" (*CC* 51).

Following other liberation theologians, however, Sobrino goes beyond the ideas of personal and original sin to speak of "structural sin." He notes that, while "Jesus stresses the personal character of sin as coming from the human heart," sin is not merely "individual"; it has "a public, social, and structural aspect" (*CC* 51–52). In other words, sin is not just something found in the hearts and lives of individuals because of humanity's fallen condition but is deeply ingrained in the systems and structures of human society:

> The Reign of God in history as a Reign of God among human beings exposes the historical wickedness of the world, and thereby the reign of sin, that negation of the Reign of God. Over and above a certain natural sin (original sin) and a personal sin (individual sin), the proclamation of the Reign and the difficulty of seeing it implanted evinces the presence of a "sin of the world," which is fundamentally historical and structural, communitarian and objective, at once the fruit and the cause of many

other personal and collective sins, and its propagation and consolidation as the ongoing negation of the Reign of God. Not that structures commit sin, as liberation theologians are sometimes accused of saying; but structures manifest and actualize the power of sin, thereby causing sin, by making it exceedingly difficult for men and women to lead the life that is rightfully theirs as the daughters and sons of God. (*ML* 355)

This means that for Sobrino, as Arthur McGovern observes, "Sin must not just be pardoned but taken away, and taking it away means eliminating opression."[5] While forgiveness is also liberating, this is because it converts us into people who forgive and accept others (*PM* 92–94).

Sobrino follows traditional Christian theology in speaking of death as the consequence of sin, but he understands this in a different sense. Without denying the idea that both physical and spiritual death follow from sin, Sobrino understands death more in terms of a life of poverty, injustice, and hardships imposed by some on others in the present world: "Sin is that which brings death to the children of God, to human beings" (*CC* xvii), and in turn

> death is what the Latin American peoples are subjected to in thousands of ways. It is slow but real death caused by the poverty generated by unjust structures—"institutionalized violence": "the poor are those who die before their time." It is swift, violent death, caused by repression and wars, when the poor threaten these unjust structures. And it is indirect but effective death when people are deprived even of their cultures in order to weaken their identities and make them more defenseless. (*PM* 50)

Similar to Ritschl, who spoke of the "kingdom of sin" (see chapter 9), Sobrino posits the existence of a type of "kingdom" opposed to the kingdom of God, namely, the "anti-kingdom" or "anti-reign." This anti-kingdom consists of those powers and structures that oppress and enslave human beings. "The anti-Kingdom determines the whole structure of society and puts many human beings to death" (*JL* 162). Thus to work on behalf of the kingdom of God inevitably involves conflict and struggle against the many forces in our world that oppose that kingdom:

> The anti-Kingdom is not just the absence or the not-yet of the Kingdom, but its formal contradiction. Building the Kingdom means destroying the anti-Kingdom; saving human beings means liberating them from their slaveries. . . . The coming of the Kingdom stands in *combative relation* to the anti-Kingdom. They are not merely mutually exclusive, but fight against one another, and this is massively evidenced in Latin America: the Kingdom is not being built from a *tabula rasa*, but in opposition to the anti-Kingdom, and the present persecution of those who are mediating the coming of the Kingdom is effective proof of this. (*JL* 126)

Funeral Services for Six Murdered Priests, 19 November 1989, San Salvador, El Salvador. In Sobrino's thought, to work for the kingdom of God inevitably involves a struggle against the forces of the anti-kingdom; and as is evident from Jesus' own life, the result of this struggle is persecution and at times even a violent death.
Photo © Reuters/Corbis.

Jesus' Work for the Kingdom

For Sobrino, the ministry of Jesus must be understood in relation to both the kingdom and the anti-kingdom. From the start, he observes that Jesus "did not make himself the focus of his preaching and mission"; rather, what was "central in Jesus' life is expressed by two terms: 'Kingdom of God' and 'Father'" (*JL* 67). These two terms are "all-embracing, since by 'Kingdom of God' Jesus expresses the whole of reality and of what is to be done, and by 'Father' Jesus expresses the personal reality that gives final meaning to his life, that in which he rests and what in turn does not allow him to rest" (*JL* 67).

As a Jew, Jesus' own understanding of the kingdom was shaped by the Old Testament tradition, where it involved the liberation of Israel from its oppressors and the establishment of justice. While "the basic general value of Jesus is that of doing justice," for Sobrino this justice should be understood not "as retributive or vindictive justice designed to give all persons and situations what is due to them by virtue of what they are," but "in the Old Testament sense," in which God "is just, not because he gives all their due, but because he tries to re-create human beings and situations, to 'save' them" (*CC* 119). It is in this sense in which justice lay at the heart of Jesus' ministry: "When he approaches the poor, the oppressed, and the sinners, he does not simply offer consolation; he offers justice. In other words, he does not propose to leave people as they are and simply console them in their plight; he proposes to re-create their present situation and thus do 'justice' to them." This involves "clearing away the barriers of class that have made them not only individuals in misery but also persons ostracized by society. The justice of Jesus, then, points towards some new form of social coexistence where class differences have been abolished, at least in principle" (CC 120).

According to Sobrino, while Jesus stressed that "God comes out of gratuitous love, not in response to human actions," and that "the Kingdom of God and its final coming do not depend on human action," he also taught that its coming required human activity, and he dedicated himself to working on its behalf (JL 76). This involved "addressing himself directly to certain people," namely, "the poor" (JL 79). Jesus preached that the kingdom of God belongs to the poor (Luke 6:20) and "saw poverty as contrary to God's original plan, as annulling it" (JL 84).

> The poor are those who are at the bottom of the heap in history and those who are oppressed by society and cast out from it; they are not, therefore, all human beings, but those at the bottom, and being at the bottom in this sense means being oppressed by those on top. . . . The poor are those close to the slow death poverty brings, those for whom surviving is a heavy burden and their chief task, and those who are also deprived of social dignity. . . . To these poor, Jesus showed undoubted partiality. (JL 80–81)

Sobrino notes that, according to the Gospels, there were many aspects to Jesus' ministry on behalf of the poor and the kingdom. He performed miracles, which were "signs against oppression" (JL 89), as well as "powerful signs springing from sorrow at the sufferings of others and, specifically, of the poor people who surrounded him" (JL 91). His activity of casting out demons also "tells us about the dimension of struggle and triumph over the anti-Kingdom implicit in the coming of the Kingdom of God" (JL 93). Besides welcoming those regarded as sinners by the society of his day (rather than merely "forgiving sins"), he called those who oppressed them to conversion, understood as "an active cessation from oppressing" (JL 96–97). The parables he told pointed to the coming of the kingdom "for the poor, the weak, and despised," giving them hope, and showed that the kingdom's coming involves crisis and conflict (JL 100–102). He also celebrated the joy associated with the kingdom, particularly through the meals he shared with the poor and the despised (JL 103). Finally, Jesus also called others to follow him in seeking justice.

In all of this, Jesus sought "to re-create the social situation, not just the concrete individual sinner" (CC 121). He carried out a prophetic "praxis," that is, a practice of ministerial activity aimed at the transformation of society in general (JL 161). His criticisms were "directed mainly at oppressive groups, collective sinners, who produce structural sin, rather than at individuals" (JL 170). This involved denouncing the use of the law to oppress people, and opposing riches as a false god or "idol" (JL 173–74). "Jesus presented people with a God who stands in complete contradiction to the existing religious situation" (CC 207).

For Sobrino, all of Jesus' praxis was rooted in his *idea of God*, which found expression in his prayer life and his own personal faith.[6] For Jesus, God is "a bountiful father in whom one can trust and rest. This experience of God's goodness permeates Jesus' activity of doing good and bestows final meaning on his person, because he sees that reality itself is charged with God's goodness" (*JL* 147). It was precisely this idea of God that led Jesus to reject the false gods of the anti-kingdom and to show mercy to the poor. Because he knew God as love, he showed that love to others. He did this in two different ways: "He manifests his love for the oppressed by being *with* them, by offering them something that might restore their dignity and make them truly human. He manifests his love for the oppressors by being *against* them, by trying to strip away all that is making them less than human" (*CC* 214).

Conflict and the Cross

Because, by nature, to work for the kingdom involves a struggle with the anti-kingdom, Jesus' ministry led to conflict and persecution. "Jesus' preaching and activity represented a radical threat to the religious power of his time, and indirectly to any oppressive power" (*JL* 196). While, initially, Jesus had merely proclaimed the kingdom and called others to place themselves at its disposal (*CC* 60), when this led to conflict, it became evident that the kingdom would not come immediately and that, instead, he would have to suffer and die. He realized that sin "is no longer something to be simply denounced and castigated, but something one has to bear" (*JL* 148). Ultimately, this meant the cross: Jesus was condemned by the religious and political authorities because the God he proclaimed was a threat to their gods.[7]

Sobrino consistently stresses the *historical reasons* for Jesus' death, namely, the conflicts his ministry generated. For Sobrino, Jesus "did not interpret his death in terms of salvation," that is, as "expiatory sacrifice or vicarious satisfaction" (*JL* 201). Rather, he merely accepted his violent death as the outcome and ultimate expression of his life of service to others and continued to place his life trustingly in the hands of his Father: "Jesus went to his death with confidence and saw it as a final act of service, more in the manner of an effective example that would motivate others than as a mechanism of salvation for others. To be faithful to the end is what it means to be human" (*JL* 204). Thus Jesus died not because atonement had to be made for human sin but because he dedicated himself to working for the kingdom: "Why Jesus was killed is very clear in the Gospels. He was killed—like so many people before and after him—because of his kind of life, because of what he said and what he did. In this sense there is nothing mysterious in Jesus' death, because it is a frequent occurrence" (*JL* 209).

For Sobrino, the question of the necessity of Jesus' death, as well as the incarnation, is understood on the basis of these same ideas. When speaking of "incarnation," however, Sobrino is referring not as much to God's Son becoming human as to the entering of a person into solidarity with others in their situation of oppression and suffering, as Jesus did. "By immersing himself in this situation, Jesus *necessarily* introduced conflict into the heart of his life. . . . If Jesus remains faithful to his incarnation, if he does not try to evade the situation in which he finds himself, then his proclamation of God will necessarily give rise to much conflict; and in the end it will lead him to the cross" (*CC* 207–8). Because Jesus was incarnate "in a world that is anti-Kingdom, which acts against the Kingdom," and "acted against this world of necessity—in the name of the Kingdom," the consequence was that "this world reacted against Jesus also of necessity"; thus Jesus' death "was the consequence of his life and this in turn was the consequence of his particular incarnation—in an anti-Kingdom which brings death—to defend its victims" (*JL* 210).

Sobrino recognizes that, following Jesus' death and their experience of him as risen, Jesus' disciples began to apply sacrificial ideas to his death (*JL* 219–32). Like other liberation theologians, however, Sobrino regards many of the traditional interpretations of Jesus' death as problematic, particularly in that they tend to regard suffering as redemptive and to isolate Jesus' death from his life. He rejects the idea that "God was pleased by or even demanded Jesus' cross," insisting instead that what pleased God was "the life of love to the end" that was manifested in Jesus (*JL* 228). He also stresses that salvation is to be attributed to Jesus' life just as much as to his death: "*The whole of* Jesus' life, not just one moment of it or another . . . , reveals God" (*CL* 116). As Roger Haight observes, this means that for Sobrino "the cross then remains negative when considered in itself. What is positive is Jesus' active fidelity, commitment, and obedience to the end."[8] Divine forgiveness is thus not the consequence of the cross; rather, the cross is an expression and consequence of God's love reaching out to forgive and accept others.

For Sobrino, then, Jesus' death is salvific primarily through what it *reveals*. Above all, the cross reveals God's love as well as what human love must consist of: "The very fact that true humanity has been revealed, contrary to all expectations, is in itself good news and therefore is already in itself salvation: we human beings now know what we are, because the truth about ourselves, which we sinfully kept captive, has been liberated. And since the central core of this true humanity is Jesus' great love for human beings, we can assert that love exists and that not only does evil make its presence felt on earth, but we are also enfolded in love" (*JL* 229–30).

Yet, following German theologian Jürgen Moltmann, Sobrino ascribes another meaning to Jesus' crucifixion: on the cross, Jesus suffered the abandonment of God, crying out, "My God, my God, why have you forsaken me?" (Mark 15:34). Sobrino relates this cry to the question of theodicy, that is, the question of why a God who is all-powerful and loving allows evil: If God is *able* to overcome evil and truly *loves* human beings, why does God not put an end to their suffering? Sobrino does not attempt to answer this question, which most theologians ultimately regard as impossible to resolve satisfactorily. Instead, he merely affirms that in Jesus, on the cross, God himself assumed the evil and suffering inherent in our human situation: "God himself has accepted, in a divine manner, to become consistently incarnate in history, to let himself be affected by it. . . . The cross should not be seen as an arbitrary plan of God's or as a cruel punishment inflicted on Jesus, but as a consequence of God's original choice, incarnation, a radical drawing near for love and in love, wherever it leads, without escaping from history or manipulating it from outside" (*JL* 244). Because "in history there is no such thing as love without solidarity and there is no solidarity without incarnation," if God "wanted to reveal his solidarity with this world's victims," he had to suffer with them (*JL* 245).

Jesus' death on the cross, therefore, not only reveals God's willingness to be *with* human beings in their suffering but also shows that the way to overcome sin is by bearing it. God wanted to save the world not from the *outside* but from *within*:

> What God's suffering on the cross says in the end is that the God who fights against human suffering wanted to show solidarity with human beings who suffer, and that God's fight against suffering is also waged in a human way. . . . [T]his fight means bearing sin. What God's suffering makes clear in a history of suffering is that between the alternatives of accepting suffering by sublimating it and eliminating it from outside we can and must introduce a new course, bearing it. (*JL* 245–46)

While, in some ways, Jesus' death was unique and unrepeatable, for Sobrino the same type of violent, unjust death is a daily occurrence in our world: "Death is what the peoples of the Third World suffer in a thousand ways. It is a slow but real death, caused by poverty" (*JL* 254). He thus follows Ignacio Ellacuría in speaking of "the crucified people," that is, those who constantly suffer "a death that is actively inflicted by unjust structures. . . . To die crucified does not mean simply to die but to be put to death. So 'cross' means that there are victims and there are executioners" (*JL* 255). "Sin is what caused the death of Jesus and sin is what continues to cause the death of the crucified people" (*JL* 260).

Just as, for Sobrino, Jesus' death is salvific primarily through what it *reveals* to human beings, so also the crucified people contribute to human salvation through what they reveal: "Those who bring salvation to the world today, or at least those who are the principle of salvation, are the crucified poor peoples" (*JL* 260). While some have raised objections to this idea,[9] it must be remembered that Sobrino understands salvation primarily in terms of the transformation of the present world; it is thus in this sense that they bring salvation. In addition to making manifest human sin and showing that the solution offered by the rich nations of the earth is bad, the crucified people offer hope for the future by making a different world possible:

> Above all, the crucified people demonstrate the existence of enormous sin and demand conversion because of it. But they also offer the possibility of conversion as nothing else in the world can. If the crucified

people are not able to turn hearts of stone into hearts of flesh, nothing can. . . . [T]he poor have a humanizing potential because they offer community against individualism, service against selfishness, simplicity against opulence. . . . The crucified people offer great love. . . . When the crucified people allow the oppressors' world to approach them, they make it possible for this world to recognize itself for what it is, sinful, but also to know that it is forgiven. In this way they introduce into the oppressors' world the humanizing reality so absent from it, grace. . . . The crucified people generate solidarity. . . . Therefore we can say that the crucified people are Christ's crucified body in history. But the opposite is also true: the present-day crucified people allow us to know the crucified Christ better. (*JL* 262–64)

The Risen Jesus as Lord

Like Jesus' life and death, for Sobrino, Jesus' resurrection is salvific through what it reveals. While the cross "tells of God's affinity with the victims," as well as "the silence, the inaction, and the consequent powerlessness or at least inoperativeness of God," Jesus' resurrection reveals and makes credible God's "liberating power" (*CL* 87–88). This understanding of Jesus' resurrection complements the idea that God showed solidarity with the "crucified people" by suffering what they suffer: what suffering people need is not merely a God who is with them in their suffering but one who *delivers* and *liberates* them from that suffering, and this is the God revealed in Jesus' resurrection. However, without the God who also suffers *with* human beings, we would be left with a God of "pure power without love, otherness without affinity, distance without closeness" (*CL* 88).

Reflection on Jesus' resurrection led the disciples to attribute a number of christological titles to Jesus, such as "High Priest," "Messiah" (or "Christ"), "Lord," "Son of God," and "Son of Man," among others. In this way, they expressed his unique significance for them as well as "the unity of Jesus with God in his life and on the cross" (*CL* 116). While these titles were taken from the Jewish and Hellenistic contexts of the time, they were filled with new meaning once they were applied to Jesus as a historical figure. Sobrino insists that the "Christ of faith," that is, the understanding of Christ that the disciples came to have after the resurrection, must always be seen in full continuity with the "Jesus of history." Thus, rather than beginning with a prior understanding of the titles to interpret Jesus, we must go "from Jesus to the titles." It is the "reality of Jesus that will explain the content of the titles, not the other way around. What the titles really mean . . . can only be known by starting from Jesus" (*CL* 119).

Perhaps the best example of this is the title "Lord," which came to be ascribed to Jesus. Sobrino argues that if we already "know what being Lord means, we do not need Jesus to tell us what it is" (*CL* 119). However, from Jesus we learn to see lordship differently, not as exercising power over others to enslave, oppress, and dominate them but as humble service that seeks to fashion the lives of others and build up community (*CL* 159–62). As Paul Ritt points out, Sobrino undoubtedly relates lordship with power, but this power "involves prophetic praxis that communicates God's love for the poor; this power is love expressed in the historical Jesus' self-surrender and service in the transformation of social reality into the kingdom of God."[10]

For Sobrino, Jesus' lordship means that he is unique as well as someone to be imitated: "Christ is the ultimate model, beyond which there is no appeal, for how we should act in all situations in our lives and in the whole of our life and death" (*CL* 162). Thus, in New Testament thought, "before Jesus we did not know fully what it was to be Lord, although we had a previous notion of it"; this notion, however, was not adequate and could be "erroneous and even contrary to how it is verified in Jesus, because it expresses exactly the opposite of what the title means as seen in Jesus" (*CL* 119). The same holds true of the other christological titles ascribed to Jesus: each one is filled with new meaning by what we see in the historical Jesus, who proves himself to be unique but also reveals a model for human life that we are called to reproduce as his disciples.

While Sobrino does not deny the divinity or preexistence of Christ as God's Son, in considering these questions he insists once more on the need to begin with the historical Jesus. Rather than starting with the affirmation that God's Son became incarnate in Jesus so as then to consider the question of his humanity, which would involve a "theology of *descent*" or Christology from *above*, it is necessary to take the historical Jesus as the starting point so as to "go in the opposite direction, from below to above" (*CC* 337–38). This is the process through which the disciples themselves passed: first they came to know Jesus as a man in a unique relation to God and then, after the resurrection, came to assert his divinity and preexistence as God's eternal Son.

The Kingdom and Utopia

Although Sobrino speaks of the kingdom of God as a "utopia" and insists that salvation must be understood as something taking place *in history*, his expectation is not that over time the world will evolve into an idyllic place of perfect peace and justice, where there is no more violence and oppression. Instead, he recognizes that "our partial efforts to establish the kingdom fail to establish it in all its fullness or even are met with outright rejection," and that "we cannot possibly realize the kingdom in all its fullness because it is a gift" (*CC* 134–35). At the same time, Sobrino does speak of the appearance of the kingdom at the "end of history," claiming that "its fullness will appear only at the end" (*JL* 129). In this regard, Sobrino tends more toward an apocalyptic eschatology, according to which our world is "a world of crisis, a mounting and increasingly violent confrontation between the God of life and the idols of death."[11]

For Sobrino, the idea of the kingdom of God as a utopia serves primarily as an ideal or "guide" by which we can judge what takes place in our history (*ML* 382), that is, a "criterion of verification" (*JL* 123). "Although the Kingdom of God cannot be achieved on this earth, the ideal of the Kingdom serves to measure, on principle, *how much* of the Kingdom there is in particular social developments" (*JL* 115). This means that, although the kingdom is a divine gift, Christians are not called to await passively the end of history; rather, as Jesus did, they are called to carry out a praxis that works toward "its actual realization in the present of history" (*JL* 129). In this way, the idea of the kingdom as "the final utopia, while beyond history, moves history here and now" (*ML* 382).

This hope, grounded in Jesus' resurrection, is the basis for Sobrino's understanding of the church's mission, which is "that justice be done to the victims of this world, as justice was done to the crucified Jesus, and so the course of action called for is to take the crucified people down from the cross" (*CL* 48). Sobrino insists that the church must be distinguished from the kingdom, avoiding "the grave danger of equating the kingdom with the church" (*JL* 123), in which case the church would become an end in itself to be served. Instead, the church is to be at the service of the kingdom. Sobrino looks to the parable of the good Samaritan (Luke 10:25-37) to define the church and its mission: "The place of the church is with the wounded one lying in the ditch along the roadside . . . , with 'the other,' and with the most radical otherness of that other—his suffering—especially when that suffering is massive, cruel, and unjust" (*PM* 21). Just as God is with the victims, so must the church be present with them as well, allowing itself "to be governed by the principle of mercy" (*PM* 25).

However, the church is not only to accompany the poor but to be a community of the poor (*JL* 28–31). As McGovern notes: "The expression 'church of the poor' is important for Sobrino. The church is not simply 'for' the poor or ethically concerned about them, but is a church 'of' the poor where the poor constitute its very basis."[12] As such, it is a place of hope, freedom, and salvation, where the coming of the kingdom is celebrated. This is expressed in the church's worship life, where one encounters "the joy of communities that, despite everything, come together to sing and recite poetry, to show that they are happy they are together, to celebrate the eucharist" (*CL* 77). In this regard, for Sobrino, the meaning of the Eucharist is to be found in Jesus' practice of eating with the marginalized: "Jesus' meals are signs of the coming of the Kingdom and of the realization of his ideals: liberation, peace, universal communion" (*JL* 103); "the shared table is a sign of the closeness of the Kingdom of God" (*CL* 61).

Evaluation

Perhaps the greatest strength of Sobrino's presentation of the Christian story of redemption is that it demands that any who claim to be Jesus' followers strive for social justice and work to overcome suffering and oppression in the world, at the same time that it moves them to mercy and thus to action. Rather than denying or dismissing the central doctrines of the Christian faith and biblical witness, Sobrino makes a conscious and concerted effort to reinterpret them in liberating terms, so as to remain in continuity with the Christian tradition. While salvation therefore involves a future hope *at the end* of history, it is still something toward which Christians must work now *in* history; Sobrino's presentation of the gospel unmasks as a betrayal of Christianity any understanding of the faith that does not lead to a commitment to combat poverty, oppression, and injustice in the world.

Probably the most common criticism of the kind of liberation theology represented by Sobrino has to do with the idea that God is partial to the poor and oppressed. This idea seems to dismiss and even demonize the rich as evil and oppressive, thus dividing human beings into two opposing groups, and to produce "an exclusiveness that limits the saving presence of God to the marginal people."[13] Liberation theologians such as Sobrino are conscious of this problem and attempt to respond to it (see, for example, *JL* 128). In their defense, it must be recognized that there is certainly a strong basis in both the Old and New Testaments for maintaining God's partiality for the poor and oppressed. In addition, once we stop focusing on the poor so as merely to proclaim that God's love is for all people equally, both rich and poor, the result seems inevitably to be that the rich and powerful end up being given preference again, as has generally occurred in the history of Christianity, while the poor fade into the distance once more to be neglected or forgotten. For Sobrino, such theology would thus end up being at the service of the anti-kingdom rather than the kingdom of God: not to opt for the poor is to accept and maintain the status quo and thus to leave the crucified people on the cross.

CHAPTER 13

Salvation as Liberation from Patriarchy in the Thought of Rosemary Radford Ruether

◆

Throughout most of Christianity's history, women in both church and society have systematically been ignored, silenced, marginalized, and excluded in structures dominated by men. This is clearly reflected in our study up to this point. All of the biblical writers and theologians considered have been male. The stories of redemption they tell speak of the salvation of "man" through a male Savior sent by a God who is consistently referred to as a "he," never a "she." Whatever women appear in those stories play only a marginal role and are subjected and subservient to males. In both theology and practice, the Christian church has been thoroughly "androcentric," placing males and masculinity at the center, as well as "patriarchal," maintaining and justifying the rule and authority of men over women through hierarchical structures in virtually every sphere of life, both inside and outside of the church.

Although nearly every period of the church's history has witnessed movements and struggles to change this situation, in recent decades the voices of women in the church have been heard more than ever before. This is not to say, of course, that those voices have always been favorably received or that the marginalization of women has ended; on the contrary, the struggles for women to achieve full equality and inclusion continue, and in many regards the obstacles to be overcome are greater than ever. Nevertheless, in academic circles both within and outside the context of the church, what has come to be known as "feminist theology" has now become firmly established, and has even taken a plurality of forms. This theology is done from the perspective of women from a wide variety of ethnic backgrounds and religious traditions, both Christian and non-Christian.

As Betty Friedan and Geoffrey Lilburne have observed, in its initial stages the Christian feminist theology done in North America concerned itself primarily with identifying and subjecting to criticism the patriarchal mentality at the root of traditional Christian theology as well as of the Christian Scriptures themselves. Following this "important but preliminary and negative work of criticism," those

Rosemary Radford Ruether

feminist theologians who chose to remain in the Christian tradition took up "the fundamental and positive task of constructing a 'post-patriarchal' understanding of the Christian faith."[1] Lilburne points to three general areas of consensus among Christian feminist theologians resulting from this work:

> first, that the received concept of God is patriarchal and thus oppressive for women; second, that the doctrinal elaboration of the person of Jesus Christ has assimilated Jesus to this patriarchal tradition and thus is equally oppressive for women; and third, that in the Jesus of history we find the example and inspiration of one who resisted patriarchy and opened up for all people, women and men, the possibility of liberation from their oppression.[2]

Among those doing Christian theology from a woman's perspective, perhaps none has been more influential than Rosemary Radford Ruether. Born in 1936 in Texas, Ruether grew up in the Roman Catholic Church and has continued to identify with that tradition, though she has also immersed herself in other religious traditions. Since receiving her doctorate in 1965 from the Claremont School of Theology in California, she has taught at several theological schools, has written extensively, and has stayed involved in the struggle for social justice. Her 1983 book, *Sexism and God-Talk*, is considered to be the first systematic theology produced by a Christian feminist, though in many ways it breaks out of the mold of the systematic theologies produced previously.[3] This work, together with several others Ruether has written, provides all of the elements necessary to reconstruct here her understanding of the Christian story of redemption.[4]

Experience, Tradition, and History

Like other feminist theologians, Ruether takes as her starting point the experience of women.[5] She notes that, in reality, all theology takes experience as a starting point (*SGT* 12). However, the experience of women provides a criterion upon which every other theology can be evaluated: "The uniqueness of feminist theology lies not in its use of the criterion of experience but rather in its use of *women's* experience, which has been almost entirely shut out of theological reflection in the past. The use of women's experience in feminist theology, therefore, explodes as a critical force, exposing classical theology, including its codified traditions, as based on *male* experience rather than universal human experience" (*SGT* 13). For Ruether, while theology is based on divine revelation, this revelation itself begins as an individual experience that is then appropriated by a group collectively and eventually develops into a tradition (*SGT* 13-16).

Precisely because tradition itself grows out of experience, Ruether also makes use of tradition as a basis for her theology, even regarding it as normative and authoritative in some sense.[6] In fact, this is true not only of the *Christian* tradition but of other religious traditions as well: alongside the Hebrew and Christian Scriptures and classical Christian theology, Ruether considers a number of other sources "usable tradition," including "marginal or 'heretical' Christian traditions," "non-Christian Near Eastern and Greco-Roman religion and philosophy," and "critical post-Christian world views such as liberalism, romanticism and Marxism" (*SGT* 22). For Ruether, all of these traditions grow out of revelatory experience. However, even these traditions must be subjected to her critical principle:

> The critical principle of feminist theology is the promotion of the full humanity of women. . . . Theologically speaking, whatever diminishes or denies the full humanity of women must be presumed not to reflect the divine or an authentic relation to the divine, or to reflect the authentic nature of things, or to be the message or work of an authentic redeemer or a community of redemption. This negative principle also implies the positive principle: what does promote the full humanity of women is of the Holy, it does reflect true relation to the divine, it is the true nature of things, the authentic message of redemption and the mission of redemptive community. (*SGT* 19)

This critical principle is derived from the "prophetic norm" found in the Hebrew and Christian Scriptures, particularly in the proclamation of the prophets of Israel and the teaching of Jesus, although there this prophetic norm was not yet fully appropriated as a "norm *for women*" (*SGT* 24). Nevertheless, the same basic principle can also be discerned in the other religious traditions to which Ruether looks, although they too must be subjected to feminist critique, since to a great extent "all of these traditions are sexist" (*SGT* 22). This means that, ultimately, Ruether's critical principle is not merely derived from tradition but represents an assumption or presupposition on her part. Of course, in this regard, Ruether's theology is no different from all other theologies, which are inevitably based on critical assumptions and presuppositions.

The importance of tradition for Ruether is particularly evident in the way she presents her theology. When dealing with any question or doctrine, she generally begins by examining the history of beliefs regarding the question or doctrine from ancient times to the present, consistently applying the critical principle she has established in order to evaluate to what extent those beliefs have been liberating or oppressive, especially toward women. In fact, at times, Ruether writes more like a historian than a theologian, though, for her, the two obviously go hand in hand. While it is not always easy to distinguish her own ideas from those she examines from other sources, she generally concludes any discussion by making her own views quite clear.

Patriarchy, Sin, and Evil

When considering human salvation, feminist theologians such as Ruether generally begin not by positing some abstract ideal to be attained, such as the human condition as it was originally intended by God in creation or Jesus' proclamation of the reign of God, but by examining critically the reality around us: "What is, is not what ought to be" (*SGT* xviii). Because that reality is one of oppression, it is sin that defines what salvation must consist of, rather than a prior notion of salvation defining how sin is to be understood; simply stated, sin is identified with patriarchy, which "has been defined as the root problem of injustice" (*IR* 117).

According to Ruether, "feminism presumes a radical concept of 'sin.' It claims that a most basic expression of human community, the I-thou relation as the relationship of men and women, has been distorted throughout all known history into an oppressive relationship that has victimized one-half of the human race and turned the other half into tyrants" (*SGT* 161). Ruether thus defines "patriarchy and other forms of domination as sin" (*IR* 69). "The domination of men over women is sinful, and patriarchy is a sinful social system" (*IR* 63). While women are the main victims of this oppressive way of thinking and males are the ones primarily responsible for originating and perpetuating it, men are also hurt by it and women play some role in its perpetuation (*SGT* 165, 174, 180–81).

As Wanda Warren Berry has observed, for Ruether, sin and evil have to do with the establishment of "hierarchical dualisms" that establish one entity as normative and superior and another as inferior; in this way, the domination of the first over the second is justified.[7] Examples of such dualisms include the placing of men over women, "man" over creation, spirit over matter, whiteness over blackness, and heaven over earth. For Ruether, this dualistic thinking finds its clearest expression in sexism: "Among the primary distortions of the self-other relationship has been the distortion of humanity as male and female into a dualism of superiority and inferiority. This is fundamentally a male ideology and has served two purposes: the support for male identity as normative humanity and the justification of servile roles for women" (*SGT* 165). This "male ideology" leads to the patriarchal "assertion of male hegemony over women" (*IR* 73). As "the distortion of relationship," sin occurs when

> some persons absolutize their rights to life and potency at the expense of others with whom they are interdependent. Thus, for example, in male-female relations men were exalted as those persons in the family system with the superior right to be valued, to receive education in preparation for gainful economic roles and political participation in society. Women were accordingly disvalued. They were denied these advantages of self-development in order to function as auxiliaries to male development. (*IR* 71–72)

This same patriarchal way of thinking finds expression in every other form of "dominating and exploitative relationship," such as racism and militarism, feeding a "cycle of violence" in which some try to subjugate others (*IR* 73). Humanity's relation to the earth has been defined in similar fashion, in terms of the subjugation of nature: "dominating and destructive relations to the earth are interrelated with gender, class, and racial domination" (*GG* 2), resulting in a "vast reign of death" (*GG* 259). Sin is thus "the misuse of freedom to exploit other humans and the earth and thus to violate the basic relations that sustain life" (*GG* 141).

Ruether rejects the doctrine of original sin as it is traditionally understood, not only because the story of the fall in Genesis cannot be regarded as historical but because it places the blame and guilt on our ancestors rather than on us: such a doctrine leads "women and men to identify themselves with a lost innocence and to fail to take responsibility for their own complicity in the evils they excoriate" (*GG* 8). Human beings have thus not lost the capacity and freedom to choose between good and evil (*IR* 69–71). Ruether also rejects the idea that death or human finitude is the result of human sin, instead affirming the ancient Hebrew view that "mortality is our natural condition": "The notion that humanity is culpable for its own finitude has laid upon Christians an untenable burden of guilt. . . . [W]hat mortality is not is sin, or the fruit of sin" (*GG* 139). Particularly abhorrent is the idea that a woman, Eve, was responsible for humanity's fall: literal acceptance of the Genesis account has led to the "continued repression and subjugation of women, as 'punishment' for her primordial 'sin' in causing the fall of 'man' and the loss of paradise" (*SGT* 169). "Women must reject a concept of the Fall that makes them scapegoats for the advent of evil and uses this to 'punish' them through historical subordination" (*SGT* 37).

In another sense, however, Ruether upholds the idea of original sin.[8] Adopting the Jewish view that there is a tendency to good as well as to evil in everyone, she affirms that our tendency to evil has been biased by historical systems of evil. The world into which we are born is not neutral, but has been deeply distorted on the side of alienation and violence. We are socialized from infancy to conform to those systems. . . . We are born into this system of patriarchal relations. . . . This is the inherited, collective, historical dimension of sin, which Christianity called "original sin". . . . We are born into sexist, racist, classist, militarist systems of society. (*IR* 70, 74; cf. *SGT* 93)

As mentioned above, however, this does not mean that we are not responsible for our complicity in these systems; as free beings, "we have the possibility of enhancing life or stifling it" (*IR* 71).

God/ess, Humanity, and Creation

According to Ruether, the patriarchal ideology is reflected in the ways Christians have traditionally spoken of God, humanity, and the world around us. In the Hebrew and Christian Scriptures, of course, God is spoken of exclusively in masculine terms, often as "Father" and "King," although in antiquity the male God Yahweh was occasionally paired with a goddess, and at times female imagery was also employed to speak of Yahweh and God's Spirit (*SGT* 54–59). Ruether chooses to speak of God in a more inclusive fashion as "God/ess" while nevertheless insisting that not only our language but our ways of conceiving God must change: "We need to start with language for the Divine as redeemer, as liberator, as one who fosters full personhood and, in that context, speak of God/ess as creator, as source of being" (*SGT* 70). Thus "our metaphors for God must include both male and female" (*IR* 86).[9] For Ruether, "God is not the power of dominating control from outside, but the matrix or ground of life-giving relations and their ongoing renewal" (*IR* 70). For this same reason, parental imagery for God is to be rejected, since even when God is spoken of as "mother," it involves placing God *over* us in a type of patriarchal relationship (*SGT* 69–70). Ruether also insists on the need to look outside of the Judeo-Christian tradition for our language and concepts of God (*IR* 66).

Naturally, Ruether rejects the use of the term *man* to refer to human beings in general, as well as any view of humanity based on an understanding of hierarchical dualisms as God's original will. Like the story of the fall, the story of creation as found in Genesis has been used to subordinate women to men. Since the man was created first and the woman was created to be man's "helper" (Gen 2:20), it is said that males are the "norms of authentic humanity" (*SGT* 19) and that the "male alone possesses the image of God normatively," in contrast to women, who possess God's image "only secondarily" (*SGT* 95). "The assumption that God was male threw in question women's capacity to be 'in the image of God' " (*IR* 11).

While various traditions speak of God creating a single "androgenous" human nature—that is, a nature that was originally both (or neither) male and female and subsequently separated into two—Ruether rejects such an idea as "implicitly androcentric," since it ultimately still posits the male as "essential humanity" (*IR*

Christa by Edwina Sandys. According to Ruether, "Christ can take on the face of every person and group and their diverse liberation struggles. We must be able to encounter Christ as black, as Asian, as Aboriginal, as woman" (*IR* 94).
Image © 1975 Edwina Sandys; photo by Adam Reich, 2006.

64–65). Furthermore, "it suggests that males and females possess both 'masculine' and 'feminine' sides to their psychic capacity," thereby perpetuating the idea that both women and men need to integrate "these 'masculine' and 'feminine' sides of themselves" (*SGT* 111). For Ruether, then, any "justification of women's subordination as due to natural inferiority" or "a divine mandate that women be subordinate in the order of creation" is to be rejected (*IR* 62).[10]

In speaking of creation, Ruether basically adopts the modern scientific worldview, though going beyond it in positing the existence of a "Great Matrix of Being" underlying the created world (*IR* 119). Thus, for example, she accepts the idea of the Big Bang, though she prefers to speak of something "such as the 'cosmic egg' or the 'superabundant nucleus,'" so as to avoid the "masculinist bias" reflected "in the choice of a metaphor of destructive violence, rather than of gestation and birth" (*GG* 57). She also recognizes that human beings "are latecomers to the earth, a very recent product of its evolutionary life" (*GG* 5).

As a theologian, however, she feels the need to go beyond science to avoid a mechanistic understanding of the universe, which separates "knowledge from wonder, reverence, and love"; instead, we must "rekindle an ethic and spirituality capable of calling us to the tasks of healing and sustaining the earth" (*GG* 57–58). This means redefining our relationship to creation: rather than seeking to dominate and exploit the earth and the various life forms it contains, reducing everything to "objects" or "things" for our "use," we must see ourselves as "cocreators" and "caretakers" of the world, "an integral part of this whole reality" (*GG* 86, 142, 227). Our relation to the created order is to be "covenantal": "Humans and other forms of life are part of one family, sisters and brothers in one community of interdependence. . . . The covenantal relation between humans and all other life forms, as one family united by one source of life, forbids this otherness from being translated into destructive hostility" (*GG* 227). This is the relation that God intended for human beings to have with creation, and we "are ultimately accountable for its welfare to the true source of life, God" (*GG* 227). All of this involves a rejection of the patriarchal mind-set that has traditionally been the basis for defining the relationship of "man" to the world.

Jesus and Patriarchy

Ruether recognizes that "patriarchy is the social context for both the Old and the New Testament" yet argues that, in spite of this, "both Testaments contain resources for the critique of patriarchy and of the religious sanctification of patriarchy." What is necessary is to appropriate the "prophetic-liberating traditions" as "normative principles of Biblical faith" and on this basis "criticize and reject patriarchal ideology" so that it "loses its normative character" (*SGT* 22–23). The essential themes of the prophetic-liberating tradition of biblical faith are "(1) God's defense and vindication of the oppressed; (2) the critique of the dominant systems of power and their powerholders; (3) the vision of a new age to come in which the present system of injustice is overcome and God's intended reign of peace and justice is installed in history; [and] (4) finally, the critique of ideology, or of religion" (*SGT* 24).

These themes are all found in the Old Testament, particularly in the prophets, though the prophetic critique of society and religion was generally not directed against patriarchy and the oppression of women. This same "prophetic critique" was "renewed in the ministry of Jesus" (*SGT* 27). Like liberation theologians, such as Sobrino, and many other feminist theologians, Ruether looks to the historical Jesus as a model for liberating praxis. Jesus rejected the patriarchal ideology reflected in the "kingly and chauvinistic understandings of the Messiah" found among many Jews of his day and instead proclaimed a message that "criticizes existing power systems and places God on the side of the oppressed. . . . This critique of power relationships is central to Jesus' radical interpretation of the prophetic-messianic tradition" (*SGT* 29–30).

For Ruether, Jesus' ministry should be understood as a criticism of the oppressive religious authorities in defense of the marginalized, and as a proclamation of the coming of God's reign, which involves the overcoming of "structures of domination and subjugation" (*SGT* 120–21). "Jesus renews the prophetic vision whereby the Word of God does not validate the existing social and religious hierarchy but speaks on behalf of the marginalized and despised groups of society," including women (*SGT* 136). Thus, in Jesus,

> we see the figure of an iconoclastic prophet of God who stands in judgment on social and religious systems that exclude subordinated and marginalized people from divine favor. Jesus' mission is one of bringing "good news to the poor," hope to despised people whom the priestly and clerical classes regarded as unworthy of redemption. Jesus' prophetic praxis confronts these male leaders for their pretences of special privilege with God and their exclusion of the unlearned and the "unclean." (*IR* 87)

Similar to Sobrino, Ruether understands Jesus' crucifixion as "the consequence of this confrontation with falsified religion at the right hand of oppressive power" (*SGT* 27). She insists that Jesus "did not seek to be killed by the powers that be, but rather to convert them into solidarity with those they had formerly despised and victimized. . . . The poor heard him gladly, but those in power refused his invitation of conversion. They sought to silence him and destroy his community of followers by subjecting him to a terrorizing public execution" (*IR* 105).

Following Jesus' death, however, his disciples had "collective experiences of Jesus' Resurrection" and came to be convinced that Jesus had been "rescued by God from death and given on-going life in the present and future" (*SGT* 122). They believed (mistakenly) that he would "return as conquering Messiah"; in the meantime, he poured out on them his "prophetic Spirit," whom they understood to be "the Risen Lord alive in their midst" (*SGT* 122–23). Ruether particularly emphasizes that, according to the Gospels, "it is the core group of [Jesus'] female followers who remain faithful at the cross and are first at the tomb, first witnesses of the resurrection, commissioned by the Risen Lord to take the good news back to the male disciples huddled in the upper room" (*IR* 88). One purpose of the story of Jesus' resurrection, told in all four Gospels, is "to make dramatically clear that despised women, last in the present social and religious order, are the faithful remnant who are first in the redeemed order" (*IR* 88).

While the earliest church tended to be more egalitarian, with both women and men being involved in ministry, this soon changed: "The ministry of women was quickly suppressed by an insurgent patriarchal concept of the church" (*IR* 88). Women began to be excluded from leadership roles in the patriarchal church, though there were some Christian groups (considered "heretical" by the patriarchal orthodoxy) in which women continued to have leadership roles.

The patriarchal ideology that gradually took over in the church was manifested in other ways as well. While Jesus had rejected the ideas of domination and subjugation associated with the Jewish concept of the reign of God and the predominant beliefs regarding the kingly Messiah, these ideas were taken up again by his male disciples (*SGT* 9–10). Most Christians also came to accept the idea that God was male and that, therefore, it had been necessary for the eternal Son of God to become a man rather than a woman; in their minds, "the human Christ must be a male in order to reveal the male God" (*IR* 82). In this way, the "Christ symbol" become "non-inclusive of women" (*IR* 85), and male humanity came to be seen as normative again. Throughout the church's history, ideas like these have continued to prevail, though there have always been groups that rejected such ideas and were more faithful to Jesus' original vision.

Yet, rather than rejecting the idea that a "male savior" can be salvific for women, Ruether affirms that we must go back to the historical Jesus so as to

> see him as paradigmatic of universal human redemption in a way that can apply to female as well as to male, to people of all ethnicities and cultures. . . . Jesus becomes paradigmatic by embodying a certain message. That message is good news to the poor, the confrontation with systems of religion and society that incarnate oppressive privilege, and affirmation of the despised as loved and liberated by God. Jesus did not speak this message; he risked his life to embody this presence of God and was crucified by those in power who rejected this message. . . . This Jesus we find as a historical figure exemplifies a way of life that is still critical, in a world where false and oppressive privilege still reign, which are still sacralized by religion. (*IR* 93)

Jesus' death also came to be understood by Christians in ways that were not in continuity with the message he had proclaimed. Many interpreted his death as atonement for human sin and considered his sufferings as redemptive in that he submitted passively to God's will that he suffer and die. Following other feminist theologians, Ruether argues that such interpretations of Jesus' death have been oppressive, particularly for women, since they teach that Christians "become Christlike by enduring suffering like Christ, who, though innocent, suffered for our sins" (*IR* 98). This understanding of the cross "has been particularly preached to Christian women to accept not only their condition of subjugation, but also arbitrary violence visited upon them by husbands. . . . Thus the cross of Christ has become an exquisite tool for justifying domestic violence and advising women to endure it without complaint" (*IR* 99–100). Combined with the beliefs that women were created to be subject to men and were responsible for the fall of "man" into sin, this led to the oppression of women in the church: they were taught to "regard the general condition of their harsh subjugation as both their 'natural' condition and as just punishment for their sin" (*IR* 99).[11]

For Ruether, Jesus' death and resurrection can be considered redemptive only when seen in the context of his prophetic "struggle for life against unjust suffering and death" (*IR* 105). Rather than "conceiving of crucifixion as something to be sought and accepted as a means of redemption," "we should say that redemption happens through resistance to the sway of evil, and in the experiences of conversion and healing by which communities of well-being are created" (*IR* 105). This is what we see in Jesus' life, death, and resurrection: "This good and holy power of life continually arises, despite the victories of unjust death, to empower new struggles for well-being. . . . The God of the resurrection did not cause the cross, but was momentarily crushed by the cross, only to rise again, overcoming it with a rebirth of protest and new hope. In the resurrection we say No to unjust death and Yes to life abundant for all of us together" (*IR* 107).

It should be clear that, for Ruether, Jesus' death does not "effect" human redemption; rather, Jesus saves and redeems others by being "paradigmatic" and "exemplifying" a way of life in accordance with God's will.[12] Such an understanding of Jesus and his death is in continuity with Abelard's understanding of Jesus as a model and example. However, Ruether goes farther by affirming that Jesus is not the *only* human being that is paradigmatic in this regard: "While Jesus is the foundational representative of this way of the cross and liberation, he is not its exclusive possibility" (*IR* 93). In this sense, Jesus is not unique. In fact, he is not the only one in whom we encounter Christ: "Christ, as redemptive person and Word of God, is not to be encapsulated 'once-for-all' in the historical Jesus" (*SGT* 138). "If we are clear that the redemption signified by Christ is both carried on and communicated through redemptive community, this means that Christ can take on the face of every person and group and their diverse liberation struggles. We must be able to encounter Christ as black, as Asian, as Aboriginal, as woman. This also means that the coming Christ, the incompleted future of redemption, is not the historical Jesus returned, but rather the fullness of all this human diversity gathered together in redemptive community" (*IR* 94). Furthermore, the "way of Christ need not and should not be seen as excluding other ways," since the "creating, inspiriting and liberating presence of God is present to all humans in all times and places" and "has been expressed in many religious cultures" (*IR* 94).[13]

The Church and the World's Salvation

For Ruether, the church is primarily a community of followers of Jesus who continue his same struggle against oppression, injustice, and patriarchy in favor of life and authentic human existence. "The Church is where the good news of liberation from sexism is preached, where the Spirit is present to empower us to renounce patriarchy, where a community committed to the new life of mutuality is gathered together and nurtured, and where the community is spreading this vision and struggle to others" (*SGT* 213).

Because the institutional churches have tended to be oppressive and patriarchal, Ruether affirms the importance of establishing smaller groups or "base communities" characterized by "celebration and resistance" (*GG* 269). "A feminist base community is an autonomous, self-gathered community that takes responsibility for reflection on, celebrating, and acting on the understanding of redemption as liberation from patriarchy" (*SGT* 205). These communities must preserve a balance between meeting the needs of their own members and reaching out to others

(*SGT* 212). In the context of the community itself, it is necessary to "dismantle clericalism, which is an understanding of leadership as rule that reduces others to subjects to be governed"; this means rejecting the clergy/laity distinction and "exercising power in a new way, as a means of liberation of one another" (*SGT* 206–7). The sacraments must also be reclaimed "as expressions of the redemptive life of the Church that the people are to administer collectively" (*SGT* 208). Baptism "involves all members of the community, who midwife each other's rebirth from alienated to authentic life," while the Eucharist is "the people, the ecclesia, who are being transformed into the body of the new humanity, infused with the blood of new life" (*SGT* 209).

The Christian community also has a mission to society "based on a vision of a transformed world beyond the alienating isms of exploitation and oppression," such as militarism (*SGT* 212). "The church becomes redemptive community, not by passively receiving a redemption 'won' by Christ alone, but rather by collectively embodying this path of liberation in a way that transforms people and social systems" (*IR* 93). This involves "a struggle to heal the world" and to "change the death system," working toward "new understandings of culture and power relations in all dimensions of society" (*GG* 268–69, 172). According to Ruether, for the church to carry out its mission, its own members must first be "converted" to a different consciousness; only then can the church reach out to the world to enable others to undergo the same conversion: "The grace of conversion from patriarchal domination opens up a new vision of humanity for women and men, one that invites us to recast and re-create all our relationships. Church, as the avant-garde of liberated humanity, should be the support system of this process" (*SGT* 193). This is Ruether's hope for the world: "To create a new society, we will need men (and women) with new psyches" (*GG* 172). Christians use a variety of means to create this new world, by forming alternative communities of resistance, struggling against all forms of injustice, and modeling new ways of living in relation to other human beings and the created order.

It is important to note that, according to Ruether's thought, salvation is something that *human beings* must accomplish, rather than something that God accomplishes *for* them. While the "grace of conversion from patriarchal domination" is undoubtedly a divine gift, ultimately it is up to us as human beings to respond to that grace and change our world. Ruether insists that we are not to expect God or Jesus to come some day from above or outside of history to save us from evil and suffering; yet neither are we to expect a gradual evolution to a utopian perfection. Each of these alternatives "contradicts the possibilities of human existence" (*SGT* 252–53). She insists that "total transformation and reconciliation will never be fully accomplished within history, since the reign of God is an eschatological norm, not a historical possibility, since both tragedy and sin will continue" (*IR* 79). Instead, what we should hope for is a more just and egalitarian world and a healed creation, which will come about only through our own efforts.

Ruether also rejects the idea of a personal salvation beyond death in some other, heavenly realm. "To be human is to be in a state of process, to change and to die. Both change and death are good. They belong to the natural limits of life. We need to seek the life intended by God/ess for us within these limits" (*SGT* 255). While admitting that it is appropriate to assume an agnostic stance toward questions having to do with life beyond death, she insists that only the "cosmic matrix of matter/energy" is "everlasting," and that, as individuals, we merely disintegrate and dissolve back into that matrix in death (*SGT* 257). Like plants and animals, "we too are fully of the earth, earthly," and "are finite centers of life who exist for a season" (*IR* 119):

> We have to accept our mortality and transience, relinquishing the illusion of permanent immortal selves that are exempt from this process. While this is a terrible word for those who see the individual self as ultimate, it can become a joyful word once we relax into knowing ourselves as an integral part of a Great Matrix of Being, that is ever renewing life in new creative forms out of the very processes of death. One generation of earth creatures die and disintegrate into the earth so another may rise from its womb. This is the real and only resurrection of the dead. (*IR* 119–20)

Evaluation

For many Christians, the greatest virtue of the work of Ruether and other Christian feminist thinkers has been its insistence that the oppression of women, as well as other forms of oppression rooted in the patriarchal ideology, cannot be justified or tolerated among faithful followers of Jesus Christ. Ruether's acceptance of traditions other than the "classical" Christian tradition also provides a basis for working with people of other traditions toward liberation and wholeness for women, men, and all of creation. At the same time, of course, this acceptance of other traditions has been criticized by many who would question whether Ruether remains in the Christian tradition, as have other aspects of her thought. Some, for example, have argued that Ruether's doctrines of God and salvation offer little hope for the future: because salvation depends on sinful human beings, there can be no assurance that sin and evil will not ultimately prevail.[14] While aware of these criticisms, Ruether nevertheless has insisted that, in the face of the injustice and oppression that millions experience daily, the only appropriate response is to look to ourselves and our own efforts for salvation, rather than to some "God of omnipotent control over history"; the fact that evil continues in our world is evidence that such a God does not exist and that "divine goodness and divine omnipotence cannot be reconciled" (*IR* 106).

CONCLUSION

It would be impossible to address here all of the questions and problems raised by our examination of the thought of the figures we have considered in this book. Nevertheless, several general observations are in order. Above all, it should be clear that all of the stories of redemption we have seen from the time of Irenaeus to the present differ in important ways from the essentially Jewish story found in Isaiah, Luke, and Paul. This means that none of them can be regarded as an entirely faithful representation of the biblical understanding of salvation in Christ; in fact, the biblical authors themselves differ from one another in certain respects, as our analysis of the writings of Luke and Paul has shown. Of course, many biblical scholars and theologians today recognize that it is neither possible nor desirable simply to attempt to reproduce the biblical understanding of redemption in Christ so as to adopt it as our own. While not all would feel comfortable speaking of the need to "demythologize" the Scriptures, as Bultmann does, many would agree with his basic point that our modern context and worldview require new ways of understanding and presenting the Christian story of salvation that, though not always in full continuity with biblical thought, nevertheless remain faithful to its basic message.

A further point to be noted is that, with the exception of Karl Barth, the theologians considered from Ritschl to the present have abandoned the idea that Christ's death and resurrection "effect" atonement or human salvation. This involves rejecting the idea of an objective redemption accomplished by Christ that affects all human beings universally. In addition, the traditional arguments for the necessity of Christ's incarnation and death based on certain definitions of divine and human nature have increasingly been called into question. Of course, it has also been argued here that arguments for necessity of that type are not actually present in the Scriptures, contrary to what many Christian theologians and biblical scholars have claimed. The New Testament affirmations regarding the necessity of Christ's death and resurrection have to do instead with the need for the divine plan prophesied in the Hebrew Scriptures to be fulfilled. Outside of more "conservative" Christian circles, where the objective understandings of Christ's work continue to be maintained, Christ's life, death, and resurrection have increasingly been seen as redemptive through what they *reveal* to us about God, humanity, and the nature of the world in which we live.[1]

Nevertheless, while it has been argued here that the objective understandings of Christ's work are foreign to the thought of Luke and Paul (and the same should be said of the other New Testament writers), it must be recognized that the idea that Christ saves human beings through what his life, death, and resurrection *reveal* to them also fails to do full justice to the teaching of the New Testament. There, Christ saves human beings not merely through the revelation he brings but by serving as God's instrument to found a new covenant community in which people may now find salvation, redemption, forgiveness, and reconciliation with God through him as their Lord. Rather than "effecting" human salvation or merely revealing important truths, Jesus' death and resurrection are redemptive in that his willingness to give up his life seeking the salvation of others in faithfulness to the task given him by God, together with God's response to that faithfulness in raising him, ensures that those who form part of the community living under him as Lord will some day attain the salvation promised of old, when he returns in glory. Therefore, because Christ died for them and was raised for them, they can now be certain of their future salvation and to some extent experience the blessings associated with that salvation in the present; by exalting him who gave up his life seeking their redemption, God has in effect already assured them of their salvation, forgiveness, and ultimate transformation in glory in Christ.

While this may be the New Testament teaching, it too is not without its difficulties. Among these are the problems of history and eschatology: many today would find it hard to believe that human history will end in the way the New Testament describes. The relation between present and future salvation also remains difficult to define: To what extent can salvation be experienced in *this* world, and in what way does any future salvation depend on what takes place in history now? Furthermore, the biblical image of God is problematic for many. Both Testaments undeniably speak of God as love but also present God as responding in wrath to human sin by punishing and condemning it, both in this life and in the next. Of course, to propose as an alternative that God simply lets human beings suffer the consequences of their own actions without intervening in human history or at a final judgment is also problematic in that we end up with a God who is no longer active either to condemn sin or to save human beings from it but who instead leaves our salvation up to us.

In the end, it seems clear that *any* understanding of God, salvation, or the work of Jesus Christ will inevitably be problematic in many respects. What is important, however, is that, in its own way, each of the stories of redemption we have considered is capable of contributing to the transformation of human beings and the world. Depending on how it is told, we can find in the story of God's saving activity in Christ assurance of forgiveness and reconciliation with God, certainty regarding the defeat of the powers of sin and evil in our fallen nature as well as the world around us, peace and healing on both a personal level and in our relationships with others, and hope for a better and more just and equitable world both within history and beyond it. Ultimately, it must be said, *all* of this is what Jesus came to bring.

ACKNOWLEDGMENTS

I would like to thank all of the people at Fortress Press who have contributed to the publication of this book; it has been a pleasure working with them once again. I am especially grateful to Editor-in-Chief Michael West for all of the guidance and support he provided for this project from the outset, and to Project Editor Joshua Messner for the many hours he dedicated to seeing the book through the editorial process.

NOTES

Chapter 1. Isaiah and the Redemption of Israel

1. For a summary of the discussion regarding the authorship of the various parts of Isaiah as well as the literary unity of the book, see Thomas L. Leclerc, *Yahweh Is Exalted in Justice: Solidarity and Conflict in Isaiah* (Minneapolis: Augsburg Fortress, 2001), 16–25.

2. See Peter D. Quinn-Mascall, *Reading Isaiah: Poetry and Vision* (Louisville, Ky.: Westminster John Knox, 2001), 18–19.

3. Rainer Albertz, *A History of Israelite Religion in the Old Testament Period*, trans. John Bowden (Louisville, Ky.: Westminster John Knox, 1994), 1:165–67.

4. On these and other images for God in chapters 40–55 of Isaiah, see especially Sarah J. Dille, *Mixing Metaphors: God as Mother and Father in Deutero-Isaiah* (London: T & T Clark International, 2004).

5. For this idea in Isaiah, see especially John J. Schmitt, *Isaiah and His Interpreters* (New York: Paulist Press, 1986), 87, 108–16.

6. Antti Laato notes that Isaiah 40–55 presents salvation unconditionally, while "Isaiah 1 shares with Isaiah 56–66 the conditional view of salvation" (*"About Zion I Will Not Be Silent": The Book of Isaiah as an Ideological Unity*, ConBNT 44 [Stockholm: Almqvist & Wiksell International, 1998], 82).

7. See John Haralson Hayes, *Isaiah, the Eighth-Century Prophet: His Times and Preaching* (Nashville, Tenn.: Abingdon, 1987), 75–78.

8. On this idea in Isaiah and elsewhere in the Hebrew Scriptures, see Donald E. Gowan, *Eschatology in the Old Testament* (Philadelphia: Fortress Press, 1986), 73–75, 87–88.

9. For these ideas in Isaiah 40–55, see Anthony Gelston, "Universalism in Second Isaiah," *JTS* 43 (1992), 377–98.

10. See Gowan, *Eschatology*, 11–14.

11. See Walter Brueggemann, *Theology of the Old Testament* (Minneapolis: Fortress Press, 1997), 149–51.

12. The translation is from Quinn-Mascall, who observes that "'I create evil' is a shocking statement that is usually softened in translations" (*Reading Isaiah*, 93).

13. Joseph Jenson, "Yahweh's Plan in Isaiah and in the Rest of the Old Testament," *CBQ* 48, no. 3 (1986): 445–46.

14. This idea is limited to Isaiah 1–39; as Joseph Blenkinsopp notes with regard to Isaiah 40–66, "nowhere in the aspirations for and dreams of a future restoration is there place for *the monarchy*" (*Isaiah 56–66: A New Translation with Introduction and Commentary*, ABC 19B [New York: Doubleday, 2003], 80).

15. See Joseph Blenkinsopp, *Isaiah 40–55: A New Translation with Introduction and Commentary*, ABC 19A (New York: Doubleday, 2002), 118.

16. See ibid., *Isaiah 40–55*, 350–53.

17. Christoph Schroeder, *History, Justice, and the Agency of God: A Hermeneutical and Exegetical Investigation on Isaiah and Psalms*, BIS 52 (Leiden: Brill, 2001), 62.

18. Particularly noteworthy among those inspired by the imagery Isaiah uses to describe a future salvation is Edward Hicks (1780–1849), who "painted more than fifty versions of the scene from Isaiah 11," generally titling his paintings *The Peaceable Kingdom* (Quinn-Mascall, *Reading Isaiah*, 53).

Chapter 2. The Divine Plan of Salvation in the Writings of Luke

1. On this discussion, see Joseph A. Fitzmyer, *The Gospel according to Luke I–IX*, ABC 28 (Garden City, N.Y.: Doubleday, 1981), 35–62. On the book of Acts, see Colin J. Hemer, *The Book of Acts in the Setting of Hellenistic History*, WUNT 49 (Tübingen: J.C.B. Mohr, 1989), 308–410.

2. See Robert L. Webb, "John the Baptist and His Relationship to Jesus," in *Studying the Historical Jesus: Evaluations of the State of Current Research*, ed. Bruce Chilton and Craig A. Evans (Leiden: Brill, 1994), 194–96.

3. See Jack Dean Kingsbury, *Conflict in Luke: Jesus, Authorities, Disciples* (Minneapolis: Augsburg Fortress, 1991), 81.

4. As I. Howard Marshall stresses, the parable is "directed against the religious leaders of the people," rather than against Israel as a whole (*The Gospel of Luke: A Commentary on the Greek Text*, NIGTC [Grand Rapids, Mich.: Eerdmans, 1978], 726).

5. See Darrell Bock, "Scripture and the Realisation of God's Promises," in *Witness to the Gospel: The Theology of Acts*, ed. I. Howard Marshall and David Peterson (Grand Rapids, Mich.: Eerdmans, 1998), 58–61.

6. On this point and what follows, see especially Charles H. Cosgrove, "The Divine δεῖ in Luke-Acts," *NovT* 26, no. 2 (1984): 168–90; John T. Squires, *The Plan of God in Luke-Acts*, SNTSMS 76 (Cambridge: Cambridge University Press, 1993), especially 1–14, 155–85.

7. See Robert C. Tannehill, "Israel in Luke-Acts: A Tragic Story," *JBL* 104, no. 1 (1985): 69–85.

8. See Peter Doble, *The Paradox of Salvation: Luke's Theology of the Cross* (Cambridge: Cambridge University Press, 1996), 3–9.

9. See Kingsbury, *Conflict in Luke*, 125.

10. On the importance of the risen Jesus' ongoing salvific activity in Luke's theology, see Robert F. O'Toole, *The Unity of Luke's Theology: An Analysis of Luke-Acts* (Wilmington, Del.: Michael Glazier, 1984), 40–61.

11. Regarding Luke's eschatology, see Robert Maddox, *The Purpose of Luke-Acts* (Edinburgh: T & T Clark, 1982), 100–157.

12. On this subject, see Rudolf Schnackenburg, *Jesus in the Gospels: A Biblical Christology*, trans. O. C. Dean Jr. (Louisville, Ky.: Westminster John Knox, 1995), 186–209.

13. On the centrality of repentance for Jesus' proclamation as presented in Luke, as well as Luke's understanding of what true repentance involves, see Guy D. Nave Jr., *The Role and Function of Repentance in Luke-Acts*, SBLAB 4 (Atlanta: Society of Biblical Literature, 2002), 159–91.

14. See Jacob Jervell, *The Theology of the Acts of the Apostles*, NTT (Cambridge: Cambridge University Press, 1996), 52–53.

15. See Heikki Räisänen, "The Redemption of Israel: A Salvation-Historical Problem in Luke-Acts," in *Luke-Acts*, ed. Petri Luomanen (Helsinki: Finnish Exegetical Society, 1991), 94–111.

16. On these points, see Frank J. Matera, "Responsibility for the Death of Jesus according to the Acts of the Apostles," *JSNT* 39 (1990): 77–93.

Chapter 3. Christ Crucified and Risen in the Letters of Paul

1. For various reconstructions of the chronology of Paul's life, see especially Calvin Roetzel, *Paul: The Man and the Myth* (Minneapolis: Fortress Press, 1999), 178–83.

2. On the question of the extent to which these epistles are "Pauline," see Ernest Best, *A Critical and Exegetical Commentary on Ephesians*, ICC (Edinburgh: T & T Clark, 1998), 36–40; John M. G. Barclay, *Colossians and Philemon*, NTG (Sheffield: Sheffield Academic Press, 1997), 18–35; James D. Miller, *The Pastoral Letters as Composite Documents*, SNTSMS 93 (Cambridge: Cambridge University Press, 1997), 138–58.

3. See my book *Paul on the Cross: Reconstructing the Apostle's Story of Redemption* (Minneapolis: Fortress Press, 2006); the current chapter is based on much of the material found in that book.

4. On this question, see James D. G. Dunn, *The Theology of Paul the Apostle* (Grand Rapids, Mich.: Eerdmans, 1998), 266–93.

5. On this question, see Victor Furnish, "The Jesus-Paul Debate: From Baur to Bultmann," in *Paul and Jesus: Collected Essays*, ed. Alexander J. M. Wedderburn, JSNTSup 37 (Sheffield: Sheffield Academic Press, 1989), 17–50.

6. See especially David Wenham, *Paul: Follower of Jesus or Founder of Christianity?* (Grand Rapids, Mich.: Eerdmans, 1995).

7. For references to these ideas in Paul's epistles, see Dunn, *Theology*, 294–315.

8. On the debate regarding the "eschatological tension" in Paul's thought, see Dunn, *Theology*, 461–98.

9. See Clinton E. Arnold, *Ephesians, Power and Magic: The Concept of Power in Ephesians in Light of Its Historical Setting*, SNTSMS 63 (Cambridge: Cambridge University Press, 1989), 145–58; Barclay, *Colossians and Philemon*, 26, 89–90; Margaret Davies, *The Pastoral Epistles*, NTG (Sheffield: Sheffield Academic Press, 1996), 52–58.

10. See especially Kent L. Yinger, *Paul, Judaism, and Judgment according to Deeds*, SNTSMS 105 (Cambridge: Cambridge University Press, 1999); Don B. Garlington, *Faith, Obedience, and Perseverance: Aspects of Paul's Letter to the Romans*, WUNT 79 (Tübingen: J.C.B. Mohr, 1994).

11. See Graham Stanton, "The Law of Moses and the Law of Christ," in *Paul and the Mosaic Law*, ed. James D. G. Dunn, WUNT 89 (Tübingen: J.C.B. Mohr, 1996), 99–116.

12. On Paul's use of "all" in relation to believers, see Douglas A. Moo, *The Epistle to the Romans*, NICNT (Grand Rapids, Mich.: Eerdmans, 1996), 343–44; John A. Ziesler, *Paul's Letter to the Romans*, TPINTC (Philadelphia: Trinity Press International, 1989), 151.

13. See the discussion in my book *Paul on the Cross*, 151–89.

14. See, for example, the discussion in John A. Ziesler, *Pauline Christianity*, rev. ed. (Oxford: Oxford University Press, 1990), 49–72.

Chapter 4. The Redemption of "Man" in the Thought of Irenaeus

1. All references to Irenaeus's writings are to *Adversus haereses* (*Against Heresies*). Quotations are taken from volume 1 of *The Anti-Nicene Fathers: Translations of the Writings of the Fathers down to A.D. 325*, ed. Alexander Roberts and James Donaldson, American Reprint (Grand Rapids, Mich.: Eerdmans, 1950). In some passages the translation has been slightly altered in order to reflect more clearly certain ideas found in the Latin or Greek original.

2. Denis Minns, *Irenaeus*, OCT (London: Geoffrey Chapman, 1994), x, 60.

3. Eric Osborn, *Irenaeus of Lyons* (Cambridge: Cambridge University Press, 2001), 74–77.

4. Ibid., *Irenaeus*, 212–14.

5. Colin E. Gunton, *The Triune Creator: A Historical and Systematic Study*, ESCT (Edinburgh: Edinburgh University Press, 1998), 55.

6. Minns, *Irenaeus*, 86–87.

7. Brian E. Daley, *The Hope of the Early Church: A Handbook of Patristic Eschatology* (Cambridge: Cambridge University Press, 1991), 29.

8. For Irenaeus's discussion regarding the fulfillment of Old Testament prophecies in Jesus' passion and death, see Daniel Wanke, *Das Kreuz Christi bei Irenäus von Lyon*, BZNW 99 (Berlin: Walter de Gruyter, 2000), 244–51.

9. On the many different aspects of "recapitulation" in Irenaeus's thought, see Yoshifumi Torisu, *Gott und Welt: Eine Untersuchung zur Gotteslehre des Irenäeus von Lyon*, SIMSVD 52 (Nettetal: Steyler Verlag, 1991), 157–79.

10. Osborn has called attention to the influence of the Platonic idea of forms and other elements of Platonism in Irenaeus, though he claims that "Irenaeus was not conscious of this Platonic pattern in his thought" (*Irenaeus*, 16; see 15–17 passim).

11. Trevor Hart rightly notes that "Irenaeus' emphasis upon the need for human faith in order for salvation to be personally appropriated would seem to fly in the face of any suggestion that he understands salvation primarily in essentially metaphysical categories, and as transmitted in some 'mysterious' and automatic manner" ("Irenaeus, Recapitulation and Physical Redemption," in *Christ in Our Place: The Humanity of God in Christ for the Reconciliation of the World*, ed. Trevor Hart and Daniel Thimell [Exeter: Paternoster, 1989], 155–56); curiously, however, he also notes that for Irenaeus "there is an ontological solidarity between this one man [Christ] and all others whereby all that he does, and indeed all that he is, may be predicated of them too" (175).

12. Gustav Aulén, *Christus Victor: An Historical Study of the Three Main Types of the Idea of Atonement*, trans. A. G. Hebert (New York: Macmillan, 1969).

13. See Gustaf Wingren, *Man and the Incarnation: A Study in the Biblical Theology of Irenaeus*, trans. Ross Mackenzie (Philadelphia: Muhlenberg Press, 1959), 129–34.

14. For this argument, see William Loewe, "Irenaeus' Soteriology: *Christus Victor* Revisited," *ATR* 67, no. 1 (1985): 1–15.

15. See Terrance L. Tiessen, *Irenaeus on the Salvation of the Unevangelized*, ATLAMS 31 (Metuchen, N.J.: Scarecrow, 1993), 188–212.

16. See Hans Boersma, "Redemptive Hospitality in Irenaeus: A Model for Ecumenicity in a Violent World," *ProEccl* 9 (2002): 219–21.

17. As Rolf Noormann notes, Irenaeus does attempt to ground his argument for the necessity of Christ's saving work in such New Testament passages as Col 1:15b, 18b, 21-22; however, no language regarding necessity actually appears in these verses (*Irenäeus als Paulusinterpret: Zur Rezeption und Wirkung der Paulinischen und Deuteropaulinischen Briefe im Werk des Irenäeus von Lyon*, WUNT 2.66 [Tübingen: J.C.B. Mohr, 1994], 441–42, 452–53).

Chapter 5. Gregory of Nyssa and the Union of Divine and Human Natures

1. Quotations are taken from volume 5 of *A Select Library of Nicene and Post-Nicene Fathers of the Christian Church*, ed. Philip Schaff and Henry Wace; Second Series, American Reprint (Grand Rapids, Mich.: Eerdmans, 1952–1957). The following abbreviations will be used to refer to Gregory's works: *GC*, *Great Catechism*; *OSR*, *On the Soul and the Resurrection*; *OMM*, *On the Making of Man*; *OV*, *On Virginity*; *AE*, *Against Eunomius*; *OBC*, *On the Baptism of Christ*; *LM*, *The Life of Moses*.

2. See Diogenes Allen, *Philosophy for Understanding Theology* (Atlanta: John Knox, 1985), 96–98; Johannes Zachhuber, "Once Again: Gregory of Nyssa on Universals," *JTS* 56, no. 1 (2005): 75–98.

3. On this question, see D. Bentley Hart, "The 'Whole Humanity': Gregory of Nyssa's Critique of Slavery in Light of His Eschatology," *SJT* 54, no. 1 (2001): 57–59.

4. On the following, see especially Ernest V. McClear, "The Fall of Man and Original Sin in the Theology of Gregory of Nyssa," *ThStud* 9, no. 2 (1948): 175–216.

5. See Raymond Winling, "Mort et résurrection du Christ dans les traités Contre Eunome de Grégoire de Nysse," *RevScRel* 64 (1990): 261–62.

6. With regard to this imagery, it is important to note, as Robert S. Paul does, that Gregory "does not present his picture as a statement of what happened but as an analogy of what happened" (*The Atonement and the Sacraments* [New York: Abingdon, 1960], 55–56).

7. See J.N.D. Kelly, *Early Christian Doctrines*, rev. ed. (San Francisco: Harper & Row, 1978), 185–86, 382–84, 387–88, 391–92, 396.

8. Adolf von Harnack, quoted in Jean Rivière, *The Doctrine of the Atonement: A Historical Essay*, trans. Luigi Cappadelta (London: Kegan Paul, Trench, Trübner, 1909), 1:183.

9. On the concept of adoption in Gregory, see Lucian Turcescu, *Gregory of Nyssa and the Concept of Divine Persons*, AARAS (Oxford: Oxford University Press, 2005), 95–102.

10. See J. Patout Burns, "The Economy of Salvation: Two Patristic Traditions," *ThStud* 37, no. 4 (1976): 605–7.

11. This is commonly referred to as the *apocatastasis*, an idea first attributed to Origen but taken up by Gregory; see John R. Sachs, "Apocatastasis in Patristic Theology," *ThStud* 54 (1993): 617–40.

12. On Gregory's eschatology, see Brian E. Daley, *The Hope of the Early Church: A Handbook of Patristic Eschatology* (Cambridge: Cambridge University Press, 1991), 85–89.

13. See, for example, Vladimir Lossky, *Orthodox Theology: An Introduction*, trans. Ian and Ihita Kesarcodi-Watson (Crestwood, N.Y.: St. Vladimir's, 1978), 95–137; John Meyendorff, "Christ's Humanity: The Paschal Mystery," *SVTQ* 31, no. 1 (1987): 5–40; Thomas F. Torrance, *The Mediation of Christ* (Edinburgh: T & T Clark, 1992), 39–41, 66–72.

14. See, for example, Daniel E. Scuiry, "The Anthropology of St. Gregory of Nyssa," *Diakonia* 18 (1983): 40; Nonna Verna Harrison, "Theosis as Salvation: An Orthodox Perspective," *ProEccl* 6, no. 4 (1997): 436.

Chapter 6. Anselm and the Satisfaction of Divine Justice

1. For the general background and context of *Cur Deus Homo*, see especially Richard W. Southern, *Saint Anselm and His Biographer: A Study of Monastic Life and Thought, 1059–c.1130* (Cambridge: Cambridge University Press, 1963), 77–121; Gillian R. Evans, *Anselm*, OCT (Wilton, Conn.: Morehouse-Barlow, 1989), 71–82.

2. Alister E. McGrath, *Iustitia Dei: A History of the Christian Doctrine of Justification* (Cambridge: Cambridge University Press, 1986), 1:24.

3. All references are to *Cur Deus Homo*. Quotations taken from volume 3 of *Anselm of Canterbury*, ed. and trans. Jasper Hopkins and Herbert Richardson (Toronto: Edwin Mellen, 1976).

4. John McIntyre, *St. Anselm and His Critics: A Re-Interpretation of the* Cur Deus Homo (Edinburgh: Oliver and Boyd, 1954), 68–69.

5. On Anselm's understanding of "man" and "human nature," see Jasper Hopkins, *A Companion to the Study of Anselm* (Minneapolis: University of Minnesota Press, 1972), 196, 198–201.

6. See Tatha Wiley, *Original Sin: Origins, Developments, Contemporary Meanings* (New York: Paulist Press, 2002), 80–82.

7. Evans, *Anselm*, 76.

8. Frederick W. Dillistone, *The Christian Understanding of Atonement* (Philadelphia: Westminster, 1968), 194.

9. Southern, *Saint Anselm and His Biographer*, 107.

10. On this subject, see Richard W. Southern, *Saint Anselm: Portrait in a Landscape* (Cambridge: Cambridge University Press, 1990), 212.

11. As D. Bentley Hart has argued, Anselm's understanding of Christ's work can even be understood as "a variant of a *Christus victor* soteriology" (*ProEccl* 7, no. 3 [1998]: 342).

12. Richard E. Weingart, *The Logic of Divine Love* (Oxford: Oxford University Press, 1970), 88.

13. On these criticisms, see especially the discussion in J. Denny Weaver, *The Nonviolent Atonement* (Grand Rapids, Mich.: Eerdmans, 2001), 126–29, 179–224.

14. Paul S. Fiddes, *Past Event and Present Salvation: The Christian Idea of Atonement* (London: Darton, Longman and Todd, 1989), 101.

15. On Anselm's understanding of necessity, see especially the observations by Roger Haight, *Jesus, Symbol of God* (Maryknoll, N.Y.: Orbis, 1999), 229–30.

16. On this discussion, which revolved around the notions of *acceptatio* and *acceptilatio*, see L. W. Grensted, *A Short History of the Atonement* (London: Longman, Greens & Co., 1920), 158–61; McGrath, *Iustitia Dei*, 2:45.

Chapter 7. Christ as Redeemer from Sin, Death, and the Devil

1. Quotations from Luther's *Small Catechism* (abbreviated as *SC*), *Large Catechism* (*LC*), and the *Smalcald Articles* (*SA*) are taken from *The Book of Concord: The Confessions of the Evangelical Lutheran Church*, ed. Robert Kolb and Timothy J. Wengert (Minneapolis: Fortress Press, 2000). References listed as *LW* are from the American edition of *Luther's Works*, ed. Jaroslav Pelikan and Helmut T. Lehmann (Philadelphia: Fortress Press; St. Louis: Concordia Publishing House, 1955–1986). Those listed as *WLS* are from Ewald M. Plass, comp., *What Luther Says: An Anthology* (St. Louis: Concordia Publishing House, 1959).

2. Henri Rondet, quoted in Thomas M. McDonough, *The Law and the Gospel in Luther: A Study of Martin Luther's Confessional Writings* (Oxford: Oxford University Press, 1963), 10.

3. Marc Lienhard, *Luther, Witness to Jesus Christ: Stages and Themes of the Reformer's Christology*, trans. Edwin H. Robertson (Minneapolis: Augsburg, 1982), 179.

4. See Paul Althaus, *The Theology of Martin Luther*, trans. Robert C. Schultz (Philadelphia: Fortress Press, 1966), 158, 220.

5. Gerhard Forde, *On Being a Theologian of the Cross: Reflections on Luther's Heidelberg Disputation, 1518* (Grand Rapids, Mich.: Eerdmans, 1997), 95.

6. William Lazareth, *Christians in Society: Luther, the Bible, and Social Ethics* (Minneapolis: Augsburg Fortress, 2001), 88.

7. On the following, see L. W. Grensted, *A Short History of the Atonement* (London: Longman, Greens & Co., 1920), 144–72.

8. Philip S. Watson, *Let God Be God! An Interpretation of the Theology of Martin Luther* (London: Epworth, 1947), 116.

9. Martin Luther, "Epistle Sermon, Twenty-Fourth Sunday after Trinity," in *A Compend of Luther's Theology*, ed. Hugh T. Kerr (Philadelphia: Westminster, 1943), 52–53; cf. *LW* 26:33.

10. On these points and those that follow, see especially Lienhard, *Luther*, 62, 109, 147, 181.

11. On the influence of mystical thought on Luther, see especially Walther von Loewenich, *Luther's Theology of the Cross*, trans. Herbert J. A. Bouman (Minneapolis: Augsburg, 1976), 152–66.

12. Alister E. McGrath, *Iustitia Dei: A History of the Christian Doctrine of Justification* (Cambridge: Cambridge University Press, 1986), 2:14; on the idea of grace as an "impersonal abstract force" and the idea of "infused righteousness," see 1:29, 34.

13. Simo Peura, "Christ as Favor and Gift (donum): The Challenge of Luther's Understanding of Justification," in *Union with Christ: The New Finnish Interpretation of Luther*, ed. Carl E. Braaten and Robert W. Jenson (Grand Rapids, Mich.: Eerdmans, 1998), 42.

14. See my article "*Sola fide* and Luther's 'Analytic' Understanding of Justification: A Fresh Look at Some Old Questions," *ProEccl* 13, no. 1 (2004): 39-57; see also Althaus, *Theology*, 238–42.

15. Robert H. Culpepper, *Interpreting the Atonement* (Grand Rapids, Mich.: Eerdmans, 1966), 96.

Chapter 8. Christ Our Righteousness in John Calvin's *Institutes*

1. On the discussion regarding the relationship between systematic and biblical theology in the *Institutes*, as well as Calvin's method and intention, see especially Richard A. Muller, *The Unaccommodated Calvin: Studies in the Foundation of a Theological Tradition* (Oxford: Oxford University Press, 2000), 101–8.

2. All quotations from the *Institutes* are taken from volumes 20–21 of *The Library of Christian Classics*, ed. John T. McNeill, trans. Ford Lewis Battles (Philadelphia: Westminster, 1960).

3. See Randall C. Zachman, "What Kind of Book Is Calvin's *Institutes?*" *CTJ* 35 (2000): 238.

4. On these two aspects of Calvin's doctrine of original sin, see Barbara Pitkin, "Nothing but Concupiscence: Calvin's Understanding of Sin and the *Via Agustini*," *CTJ* 34 (1999): 347–69.

5. On the difficulties inherent to Calvin's doctrine of divine providence and Calvin's response to these difficulties, see Paul Helm, "Calvin (and Zwingli) on Divine Providence," *CTJ* 29 (1994): 388–405.

6. For Calvin's argument for the necessity of the incarnation, see T. H. L. Parker, *Calvin: An Introduction to His Thought* (New York: Continuum, 2002), 64–66.

7. See Hans Boersma, "Calvin and the Extent of the Atonement," *EvQ* 64, no. 4 (1992): 344–45.

8. Bruce L. McCormack, "For Us and Our Salvation: Incarnation and Atonement in the Reformed Tradition," *GOTR* 43, nos. 1–4 (1998): 302–3.

9. On the importance of Christ's obedience for Calvin's teaching regarding the atonement, as well as his interpretation of Christ's death as penal substitution and expiatory sacrifice, see Robert A. Peterson, *Calvin's Doctrine of the Atonement* (Phillipsburg, N.J.: Presbyterian and Reformed, 1983), esp. 40–45, 55–76.

10. See Frederick W. Dillistone, *The Christian Understanding of Atonement* (Philadelphia: Westminster, 1968), 197–200.

11. For a review of this debate, see Roger Nicole, "John Calvin's View of the Extent of the Atonement," *WTJ* 47 (1985): 197–225.

12. On Calvin's understanding of the union of Christ with believers, see especially Dennis E. Tamburello, *Union with Christ: John Calvin and the Mysticism of St. Bernard* (Louisville, Ky.: Westminster John Knox, 1994), 84–101.

13. For Calvin's teaching regarding Christ's presence in the Lord's Supper, and his doctrine of the Eucharist in general, see Kilian McDonnell, *John Calvin, the Church, and the Eucharist* (Princeton, N.J.: Princeton University Press, 1967), 206–93.

14. See Trevor Hart, "Humankind in Christ and Christ in Humankind: Salvation as Participation in Our Substitute in the Theology of John Calvin," *SJT* 42 (1989): 78–82.

15. For a summary of Calvin's doctrine of justification, see especially Craig B. Carpenter, "A Question of Union with Christ? Calvin and Trent on Justification," *WTJ* 64 (2002): 371–84.

16. Wilhelm Niesel, *The Theology of Calvin*, trans. Harold Knight (London: Lutterworth, 1956), 137–38.

17. Graham Redding, *Prayer and the Priesthood of Christ: In the Reformed Tradition* (New York: T & T Clark, 2003), 107.

Chapter 9. Albrecht Ritschl and the Kingdom of God

1. On Ritschl's life, see especially the introduction by Philip Hefner to Albrecht Ritschl, *Three Essays*, trans. Philip Hefner (Philadelphia: Fortress Press, 1972), 3–16.

2. All references in parentheses are to page numbers from *The Christian Doctrine of Justification and Reconciliation: The Positive Development of the Doctrine*, ed. and trans. H. R. Mackintosh and A. B. Macaulay, 3rd ed., LRPT (Clifton, N.J.: Reference Book Publishers, 1966), which represents the third volume of Ritschl's *Die christliche Lehre von der Rechtfertigung und Versöhnung*, published between 1870 and 1874.

3. Stanley J. Grenz and Roger E. Olson, *Twentieth-Century Theology: God and the World in a Transitional Age* (Downers Grove, Ill.: InterVarsity, 1992), 52.

4. See Samuel Luttrel Akers, *Some British Reactions to Ritschlianism*, YSR 8 (New Haven, Conn.: Yale University Press, 1934), 34.

5. David L. Mueller, *An Introduction to the Theology of Albrecht Ritschl* (Philadelphia: Westminster, 1969), 64.

6. A. Durwood Foster, "Albrecht Ritschl," in *A Handbook of Christian Theologians*, ed. Dean G. Peerman and Martin E. Marty, enlarged ed. (Nashville, Tenn.: Abingdon, 1984), 59–60.

7. Gerhard Forde points out that Ritschl's rejection of the idea of God's wrath also leads to "a thoroughgoing rejection of the traditional doctrine of law and gospel" (*The Law-Gospel Debate: An Interpretation of Its Historical Development* [Minneapolis: Augsburg, 1969], 110).

8. Alister E. McGrath, *Iustitia Dei: A History of the Christian Doctrine of Justification* (Cambridge: Cambridge University Press, 1986), 2:163–64.

9. In this regard, Ritschl consciously distanced himself from Luther; see David W. Lotz, *Ritschl and Luther: A Fresh Perspective on Albrecht Ritschl's Theology in the Light of His Luther Study* (Nashville, Tenn.: Abingdon, 1974), 40–42.

10. In reality, this represents an oversimplification of Abelard's thought, as Richard Weingart has shown (*The Logic of Divine Love* [Oxford: Oxford University Press, 1970], esp. 94–184). On the adoption of this view by the so-called "liberal" theologians, see Alister McGrath, "The Moral Theory of the Atonement: An Historical and Theological Critique," *SJT* 38 (1985): 205–20.

11. Rolf Schäfer, *Ritschl: Grundlinien eines vast verschollenen dogmatischen Systems*, BHT 41 (Tübingen: J. C. B. Mohr, 1968), 106–8.

12. For Ritschl's understanding of Christ's divinity as well as his humanity, see James Richmond, *Ritschl, A Reappraisal: A Study in Systematic Theology* (London: Collins, 1978), 170–76.

13. Philip Hefner, *Faith and the Vitalities of History: A Theological Study Based on the Work of Albrecht Ritschl* (New York: Harper & Row, 1966), 87.

14. On the impact of Ritschl's thought in the decades following his death, as well as the primary criticisms made of his work, see especially Gerald W. McCulloh, *Christ's Person and Life-Work in the Theology of Albrecht Ritschl: With Special Attention to the* Munus Triplex (Lanham, Md.: University Press of America, 1990), 8–9, 164–97.

Chapter 10. Karl Barth's Doctrine of Reconciliation

1. Karl Barth, *Epistle to the Romans*, trans. Edwin C. Hoskyns (London: Oxford University Press, 1933), 28.

2. On the background of Barth's dialectical theology, see especially *A Map of Twentieth-Century Theology: Readings from Karl Barth to Radical Pluralism*, ed. Carl E. Braaten and Robert W. Jenson (Minneapolis: Fortress Press, 1995), 39–42.

3. All references are to Karl Barth, *Church Dogmatics*, trans. and ed. G. W. Bromiley and T. F. Torrance (Edinburgh: T & T Clark, 1936–1969).

4. On the centrality of this doctrine for the structure and hermeneutics of the *Church Dogmatics*, see especially Douglas R. Sharp, *The Hermeneutics of Election: The Significance of the Doctrine in Barth's Church Dogmatics* (Lanham, Md.: University Press of America, 1990).

5. Regarding Barth's doctrine of election and its intimate relationship to his doctrine of justification, see especially Hans Küng, *Justification: The Doctrine of Karl Barth and a Catholic Reflection* (New York: Thomas Nelson & Sons, 1964), 13–17.

6. On the "Platonic realism" in Barth's thought, and his "ontological conception" of salvation in Christ, see especially Colin Gunton, "Salvation," in *The Cambridge Companion to Karl Barth*, ed. John Webster, CCR (Cambridge: Cambridge University Press, 2000), 143–58.

7. On this subject, see especially Allen Jorgenson, "Karl Barth's Christological Treatment of Sin," *SJT* 54, no. 4 (2001): 439–62.

8. Charles T. Waldrop, referring to the nature assumed by Christ, notes that "since Barth attributes a personality, in addition to a will, to the human nature, it is clear that the human nature is personal" and that "he conceives the human nature as a concrete individual" (*Karl Barth's Christology: Its Basic Alexandrian Character*, R&R 21 [New York: Mouton, 1984], 57–58).

9. Alan J. Torrance rightly distinguishes between the idea of participation as "*koinonia*," involving "fellowship" or "communion," and the Platonic understanding of participation as "*methexis*," which has to do with an ontological union of essences; as he notes, Barth generally understands participation in the latter Platonic sense (*Persons in Communion: Trinitarian Description and Human Participation* [Edinburgh: T & T Clark, 1996], 254–55, 356n104).

10. G. C. Berkouwer, *The Triumph of Grace in the Theology of Karl Barth* (London: Paternoster, 1956), 135.

11. Barth thus combines the *Christus Victor* idea with the ideas of penal substitution and representation, although his presentation of both of these ideas departs from the traditional ones due to his understanding of the union between Christ and all men and women: just as all suffer the penalty of sin together with Christ in his death, so all rise victorious and are exalted in and with Christ. See Donald G. Bloesch, *Jesus Is Victor! Karl Barth's Doctrine of Salvation* (Nashville, Tenn.: Abingdon, 1976), esp. 43–71.

12. Frank M. Hasel, "Karl Barth's *Church Dogmatics* on the Atonement: Some Translational Problems," *AUSS* 29, no. 3 (1991): 210.

13. For Barth's ideas regarding the church's mission, see Waldron Scott, "Karl Barth's Theology of Mission," *Missiology* 3, no. 2 (1975): 209–24, who comments that for Barth "the final motive is simply that all men may know of their salvation" (219).

14. Elsewhere, Barth writes that baptism "tells us that when Christ has been dead and buried we too have been dead and buried, we the transgressors and sinners. As one baptised you may see yourself as dead. The forgiveness of sins rests on the fact that this dying took place at that time on Golgotha. Baptism tells you that that death was also your death" (Karl Barth, *Dogmatics in Outline*, trans. G. T. Thompson [London: SCM, 1949], 151).

15. Helmut Gollwitzer, "Kingdom of God and Socialism in the Theology of Karl

Barth," in *Karl Barth and Radical Politics*, ed. George Hunsinger (Philadelphia: Westminster, 1976), 95.

16. George Hunsinger, *How to Read Karl Barth* (Oxford: Oxford University Press, 1991), 131–32.

Chapter 11. Rudolf Bultmann and the Proclamation of the Word of the Cross

1. On the relation between Bultmann and Heidegger, see especially John Macquarrie, *An Existentialist Theology: A Comparison of Heidegger and Bultmann* (New York: Macmillan, 1955).

2. Nils Alstrup Dahl, *Jesus the Christ: The Historical Origins of Christological Doctrine*, ed. Donald H. Juel (Minneapolis: Augsburg Fortress, 1991), 190.

3. The following works of Rudolf Bultmann will be cited and abbreviated as indicated: *TNT, Theology of the New Testament*, trans. Kendrick Grobel (New York: Scribners, 1951); *EF, Existence and Faith: Shorter Writings of Rudolf Bultmann*, trans. Schubert M. Ogden (Cleveland, Ohio: World Publishing Company, 1960); *KM, Kerygma and Myth: A Theological Debate*, ed. Hans Werner Bartsch, trans. Reginald H. Fuller (London: SPCK, 1953); *FU, Faith and Understanding*, ed. Robert W. Funk, trans. Louise Pettibone Smith (New York: Harper & Row, 1969); *PC, Primitive Christianity in Its Contemporary Setting*, trans. Reginald H. Fuller (New York: Meridian, 1956).

4. Morris Ashcraft, *Rudolf Bultmann*, MMTM (Waco, Tex.: Word, 1972), 14. See especially *KM* 1–15.

5. See Giovanni Miegge, *Gospel and Myth in the Thought of Rudolf Bultmann*, trans. Stephen Neill (London: Lutterworth, 1960), 34, 125–26. As Miegge notes, this "translating" was first done not by Paul and John themselves but by the communities of which they formed a part.

6. On Bultmann's understanding of "inauthentic existence" and "authentic existence," along with a critique of this understanding, see Roy A. Harrisville, "Bultmann's Concept of the Transition from Inauthentic to Authentic Existence," in *Kerygma and History: A Symposium on the Theology of Rudolf Bultmann*, ed. Carl E. Braaten and Roy A. Harrisville (New York: Abingdon, 1962), 212–28.

7. A comprehensive summary of Bultmann's understanding of both sin and the salvation-event can be found in Walter Schmithals, *An Introduction to the Theology of Rudolf Bultmann* (Minneapolis: Augsburg, 1968), 71–194.

8. Otto Michel thus rightly notes that for Bultmann, "The event of salvation and of Word are not separable from each other, as though there were an event of salvation without an event of Word" ("The Event of Salvation and Word in the New Testament," in *The Theology of Rudolf Bultmann*, ed. Charles W. Kegley [New York: Harper & Row, 1966], 182).

9. Léopold Malevez, *The Christian Message and Myth: The Theology of Rudolf Bultmann* (London: SCM, 1958), 85.

10. Charles T. Waldrop, "Barth and Bultmann: Representatives of Two Ancient Theological Traditions," *PRS* 11 (1984): 16.

11. Huw P. Owen, *Revelation and Existence: A Study in the Theology of Rudolf Bultmann* (Cardiff: University of Wales Press, 1957), 26–27.

12. As Thomas C. Oden notes, for Bultmann, the indicative and imperative are "not two things, but one" and "belong together as two sides of a coin," due to their "internal unity" (*Radical Obedience: The Ethics of Rudolf Bultmann* [Philadelphia: Westminster, 1964], 95).

13. Robert D. Knudsen, "Rudolf Bultmann," in *Creative Minds in Contemporary Theology*, ed. Philip E. Hughes (Grand Rapids, Mich.: Eerdmans, 1969), 151.

14. Joseph Cahill, "The Theological Significance of Rudolf Bultmann," *ThStud* 38, no. 2 (1977): 267.

15. E. P. Sanders, *Paul and Palestinian Judaism* (Philadelphia: Fortress Press, 1977), 502, 511. Sanders, however, found Bultmann's understanding of "participation" unsatisfactory (see 522–23).

16. On the following criticisms of Bultmann's thought, see especially David Fergusson, *Bultmann*, OCT (Collegeville, Minn.: Liturgical Press, 1992), 116–17, 138–46.

Chapter 12. Jon Sobrino and the Crucified People

1. Gustavo Gutiérrez, *A Theology of Liberation*, ed. and trans. Sister Caridad Inda and John Eagleson, rev. ed. (Maryknoll, N.Y.: Orbis, 1988), 12; on the methodology proposed by Gutierrez, see 5–12.

2. For a brief summary of the history and development of liberation theology, see chapter 6 of Douglas John Hall and Rosemary Radford Ruether, *God and the Nations* (Minneapolis: Augsburg Fortress, 1995), 93–104.

3. The following works of Jon Sobrino will be cited and abbreviated as indicated: *CC*, *Christology at the Crossroads*, trans. John Drury (Maryknoll, N.Y.: Orbis, 1978); *JL*, *Jesus the Liberator: A Historical-Theological Reading of Jesus of Nazareth*, trans. Paul Burns and Francis McDonagh (Maryknoll, N.Y.: Orbis, 1993); *PM*, *The Principle of Mercy: Taking the Crucified People from the Cross* (Maryknoll, N.Y.: Orbis, 1994); *CL*, *Christ the Liberator: A View from the Victims*, trans. Paul Burns (Maryknoll, N.Y.: Orbis, 2001); *ML*, "Central Position of the Reign of God in Liberation Theology," in *Mysterium Liberationis: Fundamental Concepts of Liberation Theology*, ed. Ignacio Ellacuría and Jon Sobrino (Maryknoll, N.Y.: Orbis, 1993), 350–88.

4. Michael L. Cook, "Jesus from the Other Side of History: Christology in Latin America," *ThStud* 44, no. 2 (1983): 272, 274.

5. Arthur F. McGovern, *Liberation Theology and Its Critics: Toward an Assessment* (Maryknoll, N.Y.: Orbis, 1989), 76.

6. On the importance of these two ideas for Sobrino's Christology, see Donald E. Waltermire, *The Liberation Christologies of Leonardo Boff and Jon Sobrino: Latin American Contributions to Contemporary Christology* (Lanham, Md.: University Press of America, 1994), 60–65.

7. Marcel Dumais has criticized Sobrino on this point, noting that in the Gospels the "blasphemy" for which Jesus was condemned had to do not with his idea of God but with his claim to divine sonship ("Le sens de la croix de Jésus d'après Jon Sobrino: Questions d'exégèse et d'herméneutique," *EgT* 19 [1988]: 336).

8. Roger Haight, *Jesus, Symbol of God* (Maryknoll, N.Y.: Orbis, 1999), 346.

9. See, for example, Jürgen Moltmann, *Experiences in Theology: Ways and Forms of Christian Theology*, trans. Margaret Kohl (Minneapolis: Fortress Press, 2000), 236–37.

10. Paul E. Ritt, "The Lordship of Jesus Christ: Balthasar and Sobrino," *ThStud* 49 (1988): 720.

11. J. Matthew Ashley, "Apocalypticism in Political and Liberation Theology: Toward an Historical *Docta Ignorantia*," *Hor* 27, no. 1 (2000): 32.

12. McGovern, *Liberation Theology*, 218.

13. Winston D. Persaud, "The Article of Justification and the Theology of Liberation," *CurTM* 16, no. 5 (1989): 369.

Chapter 13. Salvation as Liberation from Patriarchy in the Thought of Rosemary Radford Ruether

1. Geoffrey R. Lilburne, "Christology: In Dialogue with Feminism," *Hor* 11, no. 1 (1984): 8.

2. Lilburne, "Christology," 10.

3. See Carter Heyward, "An Unfinished Symphony of Liberation: The Radicalization of Christian Feminism among White U.S. Women," *JFSR* 1, no. 1 (1985): 103, 106–7.

4. The following works of Rosemary Radford Ruether will be cited and abbreviated as indicated: *GG*, *Gaia & God: An Ecofeminist Theology of Earth Healing* (San Francisco: HarperSanFrancisco, 1992); *SGT*, *Sexism and God-Talk: Toward a Feminist Theology*, 10th anniversary ed. (Boston: Beacon, 1993); and *IR*, *Introducing Redemption in Christian Feminism* (Sheffield: Sheffield Academic Press, 1998).

5. On the question of theological method among feminist theologians, including Rosemary Radford Ruether, see Anne E. Carr, "The New Vision of Feminist Theology: Method," in *Freeing Theology: The Essentials of Theology in Feminist Perspective*, ed. Catherine Mowry LaCugna (San Francisco: HarperSanFrancisco, 1993), 5–29.

6. On this point, see especially Russell Pregeant, "Christological Groundings for Liberation Praxis," *ModTh* 5, no. 2 (1989): 120–23.

7. Wanda Warren Berry, "Images of Sin and Salvation in Feminist Theology," *ATR* 60, no. 1 (1978): 27–31.

8. On Ruether's understanding of original sin, see especially Tatha Wiley, *Original Sin: Origins, Developments, Contemporary Meanings* (New York: Paulist Press, 2002), 157–64, 173–77.

9. Ted Peters notes that Ruether rejects any attempt to "feminize" God or the Holy Spirit, instead insisting on inclusive imagery, yet at the same time ends up denying the doctrine of God as triune (*God—The World's Future: Systematic Theology for a New Era*, 2nd ed. [Minneapolis: Fortress Press, 2000], 120–22).

10. As Sally Asford observes, it is not always clear whether for Ruether and other Christian feminists "salvation is unification (overcoming of differentiation) or reconciliation and mutuality" between the sexes; she regards this question as "one of the great divides within feminism in general ("Sin and Atonement in Feminist Perspective," in *Atonement Today*, ed. John Goldingay [London: SPCK, 1995], 155–57).

11. For a comparison of Ruether's thought on atonement with that of other Christian feminist theologians, see J. Denny Weaver, *The Nonviolent Atonement* (Grand Rapids, Mich.: Eerdmans, 2001), 122–56.

12. On this point and what follows, see especially Mary Hembrow Snyder, *The Christology of Rosemary Radford Ruether: A Critical Introduction* (Mystic, Conn.: Twenty-Third Publications, 1988), 47–49, 69–70, 100–102.

13. As Hans Schwarz observes, Ruether's insistence that Jesus is not to be seen as "the sole and unique redeemer figure" is a common characteristic of many feminist Christologies (*Christology* [Grand Rapids, Mich.: Eerdmans, 1998], 286–87). For his discussion of Ruether's Christology in particular, see 277–79.

14. See, for example, Frederick Sontag, "Crucifixion and Realized Eschatology: A Critique of Some Proposals Concerning Feminist Theology," *AJT* 4 (1990): 66–73.

Conclusion

1. On this point, see especially George Lindbeck, "Justification and Atonement: An Ecumenical Trajectory," in *By Faith Alone: Essays on Justification in Honor of Gerhard O. Forde*, ed. Joseph A. Burgess and Marc Kolden (Grand Rapids, Mich.: Eerdmans, 2004), 183–219.

ADDITIONAL RESOURCES

Chapter 1

Further Reading

Brueggemann, Walter, *The Prophetic Imagination,* 2nd ed. (Minneapolis: Fortress, 2001). Relates the prophetic texts in their original social contexts to modern issues of justice and righteousness.

Hutton, Rodney J., *Fortress Introduction to the Prophets* (Minneapolis: Fortress, 2004). A general introduction to the nature and origins of Israelite prophecy, containing a discussion of the preexilic literary prophets.

Leclerc, Thomas L., *Yahweh is Exalted in Justice: Solidarity and Conflict in Isaiah* (Minneapolis: Augsburg Fortress, 2001). A discussion of the topic of justice throughout the book of Isaiah.

Matthews, Victor H., *Social World of the Hebrew Prophets* (Peabody, Mass.: Hendrickson, 2001). A book for students aimed at acquainting them with the social and historical contexts that influenced the lives of the Hebrew prophets and those whom they addressed.

Quinn-Mascall, Peter D., *Reading Isaiah: Poetry and Vision* (Louisville, Ky.: Westminster John Knox, 2001). A practical introduction for students to Isaiah, focusing on its poetic language and imagery.

Sweeney, Marvin A. *The Prophetic Literature,* IBT (Nashville, Tenn.: Abingdon, 2005). An overview of Hebrew prophecy and the prophetic books of the Old Testament, addressing both theological and historical questions.

http://www.cliffsnotes.com/WileyCDA/LitNote/id-103,pageNum-13.html
http://www.earlyjewishwritings.com/isaiah.html
http://www.hope.edu/bandstra/RTOT/CH10/CH10_TC.HTM

Discussion Questions

1. Isaiah defines sin primarily in terms of idolatry and injustice. How do these relate to each other?

2. In the face of injustice and oppression, do you think a God of love must also be a God of wrath? If you think not, what should God's response be when human beings oppress and harm others, especially the weak and powerless? If you think so, in what ways do you think God's wrath should manifest itself?

3. In what sense can salvation be considered *conditional*, in that it depends on what human beings do, and also *unconditional*, in that God ultimately promises to save God's people, no matter what they do?

4. Do you think Isaiah's language concerning the coming of a glorious new age, consisting of "new heavens and a new earth," should be taken literally or metaphorically?

5. In your opinion, how can the idea that God chose Israel alone to be God's special people be reconciled with the idea that God loves people from *all* nations?

6. From your perspective, what are the strengths and weaknesses of Isaiah's understanding of salvation?

Chapter 2

Further Reading

Green, Joel B., The *Theology of the Gospel of Luke,* NTT (Cambridge: Cambridge University Press, 1995). A general study of the overall theology of Luke's Gospel, including his understanding of salvation.

Jervell, Jacob, *The Theology of the Acts of the Apostles,* NTT (Cambridge: Cambridge University Press, 1996). Examines the theology of the Book of Acts with special attention to its Jewish context and the story of Israel.

Kingsbury, Jack Dean, *Conflict in Luke: Jesus, Authorities, Disciples* (Minneapolis: Fortress Press, 1991). A study of the story of Luke's Gospel focusing on Jesus' conflict with the authorities and the role that Jesus' disciples play in the narrative.

Levine, Amy-Jill, ed., *A Feminist Companion to Luke* (Cleveland, Ohio: Pilgrim, 2004). A collection of essays on the Gospel of Luke written from the perspective of women and addressing feminist concerns.

Powell, Mark Allan, *Fortress Introduction to the Gospels* (Minneapolis: Fortress Press, 1998). An introduction to the contents, background, and major theological themes of the four Gospels.

Senior, Donald, *The Passion of Jesus in the Gospel of Luke* (Collegeville, Minn.: Liturgical Press, 1992). Looks at the historical and theological aspects of the story of Jesus' passion as told by Luke.

Tannehill, Robert C., *The Shape of Luke's Story: Essays on Luke-Acts* (Eugene, Ore.: Cascade Books, 2005). An analysis of the story of salvation found in Luke and Acts, revolving around both Jesus and Israel.

http://www.bibles.com/absport/news/item.php?id=156

http://www.earlychristianwritings.com/acts.html

http://www.earlychristianwritings.com/luke.html

http://www.ntgateway.com/lukeacts/

Discussion Questions

1. According to Luke, what was it about Jesus' ministry of teaching and healing that generated such conflict, and ultimately led to his death on the cross?

2. What are some of the different ways that salvation is understood and defined in Luke's writings? How does Luke compare with Isaiah in this regard?

3. Explain and evaluate Luke's idea of a divine plan of salvation foretold in the Scriptures that contemplated Jesus' life, death, and exaltation, as well as the pouring out of the Holy Spirit and the mission to all nations.

4. According to Luke, in what sense was Jesus' death "necessary"? How does this necessity relate to Luke's idea of a divine plan of salvation?

5. In what sense does Luke regard Jesus' death as being "for others"?

6. While it may be said that the story of salvation found in Luke's writings is a *Jewish* story, some have also argued that it is *anti-Jewish* in that it represents Israel as a disobedient people who rejected and crucified the Savior sent by God and are thus deserving of divine

punishment; throughout history, many have justified the persecution of Jews on this basis. To what extent would you agree with this criticism of Luke's thought?

Chapter 3

Further Reading

Brondos, David A., *Paul on the Cross: Reconstructing the Apostle's Story of Redemption* (Minneapolis: Fortress Press, 2006). A reconsideration of Paul's understanding of salvation and the cross based on recent biblical scholarship.

Davies, Margaret, *The Pastoral Epistles,* NTG (Sheffield: Sheffield Academic Press, 1996). A literary and theological background to 1 and 2 Timothy and Titus, including a discussion of their theology, Christology, eschatology, and doctrine of salvation.

Elliot, Neil, *Liberating Paul: The Justice of God and the Politics of the Apostle* (Maryknoll, N.Y.: Orbis Books, 1994). Questions many of the traditional readings of Paul, arguing that Paul proclaimed a liberating gospel in which Jesus' cross symbolized his struggle against injustice and oppression.

Gorman, Michael J., *Cruciformity: Paul's Narrative Spirituality of the Cross* (Grand Rapids, Mich.: Eerdmans, 2001). Relates Paul's experience of God and salvation to his understanding of Jesus' death and the need for believers to be conformed to the cross.

Lincoln, Andrew T. and A.J.M. Wedderburn, *The Theology of the Later Pauline Letters,* NTT (Cambridge: Cambridge University Press, 1993). A study of the main theological themes in Paul's letters to the Ephesians and Colossians, including their understanding of Christ and salvation.

Wenham, David, *Paul: Follower of Jesus or Founder of Christianity?* (Grand Rapids, Mich.: Eerdmans, 1995). Examines the question of the relationship between Jesus and Paul, arguing that Paul was strongly influenced by the Jesus tradition.

http://www.earlychristianwritings.com/
http://www.ntgateway.com/paul/
http://www.pbs.org/wgbh/pages/frontline/shows/religion/first/missions.html
http://www.thepaulpage.com/

Discussion Questions

1. What are some of the different possibilities regarding the way Paul understood the relation between sin and death? Which of these do you find most acceptable?

2. How does Paul understand the plight of human beings, and what role does Christ play in delivering them from that plight?

3. Why do you think Paul rarely alluded to what Jesus said and did during his ministry, and instead focused primarily on Jesus' death, resurrection, and exaltation?

4. Explain the difference between affirming that Jesus' death itself saves and redeems people and reconciles them to God, and saying that people are saved, redeemed, and reconciled to God *through* Jesus' death, that is, through his faithfulness unto death in seeking the salvation and redemption of others.

5. According to Paul, what does Jesus do in relation *to God* to save human beings? What does Jesus do in relation *to human beings* themselves to save them? How do these two aspects of Christ's work relate to each other?

6. How do you understand Paul's affirmations that believers are "in Christ" and have "died with Christ"? In your opinion, are these expressions to be understood literally in some sense, or only figuratively and metaphorically?

Chapter 4

Further Reading

Donovan, Mary Ann, *One Right Reading? A Guide to Irenaeus* (Collegeville, Minn.: Liturgical Press, 1997). A companion to the study of Irenaeus's *Against Heresies,* relating his thought to contemporary questions and concerns.

Grant, Robert M., *Irenaeus of Lyons,* ECF (London: Routledge, 1997). A new translation of important passages of Irenaeus's work, along with a general introduction to his thought.

Minns, Denis, *Irenaeus,* OCT (London: Geoffrey Chapman, 1994). A general introduction to Irenaeus's thought, accessible for readers of all levels.

Osborn, Eric, *Irenaeus of Lyons* (Cambridge: Cambridge University Press, 2001). Examines Irenaeus's life and theology, including particularly his doctrines of recapitulation and participation.

Wingren, Gustaf, *Man and the Incarnation: A Study in the Biblical Theology of Irenaeus,* trans. Ross MacKenzie (Eugene, Ore.: Wipf & Stock, 2004). Originally published in English in 1959, this book relates the central themes of Irenaeus's doctrine of salvation to Scripture.

http://dlibrary.acu.edu.au/research/theology/ejournal/aet_1/Casey.htm
http://www.earlychristianwritings.com/irenaeus.html
http://www.ntcanon.org/Irenaeus.shtml

Discussion Questions

1. Share your perspective on Irenaeus's idea that the first human beings were not created in a state of full perfection, but as "infants" who still needed to grow and mature.

2. Explain and evaluate Irenaeus's use of the word "man" in his doctrine of salvation.

3. What are the different ways in which Irenaeus presents the plight of human beings, and in what ways does Jesus "save" human beings in his thought?

4. In your opinion, is it possible to reconcile Irenaeus's idea that *all* people were saved objectively through Christ's incarnation, life, death, and resurrection with Irenaeus's teaching that those who do not respond subjectively in faith to what God did in Christ are *not* saved?

5. What are the different arguments that Irenaeus uses to claim that it was impossible for human beings to be saved without Christ? How do Irenaeus's arguments for the necessity of Christ's incarnation and death compare with the arguments for necessity found in Luke's writings?

6. What are the main similarities and differences between Irenaeus's understanding of salvation and those we have seen in the first three chapters? Would you agree that in some ways Irenaeus's story of salvation is no longer a Jewish story?

Chapter 5

Further Reading

Anatolios, Kahled, *Athanasius,* ECF (London: Routledge, 2004). An introduction to the life and theology of the fourth-century church father Athanasius, whose understanding of Christ and salvation heavily influenced Eastern Christian thought; includes selections from his work.

Coakley, Sarah, ed., *Re-thinking Gregory of Nyssa* (Malden, Mass.: Blackwell, 2003). A collection of essays on different aspects of Gregory's theology.

Kelly, J. N. D., *Early Christian Doctrines,* rev. ed. (New York: Continuum, 2000). A history of the development of early Christian thought, originally published in 1959.

Meredith, Anthony, S.J., *Gregory of Nyssa,* ECF (London: Routledge, 1999). Selections from Gregory's most important writings, along with an introduction to his life and theological system.

Studer, Basil, *Trinity and Incarnation: The Faith of the Early Church,* trans. Matthias Westerhoff, ed. Andrew Louth (Collegeville, Minn.: Liturgical Press, 1993). Examines the teachings of many of the church fathers from the second to the sixth century on the subject of the triune God, Christ, and salvation.

Wilkin, Robert Lewis, *The Spirit of Early Christian Thought: Seeking the Face of God* (New Haven, Conn.: Yale University Press, 2005). Accessible to laypeople, this book looks at the theology of Gregory of Nyssa and other church fathers in the context of their intellectual and spiritual world and the early years of the church.

http://en.wikipedia.org/wiki/Eastern_Orthodox_Church
http://www.iep.utm.edu/g/gregoryn.htm
http://www.newadvent.org/fathers/

Discussion Questions

1. What is the relation between Gregory's doctrine of a "double creation" and his understanding of a single human nature in which all individual human beings share?

2. Explain and evalute Gregory's view that death is not a *punishment* for human sin but rather a means for purifying human beings from their fallen state and enabling them to be transformed into a new condition.

3. According to Gregory, in what ways does Christ save human beings? In Gregory's thought, why does the incarnation of God's Son seem to be more important than his death?

4. Would you agree with Harnack's criticism that Gregory made salvation a "physico-pharmacological process," according to which Christ's incarnation, death, and resurrection "work" to produce salvific "effects" in the same ways that chemicals or medicines "work"? Do you think Gregory presents salvation as something automatic and universal?

5. Share your perspective on Gregory's idea that all people (and perhaps even the devil) will ultimately be saved, in some cases after passing through a fiery process of purification after death.

6. What do you think of Gregory's claim that he has made the Holy Scriptures the "rule and measure of every tenet" of his doctrine of salvation? Do you think it is valid for Christians to take ideas from sources other than Scripture in developing their understanding of Christ and his saving work?

Chapter 6

Further Reading

Brower, Jeffrey E. and Guilfoy, Kevin, *The Cambridge Companion to Abelard,* CCP (Cambridge: Cambridge University Press, 2005). Essays on the life and theology of Abelard, whose understanding of Christ's saving work came to be seen as an alternative to that of Anselm.

Davies, Brian and Leftow, Brian, eds., *The Cambridge Companion to Anselm,* CCP (Cambridge: Cambridge University Press, 2005). A collection of essays on Anselm's most important philosophical and theological ideas.

Denney, James, *The Death of Christ: Its Place and Interpretation in the New Testament*

(Eugene, Ore.: Wipf & Stock, 2005). A classic defense of the Anselmian understanding of Jesus' death as an atonement for human sin, written in 1900.

Evans, Gillian R., *Anselm,* OCT (Wilton, Conn.: Morehouse-Barlow, 1989). A general introduction to the thought of Anselm, considered in the context of his life and world.

Southern, Richard W., *Saint Anselm: Portrait in a Landscape* (Cambridge: Cambridge University Press, 1990). An in-depth biographical study of Anselm.

http://plato.stanford.edu/entries/anselm/

http://www.enotes.com/classical-medieval-criticism/st-anselm-canterbury

http://www.newadvent.org/cathen/01546a.htm

http://www.utm.edu/research/iep/a/anselm.htm

Discussion Questions

1. Summarize and evaluate Anselm's argument that no one can possibly be saved without Christ. Do you find that argument convincing?

2. In your opinion, is it possible to reconcile the idea that human beings sin because they are born into a fallen condition in which they are enslaved to sin and the devil with the claim that human beings have no one to blame but themselves for the sins they commit?

3. What is your opinion of Anselm's conception of God and God's nature? Do you think the image of God presented by Anselm is in continuity with biblical thought?

4. Would you agree with Anselm's claim that God's justice and righteousness would be compromised if God simply forgave human sins freely without demanding either punishment or satisfaction, such as that offered to God by Christ in his death?

5. Compare and contrast Anselm's understanding of salvation as deliverance from the punishment of sins with Gregory of Nyssa's understanding of salvation as the transformation of human nature. Which do you find more acceptable, and why?

6. In your opinion, what are the strengths and weaknesses of Anselm's understanding of salvation through Christ and his death?

Chapter 7

Further Reading

Althaus, Paul, *The Theology of Martin Luther,* trans. Robert C. Schultz (Minneapolis: Fortress Press, 1966). Written in 1961, this book is still one of the clearest and most accessible summaries of Luther's theological thought.

Aulén, Gustav, *Christus Victor: An Historical Study of the Three Main Types of the Idea of Atonement,* trans. A. G. Hebert (New York: Macmillan, 1969). First published in English in 1931 and now considered a classic, Aulén looks at the Christus Victor idea as found especially in the writings of Paul, Irenaeus, and Luther.

Forde, Gerhard, *On Being a Theologian of the Cross: Reflections on Luther's Heidelberg Disputation, 1518* (Grand Rapids, Mich.: Eerdmans, 1997). A basic, easy-to-read study on Luther's theology of the cross and its significance for contemporary life.

Lazareth, William H., *Christians in Society: Luther, the Bible, and Social Ethics* (Minneapolis: Fortress, 2001). Presents the basic themes of Luther's understanding of the story of salvation, relating this to his theological ethics.

Lohse, Bernard, *Martin Luther's Theology: Its Historical and Systematic Development,* trans. Roy A. Harrisville (Minneapolis: Fortress Press, 1999). An analysis of the development of Luther's theological thought, including a systematic survey of topics.

Marty, Martin, *Martin Luther,* PL (New York: Penguin Books, 2004). A brief and readable biography of Martin Luther, focusing on the struggles that characterized his life.

http://www.educ.msu.edu/homepages/laurence/reformation/Luther/Luther.htm
http://www.island-of-freedom.com/luther.htm
http://www.pbs.org/empires/martinluther/

Discussion Questions

1. For Luther, what role does God's law play in human salvation?

2. According to Luther, why must human beings be driven to despair before they can be saved? Would you agree with Luther on this point?

3. In Luther's thought, in what ways does Christ save human beings?

4. Explain and evaluate Luther's understanding of the "joyous exchange" between Christ and believers. What is your opinion of this idea?

5. How does Luther understand the doctrine of justification? For Luther, what is the relation between justification, faith, and good works?

6. Would you agree with the criticism that Luther is "too literalistic in his interpretations and too extreme in his expressions" and makes use of "grotesque imagery" in depicting Christ's saving work, or do you instead consider that Luther did not intend for his graphic language concerning Christ's victory over the law, sin, death, and the devil to be taken literally?

Chapter 8

Further Reading

Bouwsma, William J., *John Calvin: A Sixteenth Century Portrait* (New York: Oxford University Press, 2007). A contemporary portrayal of the life of John Calvin, including ample quotations from his writings.

Johnson, William Tracy, and John H. Leith, eds., *Reformed Reader: A Sourcebook in Christian Theology: Classical Beginnings, 1519–1799* (Louisville, Ky.: Westminster John Knox, 1993). Readings from the time of Calvin and the other Reformers to the end of the eighteenth century on the most important Reformed doctrines, including the doctrines of creation, redemption, and eschatology.

Lewis Battles, Ford, *Interpreting John Calvin,* ed. Robert Benedetto (Grand Rapids, Mich.: Baker Books, 1996). An introduction to the theology of Calvin in its historical context by one of the most highly respected Calvin scholars.

Parker, T. H. L., *Calvin: An Introduction to His Thought* (New York: Continuum, 2002). A basic summary of Calvin's doctrines of God, Jesus Christ, the Holy Spirit, and the church.

Peterson, Robert A., *Calvin's Doctrine of the Atonement* (Phillipsburg, N.J.: Presbyterian and Reformed, 1983). A study of the various understandings of Christ's saving work in the writings of Calvin.

http://www.calvin.edu/about/about_jc.htm
http://www.educ.msu.edu/homepages/laurence/reformation/Calvin/Calvin.Htm
http://www.island-of-freedom.com/CALVIN.HTM

Discussion Questions

1. Given the context in which Calvin wrote, why do you think the notion of certainty or assurance regarding salvation was so important for his teaching regarding salvation? Do you think he is successful in providing such assurance?

2. Explain and evaluate Calvin's teaching regarding original sin. Do you think Calvin's view of fallen human nature is too negative, or would you regard him as being a realist in this regard?

3. According to Calvin, how does Jesus' death save human beings? What do you regard as the strengths and weaknesses of his teaching on this subject?

4. Share your perspectives on Calvin's views concerning God's sovereignty, God's wrath, and God's grace. Do you believe Calvin's portrayal of God is faithful to Scripture?

5. Compare and contrast Calvin's understanding of Christ's work and his relation to believers with that of Luther. Where do they agree and disagree?

6. What is your opinion of Calvin's presentation of the doctrine of election or predestination? Would you agree with the claim made in the evaluation that, in order to give assurance of salvation, it is not necessary to claim that God has the *only* word, but merely that God has the *last* word?

Chapter 9

Further Reading

Hodgson, Peter C., *Liberal Theology: A Radical Vision* (Minneapolis: Fortress Press, 2007). A look at Protestant liberal theology from the nineteenth century to the present, addressing its continued relevance for today.

Jodock, Darrell, ed., *Ritschl in Retrospect: History, Community, and Science* (Minneapolis: Fortress Press, 1995). Essays discussing the most important aspects of Ritschl's thought, including his understanding of the kingdom of God and the church.

McCulloh, Gerald W., *Christ's Person and Life-Work in the Theology of Albrecht Ritschl: With Special Attention to Munus Triplex* (Lanham, Md.: University Press of America, 1990). Discusses Ritschl's presentation of Jesus' work as prophet, priest, and king, along with other aspects of Ritschl's thought.

Mueller, David L., *An Introduction to the Theology of Albrecht Ritschl* (Philadelphia: Westminster, 1969). Originally published in 1939, this book still represents one of the best introductions to Ritschl's understanding of sin, justification, and reconciliation.

Schweitzer, Albert, *The Quest of the Historical Jesus,* trans. William Montgomery (Baltimore, Md.: Johns Hopkins University Press, 1998). The classic study of the nineteenth-century reconstructions of Jesus, originally written in 1906.

Welch, Claude, *Protestant Thought in the Nineteenth Century,* 2 vol. (Eugene, Ore.: Wipf & Stock, 2003). An introduction to the Protestant theology of the 1800s, including the liberal theologians such as Ritschl.

http://people.bu.edu/wwildman/WeirdWildWeb/courses/mwt/dictionary/mwt_themes_675_ritschl.htm#Albrecht%20Ritschl%20(1822-1889)

http://www.bible.org/page.php?page_id=177

http://www.bookrags.com/Albrecht_Ritschl

http://www.newadvent.org/cathen/13086a.htm

Discussion Questions

1. Explain and evaluate Ritschl's understanding of the kingdom of God as something to be realized (perhaps gradually) *in* history rather than *beyond* history.

2. Would you agree with Ritschl's claim that before we can define what sin is, we must first define what salvation is? Or do you think we must define sin and the human plight before attempting to define what salvation consists of?

3. Share your perspectives on Ritschl's affirmation that it is impossible to speak of sinners being objects of God's love and God's wrath at the same time. Do you find the idea of a wrathful God problematic, as Ritschl did?

4. According to Ritschl, how does what Christ did make salvation possible?

5. How does Ritschl understand the relationship between Jesus' death and his life or "vocation"? What do you think of Ritschl's ideas in this regard?

6. Do you think Ritschl's understanding of salvation contains ideas that are still applicable for today, or would you regard his views as outdated?

Chapter 10

Further Reading

Braaten, Carl E., and Robert W. Jenson, eds., *A Map of Twentieth-Century Theology: Readings from Karl Barth to Radical Pluralism* (Minneapolis: Fortress Press, 1995). Passages from the writings of the key theologians of the twentieth century aimed at introducing students to the background and main themes of the period.

Bromiley, Geoffrey W., *An Introduction to the Theology of Karl Barth* (Edinburgh: T & T Clark, 1991). Following the structure of Barth's Church Dogmatics, this introduction summarizes in accessible terms Barth's thought regarding the doctrines of God, the Word of God, creation, and reconciliation.

Busch, Eberhard, *The Great Passion: An Introduction to Karl Barth's Theology* (Grand Rapids, Mich.: Eerdmans, 2004). Written by one who knew Barth well, this book looks at the central themes of Barth's theology against the background of his life and context.

Hunsinger, George, *How to Read Karl Barth: The Shape of His Theology* (New York: Oxford University Press, 1991). Presents the main motifs of Barth's *Church Dogmatics,* including his doctrines of salvation and revelation.

Webster, John, ed., *The Cambridge Companion to Karl Barth,* CCR (Cambridge: Cambridge University Press, 2000). Written by a variety of specialists in Barth's theology, this work examines Barth's understanding of doctrines such as revelation, Scripture, creation, Christ, and salvation.

http://libweb.ptsem.edu/collections/barth

http://people.bu.edu/wwildman/WeirdWildWeb/courses/mwt/dictionary/mwt_themes_750_barth.htm#top

http://www.faithnet.org.uk/Theology/barth.htm

Discussion Questions

1. Compare and contrast Barth's understanding of the doctrines of election and predestination with that of Calvin. Which of the two thinkers do you consider to be more biblical in this regard? Do you find the views of one or the other more acceptable, or would you reject out of hand any idea of election and predestination?

2. How does Barth understand the concept of "man," and what role does this understanding play in his doctrine of salvation?

3. Would you agree with the criticism that Barth's understanding of salvation is too objective, automatic, mechanical, and universal?

4. Compare and contrast Barth's "neo-orthodox" understanding of salvation in Christ with the "liberal" understanding of Ritschl. Where do they agree and disagree? To what extent is the idea that Christ saves human beings through the revelation he brings central for both?

5. Would you agree with Barth in claiming that what took place in Christ's incarnation, life, death, and resurrection had some saving effect on human beings of all times and places?

6. From your perspective, is Barth's understanding of Christ's saving work too abstract? Or do you think it has important practical applications for the contexts we live in today?

Chapter 11

Further Reading

Fergusson, David, *Bultmann,* OCT (Collegeville, Minn.: Liturgical Press, 1992). A general introduction to Bultmann's life and thought.

Inwood, Michael, *Heidegger,* PMast (New York: Oxford University Press, 1997). An introduction to the life and the existentialist philosophy of Bultmann's friend and associate Martin Heidegger, whose work heavily influenced that of Bultmann.

Johnson, Roger A., ed., *Rudolf Bultmann: Interpreting Faith for the Modern Era,* MMT (Minneapolis: Fortress Press, 1991). Selected texts from Bultmann's writings with a brief introduction to his life and thought.

Kay, James F., *Christus Praesens: A Reconsideration of Bultmann's Christology* (Grand Rapids, Mich.: Eerdmans, 1994). Examines Bultmann's understanding of Christ's presence in the proclamation of the word of God, including his interpretations of St. Paul and St. John on the subject.

Schweitzer, Albert, *The Mysticism of Paul the Apostle,* trans. William Montgomery (Baltimore: Johns Hopkins, 1998). A classic study of Paul's understanding of Christ and salvation, originally published in English in 1931, discussing many of the same questions and themes as the work of Bultmann.

http://people.bu.edu/wwildman/WeirdWildWeb/courses/mwt/dictionary/mwt_themes_760_bultmann.htm

http://theologytoday.ptsem.edu/jul1958/v15-2-article2.htm

http://www.religion-online.org/showarticle.asp?title=1827

Discussion Questions

1. Explain and evaluate Bultmann's ideas regarding the need to "demythologize" Scripture in order to make it meaningful and acceptable for modern human beings.

2. How does Bultmann define sin and death, and the relation between the two? To what extent is his thought influenced by existentialism?

3. According to Bultmann, how are human beings saved by Christ and his death and resurrection? How does his thought in this regard compare to that of Barth?

4. In Bultmann's thought, what should the relationship of the believer to the world be? How is it to be different from the relationship of the unbeliever to the world? Do you agree with Bultmann's views?

5. Share your perspectives on Bultmann's eschatology, according to which every moment of our life represents the "end" in some sense, since we are constantly deciding between life and death.

6. Would you agree with the criticism that Bultmann undermines the Christian faith because he no longer bases it on historical events, such as Jesus' resurrection? Or do you believe that one can be a faithful Christian without believing literally in Jesus' bodily resurrection?

Chapter 12

Further Reading

Boff, Leonardo, *Jesus Christ Liberator: A Critical Christology for Our Time,* trans. Patrick Hughes (Maryknoll, N.Y.: Orbis Books, 1978). A Latin American study of Jesus' life and death addressing many of the same themes as the work of Sobrino, written from a similar perspective.

Burke, Kevin F., *The Ground Beneath the Cross: The Theology of Ignacio Ellacuría* (Washington, D.C.: Georgetown University Press, 2000). An introduction to the life and thought of Ignacio Ellacuría, who played an important role in the development of Sobrino's understanding of the cross as his close friend and associate before he was murdered in 1989 during the civil war in El Salvador.

Ellacuría, Ignacio, and Jon Sobrino, eds., *Mysterium Liberationis: Fundamental Concepts of Liberation Theology* (Maryknoll, N.Y.: Orbis Books, 2004). A systematic theology with chapters on the basic doctrines of the Christian faith written by prominent Latin American liberation theologians.

Moltmann, Jürgen, *The Crucified God: The Cross of Christ as the Foundation and Criticism of Christian Theology,* trans. Margaret Kohl (Minneapolis: Fortress Press, 1993). Originally written in 1972, this study on the relation of the theology of the cross to human liberation was influential in the work of Sobrino.

Pope-Levison, Priscilla, and Jon Levison, *Jesus in Global Contexts* (Louisville, Ky.: Westminster John Knox, 1992). Examines the new understandings of Jesus and his life and death proposed by theologians in Latin America, Asia, Africa, and North America from a liberationist perspective.

Waltermire, Donald E., *The Liberation Christologies of Leonardo Boff and Jon Sobrino: Latin American Contributions to Contemporary Christology* (Lanham, Md.: University Press of America, 1994). Summarizes and analyzes the thought of Leonardo Boff and Jon Sobrino regarding the person and work of Christ.

http://theologytoday.ptsem.edu/oct1994/v51-3-churchworld1.htm

http://www.iep.utm.edu/e/ellacuria.htm

http://www.liberationtheology.org/

Discussion Questions

1. How does Sobrino's understanding of sin, death, and salvation differ from those of the figures we have seen previously in this book?

2. Do you agree with Sobrino's claim that the Bible presents both God and Jesus showing partiality to the poor? Should faithful Christians and the church show such partiality to the poor today?

3. According to Sobrino, what was Jesus attempting to accomplish in his ministry, and why did it lead to his death?

4. For Sobrino, in what way does Jesus' death contribute to human salvation? What does it reveal?

5. Explain and evaluate Sobrino's claim that the crucified people bring salvation to the world.

6. What role does the idea of "utopia" play in Sobrino's understanding of salvation? Would you consider Sobrino utopian?

Chapter 13

Further Reading

Brown, Joanne Carlson, and Carol R. Bohn, eds., *Christianity, Patriarchy, and Abuse: A Feminist Critique* (New York: Pilgrim Press, 1989). A collection of essays examining how Christian theology, and especially the traditional understandings of Jesus and his death, have contributed to injustice and violence toward women.

Darby, Kathleen Ray, *Deceiving the Devil: Atonement, Abuse, and Ransom* (Cleveland, Ohio: Pilgrim Press, 1998). Addresses the subjects of sin, evil, salvation, atonement, and the death of Christ from a critical feminist perspective.

Grey, Mary, *Feminism, Redemption, and the Christian Tradition* (Mystic, Conn.: Twenty-Third Publications, 1990). Challenges the traditional definitions of women and God handed down by the church, and explores how to reinterpret the traditional Christian views regarding redemption and atonement in ways that are meaningful and liberating for women.

Heyward, Carter, *Saving Jesus from Those Who Are Right: Rethinking What It Means to Be Christian* (Minneapolis: Fortress Press, 1999). A feminist reflection on the significance of Jesus for us today as we address contemporary problems and concerns.

LaCugna, Catherine Mowry, ed., *Freeing Theology: The Essentials of Theology in Feminist Perspective* (San Francisco: HarperSanFrancisco, 1993). Essays by women theologians on the classical themes of Christian systematic theology.

Snyder, Mary Hembrow, *The Christology of Rosemary Radford Ruether: A Critical Introduction* (Mystic, Conn.: Twenty-Third Publications, 1988). A study of Ruether's understanding of Jesus' person and work, as well as her personal history and theological methodology.

http://people.bu.edu/wwildman/WeirdWildWeb/courses/mwt/dictionary/mwt_themes_908_ruether.htm#top

http://womenshistory.about.com/od/rosemaryruether/Rosemary_Radford_Ruether_Feminist_Theologian.htm

http://www.bookrags.com/biography/rosemary-radford-ruether/

http://www.theology.ie/theologians/ruether.htm

Discussion Questions

1. What is the starting point and the critical principle of Ruether's understanding of salvation? To what extent is this derived from Scripture? Do you agree with Ruether on this point?

2. How does Ruether define sin and salvation? How does her view of salvation, and especially eschatology, differ from traditional Christian thought?

3. For Ruether, what is the relation between the patriarchal oppression of women and the ecological damage being done to the earth by human beings?

4. Would you agree with Ruether's affirmation that we must include both male and female metaphors in speaking of God (or God/ess), rather than using exclusively masculine language for God as in the Bible and Christian tradition? Should we refer to God as a "he," as a "she," as both "he" and "she" alternatively, or avoid using personal pronouns entirely?

5. According to Ruether, in what way does Jesus contribute to human salvation? In what sense is he unique as Christ, and in what sense is he *not* unique as Christ? Do you find Ruether's ideas acceptable?

6. In Ruether's thought, to what extent does God save human beings, and to what extent must we seek to save ourselves rather than expecting an all-powerful God to come and save us? What is your perspective in this regard?

GLOSSARY

Anabaptist: belonging to one of the religious groups that arose in the Reformation period in opposition to both Roman Catholicism and Protestantism; these groups rejected infant baptism, teaching that those who had been baptized as infants needed to be rebaptized ("ana-" is of Greek origin, meaning "again"), and generally practiced pacifism

apocalyptic: a view of history according to which God is in control of the course of human events and will bring about a sudden, cataclysmic end to the present age in order to inaugurate a new one; apocalyptic thought also stresses that this world lies under the influence of evil and demonic powers that will ultimately be defeated

apostasy: a revolt against God rooted in a rejection of faith in God

Arianism: a movement arising in the fourth century CE that adhered to the views of Arius, who rejected the belief that God's Son was fully divine; Arius' teaching was condemned as heretical by orthodox Christians

biblical theology: a theology that attempts to reconstruct the beliefs of the biblical writers in their original historical contexts, inquiring as to what biblical texts originally meant (rather than their meaning for us today)

***Christus Victor* idea:** an understanding of Christ's work that centers on his triumph over the devil and the forces of evil through his life, death, and resurrection

concupiscence: the innate inclination or desire to sin found in all fallen human beings, according to certain understandings of original or inherited sin

corruption: a condition characteristic of fallen human beings, according to which their bodies gradually grow old, die, and decay

crusade: one of the military expeditions made by European Christians between 1095 and 1291 aimed at taking back the Holy Land from the Muslims

cultic: related to worship and the rituals associated with worship, such as the offering of sacrifices

determinism: the doctrine that the course of history as a whole was determined by God ahead of time; absolute determinism involves the belief that God alone has preordained everything that takes place, so that human beings have no real free will

dialectic: the use of dialogue, reason, or logic to examine beliefs and ideas, often involving the claim that the truth can only be expressed fully by letting apparently contradictory statements stand in tension alongside one another

dogma: a doctrinal formulation that must be accepted as true because it has been established by the authority of the church

Eastern Orthodoxy: the historical expression of Christianity that became predominant in Eastern Europe and areas around the eastern part of the Mediterranean Sea, which traces its roots back to the time of the apostles and accepts as authoritative the creedal formulations of the seven ecumenical councils and the writings of the church fathers

Enlightenment: the eighteenth-century intellectual movement that emphasized reason, science, individualism, and human freedom over against tradition, irrationality, and tyranny

eschatology: the part of theology having to do with the end of the present world and the final destiny of humanity, both on an individual and a universal level

excommunicate: to officially exclude a person from the fellowship of the church and participation in the sacraments

existentialism: a philosophy that teaches that each individual person has the freedom and responsibility to determine his or her own development and create meaning for his or her life

feudal: pertaining to the social system of medieval Europe in which the common people were subject to a lord, who provided them with land and protection in exchange for their service and allegiance

fiat: a Latin word meaning "Let it be done"; in theology, this generally refers to God's power to bring some reality into being merely by willing it to be so

forensic: having to do with a court of law; when used in connection with the doctrine of justification, it refers to God's gracious decision to declare sinners righteous in spite of the fact that they have no actual righteousness of their own

Gnostic: pertaining to a system of beliefs that arose in the first or second century CE, according to which salvation involves receiving esoteric knowledge (Greek: "gnosis") regarding the nature of reality through a figure sent from God; most Gnostics also posited the existence of divine beings other than the one supreme God, and believed that the material world was evil

Hellenistic: relating to ancient Greek life, thought, and culture from the fourth century BCE to the time of the Roman Empire

hermeneutics: the study of the interpretation of texts, especially those from the Bible

historical Jesus: a reconstruction of the man Jesus of Nazareth as he "really was" made by historians using the historical method

historical-critical method: a methodology based on scientific presuppositions and theories used to study the origin of the biblical writings and to attempt to understand them in their original contexts

imputation: the act of reckoning or accounting something to someone; when used in connection with the doctrine of justification, this involves graciously reckoning the righteousness of Christ to believers, rather than imparting to them or infusing into them an actual righteousness coming from God

incorruption: a condition into which those human beings saved by God will be transformed following the resurrection of the dead, in which their bodies will no longer grow old, die, or decay

juristic: relating to legal matters, including the relation of human beings to God as their judge

justification: the divine act of declaring believers righteous and thus acceptable before God, in spite of their sins

kerygma: the content of the gospel as it was proclaimed by Jesus' first followers

liberal theology: the Christian theology that originated in the eighteenth and nineteenth centuries emphasizing the freedom of theologians to question and reformulate traditional Christian teachings and bring them into harmony with the modern scientific worldview

mediator: one who intervenes between two parties, such as God and humanity, in order to bring about unity or reconciliation between them

metaphysical: having to do with the ultimate nature of reality, particularly that which lies beyond what is perceptible to the senses

Mosaic law: the law of Moses or Torah, as found in the first five books of the Bible

mystery religions: religions of antiquity characterized by a belief that one could gain access to divine mysteries or to a hidden wisdom regarding the nature of the world and the divine after a ceremonial initiation into the group in which one was thought to die and rise again in some sense

ontological: having to do with the being, essence, or existence of something or someone

parousia: the second coming of Christ to judge the living and dead and inaugurate a new age

patristic: having to do with the church fathers, especially those of the first five centuries of the church's existence

praxis: action, especially oriented toward ministering to others, carried out on the basis of one's faith

penal substitution: the suffering of a penalty deserved by others in their place, with the result that they are no longer subject to that penalty

presbyter: an ordained minister of the church

propitiate: to carry out an act that appeases or placates the wrath of another, such as God

Protestant orthodoxy: a movement in the churches of the Reformation that understood the Christian faith primarily in terms of a system of doctrines that had to be kept pure; this movement was opposed to Protestant liberal theology

purgatory: a realm or state into which one enters immediately after death in order to be purified from one's sinful condition by means of some type of suffering prior to being taken into an eternal blessed existence in heaven

recapitulation: the act of bringing all things together under a single head, such as God or Christ

reconciliation: the restoration of a right relationship brought about by the overcoming of estrangement and enmity

redemption: the salvation or deliverance of people and the world in which they live from a condition of slavery or oppression

Reformed: belonging to a church that developed out of the Reformation movement led by Calvin and other Reformers in Switzerland

sanctification: the process of becoming holy in life and deed, generally said to follow upon the justification and regeneration of believers

satisfaction: a payment or compensation made to another person to make up for having wronged that person in some way

sovereignty: absolute power and authority over all people and things

summum bonum: Latin for the "greatest good," that is, what is to be valued above all else

Synoptic Gospels: the New Testament Gospels according to Matthew, Mark, and Luke, which share many features in common that distinguish them from the Gospel according to John

tabernacle: to make one's dwelling in a certain place in order to be worshiped there

transcendence: the quality of existing far above all people and things

INDEX

Abelard, 85, 92-93, 123-24, 150, 179, 194
Adam, 36-38, 48, 50-51, 56, 58, 65-67, 73, 77-
    80, 90, 99, 105, 110, 119, 121, 134
Akers, Samuel Luttrel, 194
Albertz, Rainer, 6, 187
Allen, Diogenes, 199
Althaus, Paul, 192-93
angels, 19, 23-25, 66, 78-79
Anselm, 76-87, 95, 108, 110, 191-92
Arianism/Arius, 64, 68
apocalyptic, 51, 63, 152, 166
Apollinarius, 64, 68
apostles (disciples), 20, 22-32, 34, 36, 42-43,
    49, 56, 59, 125, 150, 163, 166, 177-78
Arnold, Clinton E., 189
Asford, Sally, 198
Ashcraft, Morris, 142, 196
Ashley, J. Matthew, 197
Athanasius, 64
atonement, 1-2, 89, 94-95, 102, 109, 111, 149,
    153, 162, 178, 183, 198
Augustine, 76, 105, 121
Aulén, Gustav, 56, 190

baptism, 2, 20, 23-24, 27, 30, 47, 54-55, 72-
    73, 101, 114, 128, 139, 148-49, 154,
    180, 195
Barclay, John M. G., 189
Barth, Karl, 130-41, 149, 183, 195-96
Basil, 64-65
Berkouwer, G. C., 137, 195
Berry, Wanda Warren, 172, 198
Best, Ernest, 189
biblical theology, 141-42, 183, 193
Blenkinsopp, Joseph, 187
Bloesch, Donald G., 195
Bock, Darrell, 188
Boersma, Hans, 190, 193
Brondos, David, 189, 193

Brueggemann, Walter, 187
Bultmann, Rudolf, 141-53, 183, 196-97
Burns, J. Patout, 191

Cahill, Joseph, 152, 196
Calvin, John, 103-115, 121, 124, 131-32, 193-
    94
Carpenter, Craig B., 194
Carr, Anne E., 198
Christus Victor idea, 46, 56-58, 60-61, 85, 92,
    94, 97, 123, 184, 192, 195
church, 2, 23-24, 26-28, 30, 33-34, 36, 39, 43-
    47, 49, 59, 64, 72-74, 76-77, 87-89, 92,
    98, 101, 103-4, 111-12, 114-18, 122-29,
    139, 144-45, 147, 149, 152-54, 165-71,
    177-80, 184, 195
    definitions of, 23, 47, 59, 114, 127-28, 139,
        152-53, 167, 179-80
    mission of, 26-27, 59, 101, 114, 128, 139,
        152-53, 167, 170, 179-80, 195
commandments. See law
community. See church
condemnation, 15, 30, 33, 48, 56-57, 59, 83-84,
    89-90, 92-93, 95-96, 98, 105-8, 110-11,
    121, 137-38, 184
Cook, Michael L., 157, 197
Cosgrove, Charles H., 188
covenant, 11, 13, 26, 28, 40, 43-45, 48, 131,
    134-35, 139, 184
creation, 1, 12, 14-15, 35-36, 38-39, 49-51, 55,
    58, 60-62, 65-67, 77-78, 80, 86, 89-90,
    92, 104-6, 118, 127, 131-34, 142, 144-
    45, 158, 172-76, 178-81
Culpepper, Robert H., 193

Dahl, Nils Alstrup, 196
Daley, Brian E., 51, 190-91
Darwin, Charles, 116
Davies, Margaret, 189

death (human), 8, 10, 17, 26, 36-38, 47-48, 51,
    55-57, 60-61, 67-70, 74, 79, 81-82, 87,
    89-90, 92-95, 97-98, 100-101, 107-8,
    121, 132, 135-38, 145-49, 151-53, 159,
    161, 163-66, 173, 178-81
demons. See evil powers
devil, 14, 20, 31-32, 36-38, 48, 51-52, 56-61,
    67, 70-73, 77-79, 83-85, 88-90, 92-94,
    97-98, 101-2, 105-8
Dille, Sarah J., 187
Dillistone, Frederick W., 192-93
disciples. See apostles
Doble, Peter, 188
Dumais, Marcel, 197
Dunn, James D. G., 189

election, 12-14, 16, 18, 33, 35-36, 78, 104, 106-
    7, 111-13, 115, 127, 131-32, 135, 195
Ellacuría, Ignacio, 155, 163, 197
eschatology, 1, 11-12, 14-18, 29-30, 33, 36, 39,
    42, 44, 46, 48, 50-51, 61, 63, 73, 75, 78,
    100-101, 112-13, 116, 118-19, 121, 128,
    138-40, 147-49, 151-53, 158, 166-67,
    176-77, 180-181, 184
eternal life, 25, 42, 47, 51, 68-69, 73, 78, 87,
    98-100, 112-13, 119, 127, 139-40, 151,
    153, 180
Eucharist. See Lord's Supper
Evans, Gillian R., 191
evil powers, 1, 14, 20, 22, 31, 36-38, 46, 48, 63,
    79, 142, 157-58
existentialism, 141-43, 152

faith, 1, 23, 26-30, 35-36, 40-43, 45-47, 49, 55,
    57, 59, 63-64, 72, 74, 84-85, 87-89, 91-
    93, 97-104, 111, 113-18, 122-23, 127,
    138-40, 142, 144, 147-53, 167-68
fall (of humanity into sin), 36, 51, 60, 66-68,
    78-79, 90-92, 104-7, 119, 121, 131-32,
    134, 144-45, 147, 149, 173-74, 178
Fergusson, David, 197
Fiddes, Paul S., 86, 192
Fitzmyer, Joseph A., 188
flesh, 45, 50-51, 53-56, 66, 69-71, 75, 82, 94,
    97, 100, 108, 110, 112, 145-47, 152
Forde, Gerhard, 91, 192, 194
forgiveness, 1, 9-11, 20, 22, 25-26, 28-31, 35,
    41, 43-45, 59, 81, 83-85, 87-88, 99, 101,
    103, 108, 110-11, 113-14, 122-28, 150-
    51, 159, 163, 165, 184, 195
Foster, A. Durwood, 121, 194
Friedan, Betty, 169

Furnish, Victor, 189

Garlington, Don B., 189
Gelston, Anthony, 187
Gentiles (nations), 7, 10, 12-16, 19, 24-27, 30-
    38, 42-43, 45, 48-49, 74, 128-29
Gnosticism, 143, 148
God,
    as creator, 1, 12, 14-15, 35-36, 38, 50-51,
        55, 60-62, 64-67, 77-78, 86, 89-90, 92,
        104-6, 131-34, 144-45, 158, 172, 174-
        76, 178-79, 187
    grace of, 10-11, 15, 26, 30, 40-41, 88-89,
        91-92, 98-101, 108-13, 115, 118, 122-
        25, 147, 150-51, 158, 180, 193
    image of, 50-51, 65-67, 73, 90, 100, 105,
        174, 184
    justice/righteousness of, 17, 45, 56, 61-62,
        70, 75, 79, 81-83, 85-86, 94-95, 102,
        107-11, 132, 160
    love of, 2, 8-10, 15, 17, 21-22, 41, 44, 67-
        68, 75, 89, 91, 93, 99, 102, 110, 118,
        121-26, 132, 134, 152, 161-66, 168,
        178, 184
    omnipotence of, 14, 56, 60-62, 65, 68, 81,
        86, 95, 104, 106, 108, 130, 163-65, 181
    sovereignty of, 14-15, 104, 106-7, 115, 118,
        130, 144
    spirit of. See Holy Spirit
    wrath of, 2, 7-8, 10, 12-13, 33, 44, 48, 59,
        83, 88, 90-98, 102, 108-112, 121-24,
        129, 131-32, 134, 138, 184, 194
Gollwitzer, Helmut, 139, 195
gospel, 24-27, 33-34, 36, 39, 43, 46, 63, 88-89,
    92, 101, 111, 113-14, 128, 130, 139,
    142-44, 147, 168, 194
Gospels, 19-33, 35, 38-39, 41-43, 46-48, 61,
    63, 108, 117, 124, 144-49, 151-52, 157,
    161-63, 177, 197
Gowan, Donald E., 187
Gregory Nazianzus, 65, 70
Gregory of Nyssa, 64-78, 82, 85-86, 93, 190-
    91
Grensted, L. W., 192
Grenz, Stanley J., 118, 194
guilt, 1, 11, 18, 38, 79, 81, 83-84, 88, 90, 92, 94,
    98, 105, 108, 113, 121-23, 149-50, 172
Gunton, Colin E., 190, 195
Gutierrez, Gustavo, 155, 197

Haight, Roger, 163, 192, 197
Hall, Douglas John, 197

Harnack, Adolf von, 72, 191
Harrison, Nonna Verna, 191
Harrisville, Roy A., 196
Hart, D. Bentley, 191-92
Hart, Trevor, 190, 193
Hasel, Frank, 137, 195
Hayes, John Haralson, 187
heaven, 12, 23, 29, 36, 39, 50-51, 78, 100, 111-13, 127, 137, 149, 172, 180
Hefner, Philip, 127, 194
Heidegger, Martin, 141, 196
hell, 73, 83, 90, 93, 95, 97, 108-9, 149
Helm, Paul, 193
Hemer, Colin J., 188
heresy, 49, 54, 62, 64, 68, 88, 171, 177
Heyward, Carter, 198
Hicks, Edward, 188
history, 1, 11-12, 14-15, 18, 30, 35, 39, 51, 63-64, 104, 115-19, 121, 127, 129-130, 132, 136-37, 139-40, 142-44, 147, 150, 152-53, 156-158, 161-62, 164-74, 176, 178-81, 184
Holl, Karl, 100
Holy Spirit, 2, 11, 16, 20, 23-25, 27-28, 30-31, 38-42, 44-45, 47, 50, 55-56, 61-65, 72-73, 87, 99-101, 111-15, 128, 131, 139, 153, 174, 177, 179, 198
Hopkins, Jasper, 191
Hume, David, 116
Hunsinger, George, 196

idolatry, 6-7, 10-11, 161, 166
immortality, 51, 55, 59-61, 66-74, 77-79, 151, 181
incorruptibility, 50, 54-56, 58-61, 68-69, 73
injustice, 5-8, 10, 16-18, 20, 79, 81, 86, 105, 107, 154-61, 163-64, 167-68, 170, 172-74, 176-81
Irenaeus, 49-63, 68, 70, 76, 78, 85, 132, 183, 189-90
Isaiah, 5-20, 26, 29-33, 48, 62, 86-87, 183, 187-88
Israel, 1, 5-20, 22-26, 28-31, 35, 38, 40-43, 45, 48, 63, 74-75, 134, 160, 171

Jenson, Joseph, 187
Jervell, Jacob, 188
Jesus Christ,
  as king, 19, 32, 111-12, 124-25
  as Messiah, 19-20, 22-23, 25, 29-31, 47, 74, 147, 165, 176-77
  as priest, 59, 111-12, 124-25, 165
  as prophet, 22, 26-27, 41, 111-12, 124, 151, 161, 166, 171, 176-78
  ascension of, 23, 28, 112, 114
  birth of, 5, 19, 26, 38, 69, 98, 112
  blood of, 26-28, 35, 43-46, 53, 70, 83, 85-86, 95, 101, 108-110, 154
  conflict with authorities, 20-24, 32, 41, 126, 159, 161-63, 177
  death, crucifixion, cross of, 1-2, 22-30, 32-36, 38-49, 51-52, 55-63, 68-70, 72, 74, 77, 81-87, 92-98, 102, 107-15, 122-23, 126-29, 131-32, 135-39, 144, 147-54, 162-66, 177-79, 183-84
  divinity of, 35, 49, 55-57, 59, 61, 64, 68-74, 81-82, 94-95, 108, 117, 124, 127, 131, 135, 150, 163-64, 166, 194
  Godward activity of, 44, 59, 100-101, 111-12, 124-25
  historical, 38-39, 117, 127, 144, 156-57, 162, 165-66, 176-79
  incarnation of, 2, 51-64, 68-72, 74, 77, 81-83, 85, 94-95, 97, 108, 131-37, 162-64, 166, 178-79, 183
  life and ministry of, 1-2, 19-23, 26-30, 38-45, 48, 51, 55, 58-59, 63, 71-75, 87, 95-96, 111, 122-28, 144, 147, 157-163, 165-66, 176-79, 183-84
  lordship of, 19-20, 23, 30, 36, 39, 41-42, 44, 47, 89, 94, 97, 101, 123-27, 144, 147, 150, 152, 165-66, 177
  obedience of, 44-45, 57, 81, 83, 95-97, 110, 113, 125, 132, 138, 163
  passion of, 22-26, 43, 47, 52, 60, 69, 96, 131, 154, 162-64, 178, 190
  preexistence of, 35, 127-28, 144, 148, 166
  presence of, 27-28, 97-99, 101, 112, 147, 149-50, 179
  present/ongoing work of, 27-29, 44, 97-101, 111-13, 119, 127
  rejection of, 22, 24, 26-27, 31, 43, 132, 177
  resurrection of, 1-2, 22-25, 27-31, 36, 38-40, 44-47, 51-52, 55-57, 63, 68-70, 72, 74, 87, 93, 97-98, 114, 116-17, 127, 132, 137, 139, 142, 147-53, 157, 165-67, 177-79, 183-84
  second coming of, 27-29, 39, 43-47, 52, 63, 139-140, 142, 152, 177, 179-80, 184
  teaching of, 20, 22-23, 27, 31, 38-41, 44, 48, 58, 71-72, 124, 147, 157, 161, 171
John (Evangelist), 142-149, 151-52
John the Baptist, 19-20

Jorgenson, Allen, 195
judgment, 15, 30, 36-37, 40, 48, 88, 99, 112-13, 132, 136-37, 144
justice, 6, 10-11, 15-17, 20-21, 56, 62, 70, 75, 79, 81-86, 94-95, 102, 105, 108, 110, 132, 153, 155, 157-61, 164-168, 170, 172-73, 179-81, 184
    social, 6, 17, 128, 152-53, 155, 157-61, 164-168, 170, 172-73, 176-77, 179-81
justification, 31, 35, 39-41, 45-46, 98-101, 113-15, 122-23, 125, 128, 137-40, 147

Kant, Immanuel, 116, 118
Kelly, J. N. D., 191, 201
kingdom (reign) of God, 15-16, 19-20, 23, 26-30, 39, 43-44, 81, 112-13, 118-20, 122, 124-30, 139-40, 147, 152, 158-63, 166-68, 172, 176-78, 180
Kingsbury, Jack Dean, 20, 188
Knudsen, Robert D., 196
Küng, Hans, 195

Laato, Antti, 187
law, 6-11, 14, 20-22, 24-25, 28, 31, 33, 38, 40-41, 43, 45, 48, 59, 86, 89-97, 99-100, 108, 111, 124, 145-47, 149, 151, 161, 194
Lazareth, William, 92, 192
Leclerc, Thomas L., 195
Lienhard, Marc, 89, 192
Lilburne, Geoffrey R., 169-70, 197
Lindbeck, George, 198
Loewe, William, 190
Loewenich, Walter von, 192
Lord's Supper, 2, 26-28, 43, 47, 55, 63, 72, 101-2, 112, 114, 128, 139, 148-49, 167, 180, 193
Lossky, Vladimir, 191
Lotz, David W., 194
Luke, 19-35, 39-41, 43, 46-48, 50, 52, 62, 87, 161, 167, 183-84, 188
Luther, Martin, 88-103, 108, 110, 113, 115, 122, 151, 192-93

McClear, Ernest V., 191
McCormack, Bruce L., 110, 193
McCulloh, Gerald W., 194
McDonnell, Kilian, 193
McGovern, Arthur F., 159, 167, 197
McGrath, Alister E., 99, 123, 191-92
McIntyre, John, 79, 191

Macquarrie, John, 196
Maddox, Robert, 188
Malevez, Léopold, 150, 196
"man", 2-3, 50-63, 65-69, 71-73, 77-81, 83-84, 105, 131-40, 169, 172-74, 176, 178
Marshall, I. Howard, 188
Matera, Frank J., 188
Messiah, 15-16, 19-20, 22-23, 25, 29-31, 48, 61, 74, 147, 165, 176-77
Meyendorff, John, 191
Michel, Otto, 196
Miegge, Giovanni, 196
Miller, James D., 189
Minns, Denis, 50, 189-90
Moltmann, Jürgen, 163, 197
Moo, Douglas A., 189
Mueller, David L., 119, 194
Muller, Richard A., 193
mystery. See plan (of salvation)
mystery religions, 143, 148
mystical union. See union with Christ
myth, 49, 58, 123, 142-44, 148-50, 152, 183

nations. See Gentiles
nature, 3, 11, 37-38, 53-56, 60-62, 65-75, 77-79, 82, 84-86, 90-93, 95, 101, 105, 108, 110, 116, 121, 130, 134-36, 173-75, 178, 181, 183-84
    divine, 54-56, 60-62, 65-74, 82, 86, 95, 108, 110, 183
    human, 3, 37-38, 53-56, 60-62, 65-75, 77-79, 82, 84-85, 90-93, 101, 105, 108, 121, 130, 134-36, 174, 181, 183-84
Nave, Jr., Guy D., 188
necessity (arguments for), 1, 25-27, 48, 59-62, 68-70, 77, 81-83, 85-86, 94-95, 108, 110, 115, 122, 126-27, 132, 134, 153, 162-63, 178, 183
new covenant, 26, 28, 40, 43-45, 184
New Testament, 5, 19-52, 60, 62-63, 74-75, 77, 87, 108-9, 111, 140-53, 156-57, 166, 168, 176, 183-84
Nicole, Roger, 193
Niesel, Wilhelm, 194
Noormann, Rolf, 190

O'Toole, Robert F., 188
obedience (of believers), 1, 8, 10-11, 14, 17, 20, 28, 30, 33, 36, 40-41, 44-45, 50, 57-58, 79, 81, 87, 90, 97, 106, 110-11, 118, 139, 146, 151

Oden, Thomas C., 196
Old Testament, 5-18, 32, 52, 110, 142, 160, 168, 176, 184
Olson, Roger E., 194
Osborn, Eric, 50, 189-90
Owen, Huw P., 151, 196

paradise, 12, 51, 65, 67, 73, 78-79, 81, 173
Parker, T. H. L., 193
patriarchy, 169-70, 172-74, 176-81
Paul, 19, 23-27, 31, 34-48, 50, 52-53, 62-63, 87-88, 98, 130, 142-49, 151, 153, 183-84, 189
Paul, Robert S., 191
penal substitution, 17, 38, 46, 94-97, 102, 108-11, 113, 122-23, 129, 136-37, 153, 193
Pentecost, 23, 25
Persaud, Winston D., 197
persecution, 23-24, 26, 33, 49, 64, 103, 159, 162
Peters, Ted, 198
Peterson, Robert A., 193
Peura, Simo, 99, 193
Pitkin, Barbara, 193
plan (of salvation), 1, 14-15, 24-27, 32-33, 35-36, 43, 45, 48, 50-51, 60, 62, 80-81, 89, 106-7, 131, 144, 161, 164, 183
Platonism, 53-54, 62, 65, 74-75, 132-33, 135, 190
poverty, 6, 8, 15, 20, 29, 33, 154-56, 158-62, 164-68, 177-78
predestination. See election
Pregeant, Russell, 198
punishment, 2, 7-10, 12-18, 33, 38, 51, 67, 75, 79-81, 85-87, 94-97, 102, 105, 108-13, 121-23, 136, 145, 149, 164, 173, 178, 184
purgatory, 73, 88
purification, 8-9, 11, 14, 17-18, 45, 67-68, 73, 75, 110

Quinn-Mascall, Peter D., 187

Räisänen, Heikki, 188
ransom, 46, 70, 77, 94, 111
recapitulation, 36, 50, 52, 55, 63, 190
reconciliation, 17, 35, 39, 43-46, 55, 109-10, 113, 119, 122-25, 128, 131-32, 137-40, 151, 158, 180, 184
redemption, 1-3, 5, 9-10, 13-14, 17, 19, 26, 29, 31, 34-35, 39, 44-51, 53-59, 62-63, 70,

73-74, 77, 83-85, 87, 89, 92, 94, 100, 104, 112, 118, 122, 131-32, 137, 148, 153, 163, 167-71, 174, 177-80, 183-84
magical views of, 55, 74, 153
mechanical views of, 74, 98, 110, 128, 140
Redding, Graham, 115, 194
repentance, 5-6, 8, 10-11, 14, 19-20, 22-23, 25-27, 30-31, 33, 41, 74, 84-85, 93, 111, 121, 127, 138, 188
revelation, 26, 30, 36, 38, 43-44, 49, 52-53, 58-62, 91, 93, 98, 104, 107, 117, 119-20, 122-26, 128-29, 134, 139-40, 145, 148-49, 152, 163-66, 171, 178, 183-84
Richmond, James, 194
Ritschl, Albrecht, 116-29, 134, 150, 152, 159, 183, 194
Ritt, Paul E., 166, 197
Roetzel, Calvin, 189
Rondet, Henri, 89, 192
Ruether, Rosemary Radford, 2, 169-81, 197-98

Sachs, John R., 191
sacraments, 2, 73-74, 87, 101-2, 114, 128, 139, 148-49, 180
sacrifice, 6, 10-11, 16-17, 28, 44-45, 59, 95, 107-15, 122, 138, 147-50, 162-63, 193
salvation, 1-3, 5, 10-21, 24-33, 35-36, 38-48, 50-63, 68-77, 82-100, 105-15, 118-19, 122-32, 134-40, 142, 147-53, 157-58, 160-69, 171-72, 176-81, 183-84
definitions of, 1, 11-14, 29-30, 39, 51, 68-69, 85, 104-5, 112-13, 119, 139, 149-51, 157-58, 164, 172
objective, 1, 33, 46, 55, 57-58, 63, 69, 74, 84, 111, 113, 123, 135-40, 150-51, 183-84
subjective, 1, 46, 55, 58, 84, 87, 113, 123, 138-39, 151
sanctification, 101, 113-14, 138-39
Sanders, E. P., 153, 197
Satan. See devil
satisfaction, 17, 80-87, 94-97, 102, 108-11, 122, 127, 162
Schäfer, Rolf, 123, 194
Schleiermacher, Friedrich, 116-17
Schmithals, Walter, 196
Schmitt, John J., 187
Schnackenburg, Rudolf, 188
Schroeder, Christoph, 17, 188

Schwarz, Hans, 198
Scott, Waldron, 195
Scotus, Duns, 108
Scriptures, fulfillment of, 16, 19, 24-26, 32,
    36, 44-45, 48, 52, 62, 183, 190
Scuiry, Daniel E., 191
Sharp, Douglas R., 195
sin, 1-2, 5-12, 14-18, 20, 26, 28-31, 33, 36-39,
    41, 43-46, 48, 51, 55-56, 58-61, 66-68,
    72-73, 80-102, 105-14, 119-28, 131-38,
    144-51, 153, 157-59, 161-64, 172-73,
    176-81, 184
    as injustice, oppression, 5-7, 157-59, 161-
        65, 172-74, 176-79
    consequences of, 9-10, 38, 68, 79, 121, 145,
        159
    definitions of, 6-7, 31, 79, 119-20, 134,
        145, 159, 172-73
    extrinsic/intrinsic distinction, 9-10, 38,
        79, 121
    original/inherited, 37, 79, 82, 90-92, 105,
        121, 145, 158, 173-74
    penalty of, 1, 38, 79, 87, 94-97, 102, 105,
        108-11, 113, 122-23, 136, 149
    power of, 1, 37, 48, 56, 58, 60-61, 74, 84,
        88, 93-95, 99, 105, 107-8, 113, 145-47,
        149-50, 153, 159, 184
    structural, 158-59, 161, 169, 177
Snyder, Mary Hembrow, 198
Sobrino, Jon, 154-68, 176-77, 197
Sontag, Frederick, 198
Southern, Richard W., 79, 191-92
Squires, John T., 188
Stanton, Graham, 189
suffering, 7-10, 12, 14, 16-18, 22, 25-26, 29,
    31, 33, 43, 47, 49, 58-60, 67-68, 79,
    81-83, 94-98, 105, 108, 110-12, 121-

22, 126, 130-32, 136-38, 140, 146, 148,
    154, 158, 161-65, 167, 178, 180, 184
suffering servant, 16-17

Tamburello, Dennis E., 193
Tannehill, Robert C., 188
temple, 14-15, 20, 22, 24-25, 29
Tiessen, Terrance L., 190
Torisu, Yoshifumi, 190
Torrance, Alan J., 195
Torrance, Thomas F., 191
Turcescu, Lucian, 191

union with Christ, 47, 55-56, 58-59, 62-63, 93,
    97-99, 101-2, 104, 112-15, 132-37, 148

Waldrop, Charles T., 150, 195-96
Waltermire, Donald E., 197
Wanke, Daniel, 190
Watson, Philip S., 93, 192
Weaver, J. Denny, 192, 198
Webb, Robert L., 188
Weingart, Richard E., 192, 194
Wenham, David, 189
Wiley, Tatha, 191, 198
Wingren, Gustaf, 190
Winling, Raymond, 191
word of God, 2, 14, 25, 50, 52-54, 56, 58, 60-
    62, 64-65, 92, 100-101, 104, 107, 147,
    149-53, 155, 177, 179

Yinger, Kent L., 189

Zachhuber, Johannes, 190
Zachman, Randall C., 193
Ziesler, John A., 189